The Lost Synagogues of Brooklyn

The stories behind how and why many Brooklyn synagogues, now old "ex-*shuls*," were converted to other uses, primarily as Christian churches.

by Ellen Levitt

Avotaynu
Bergenfield, N.J.
2009

Requests for permission to make copies of any part of this publication should be addressed to:
Avotaynu, Inc.
155 N. Washington Ave.
Bergenfield, NJ 07621

Printed in the United States of America

Cover: Independent Chevra Sphard of Perryslaw
247 Snediker Avenue, East New York
(now Brooklyn Christian Center)

Library of Congress Cataloging-in-Publication Data

Levitt, Ellen.
 The lost synagogues of Brooklyn : the stories behind how and why many Brooklyn synagogues, now old "ex-shuls," were converted to other uses, primarily as Christian churches / by Ellen Levitt.
 p. cm.
Includes bibliographical references.
ISBN 978-1-886223-39-4 (alk. paper)
 1. Synagogues—New York (State)—New York—History. 2. Synagogues—New York (State)—New York—Pictorial works. 3. Jews—New York (State)—New York—History. 4. Church buildings—New York (State)—New York—History. 5. Church buildings—New York (State)—New York—Pictorial works. 6. Brooklyn (New York, N.Y.)—Buildings, structures, etc. 7. Brooklyn (New York, N.Y.)—Buildings, structures, etc.—Pictorial works. I. Title.

NA4690.L48 2009
726'.30974723—dc22
  2009003062

For Jessica, Michelle and Howard

"Mommy, we in Brooklyn!"
—Jessica, age two, on the F train

Contents

Acknowledgements ix

Introduction 1

How I Conducted My Research 5

What Else Is Gone? 7

Scholarly Note 8

The Rise and Fall of Jewish Life in Brownsville and Area Neighborhoods 10

The Synagogue—Its Historical Development, Evolution in America and Especially Brooklyn ... 21

Shaari Israel: An In-Depth Study of an Ex-Shul of Brooklyn 29

Pleading With History: Memories of Brooklyn's Ex-*Shuls* 41

Meeting Amongst the Faithful: My Visits With Congregants of Converted Ex-Shuls 56

More Visits with People at Synagogues That Became Churches 67

What Does Jewish Law Say About All This? 70

Conclusion 74

Survey of the Buildings 77

Taking a Tour: Photographs and Text on Ex-Shuls of Brooklyn 79

Map of Brooklyn Showing Location of Lost Synagogues 82

    Congregation Adath Yeshurun, 1403 Eastern Parkway at Lincoln Place, Brownsville 84

    Congregation Agudas Achim Ansche Bobruisk, 729 Saratoga Avenue, Brownsville 85

    Agudas Achim Anshei Mishnitz, 726 Driggs Avenue, Lower Williamsburg 86

    Agudas Achim Anshei New Lots, 43 Malta Street, New Lots 87

    Agudath Achim Anshei David Horodok, 855 Saratoga Avenue, Brownsville 88

    Congregation Ahavath Achim of Bedford Section, 404 (402) Gates Avenue, Bedford-Stuyvesant 89

    Agudath Achim Bnei Jacob of East New York, 503 Glenmore Avenue, East New York 90

    Congregation Ahavas Achim B'nai Abraham, 394–396 Logan Street, East New York 92

    Ahavath Achim Anshei Brownsville, 105 Riverdale Avenue, Brownsville 93

    Congregation Ahavas Achim of East Flatbush, 203 East 37th Street, East Flatbush 94

    Congregation Ahavath Chesed Day Nursery, 394 Hendrix Street, East New York 95

    Ahavath Chesed, 740-742 Jefferson Avenue, Bedford-Stuyvesant 96

    Ahavath Israel, 760 Sackman Street, East New York/New Lots 97

    Ahavath Reyim, 209 Rochester Avenue, Northern Crown Heights 98

    Anshei Azaritz/Azaritz Young Friends, 885–887 Thomas Boyland (Hopkinson) Street, Brownsville 99

    Anshei Krashnik of East New York Nusach Sfard, 473 Vermont Street, East New York 100

    Congregation Beth Abraham, 770 Howard Avenue near Livonia Avenue, Brownsville 101

    Beth Hamedrash HaGadol, 777–779 Schenectady Avenue (East 47th Street), East Flatbush 102

    Beth Hamedrash Hagadol Nachloth Zion of South Flatbush, 2175 East 22nd Street, Sheepshead Bay 103

    Beth Hemidrash Hagadol, 611 Williams Street, East New York/New Lots 104

    Congregation Beth Israel, 771 Sackman Street, Brownsville 105

    Congregation Beth Israel, 8910 Remsen Avenue/ 650 Avenue A, Remsen Heights/ East Flatbush 106

    Beth Israel, 231–233 Ainslie Street, Williamsburg 107

    Bikur Cholim, 3 (or 3–5–7) Lewis Avenue, Northern Bedford-Stuyvesant 108

Congregation Bikur Cholim Bnai Jacob, 2134 Dean Street, Weeksville-Bedford-Stuyvesant.....................109

B'nai Israel Jewish Center, 9517 Kings Highway, East Flatbush/Brownsville border 110

Chevra Ahavath Israel Anshei Ostrolenker, 375 Bristol Street, Brownsville 111

Chevra Poelei Tzedek Anschei Glubucker of Brownsville, 167–169 Chester Street, Brownsville.............. 112

Congregation Chevra Tehillim Nusach Ashkenaz, 511 Elton Street, East New York................................ 113

Chevra Torah Anshei Radishkowitz, 135–139 Amboy Street, Brownsville.. 114

Chevre Anshei Zedek/ Talmud Torah Anshei Zedek of East New York, 308–310 Atkins Avenue,
    East New York 115

Daughters of Zion, 130 Boerum Street, East Williamsburg.. 116

Congregation Dorshe Tov Anshei New Lots, 21 Louisiana Avenue, New Lots 117

Congregation Eliezer of East New York, 133 Hinsdale Street, East New York 118

Etz Chaim Machzikei Hadath, 1477 Lincoln Place, Brownsville 119

Ezrath Israel, 496 Gates Avenue, Bedford-Stuyvesant 120

Congregation Friends Oholei Torah, 890 Lenox Road, East Flatbush 121

Gates of Prayer/Community Center Congregation and Talmud Torah/Odessa Benevolent,
    180–182 Van Buren Street, Bedford-Stuyvesant..122

Glenwood Jewish Center-Lila R. Korf Talmud Torah, 888 East 56th Street, Old Mill Basin 123

H.E.S. (Hebrew Educational Society), Thomas Boyland (Hopkinson) Street at Sutter Avenue,
    Brownsville 125

Hebrew Ladies Day Nursery, 521 Thomas Boyland Street, Brownsville...126

Hebrew School of Williamsburg, 310 South 1st Street, Williamsburg..127

Hessed Ve Emeth Society of Castorialis, 69–71 Malta Street, East New York 128

Independent Chevra Sphard of Perryslaw, 247 Snediker Avenue, East New York 129

Congregation Independent Esrath (or Ezrath) Achim, 144 Newport Street, Brownsville.........................130

Israel Elioe Brethren of Yale, 474–476 Kosciuszko Street, upper Bedford-Stuyvesant 131

Jewish Center of Hyde Park, 779 East 49th Street, East Flatbush 132

Judea Center, 2059 Bedford Avenue, East Flatbush 133

Congregation Kachlow Israel, 220–222 Hegeman Avenue, Brownsville-East New York...........................134

Kenesseth Israel Beth Jacob, 35 Blake Avenue, Brownsville..135

Kesser Torah, 2310 Cortelyou Road at East 23rd Street, Flatbush 136

"Kevelson's" Shul, 1387 East 96th Street, Canarsie 137

Machzikei Torah Bnei David, 175 Hart Street, Bedford-Stuyvesant 138

Men of Justice, 1676–1678 Park Place, Brownsville/East New York...139

New Hebrew School of Brooklyn/ Bnos Israel Malbush Arumim, 146 Stockton Street,
    Bedford-Stuyvesant 140

New Lots Talmud Torah, 330–370 New Lots Avenue at Pennsylvania Ave., East New York..................... 141

Ohev Shalom (Bais Harav Midrash Eliyahu Anshei Charney?), 744 Dumont Avenue, East New York.....142

Ohev Sholom Anshei Sfard, 157 Leonard Street at Stagg Street, East Williamsburg...............................144

The Parkway Theater, 1768 St. John's Place, Brownsville...145

Congregation Petach Tikvah, 261 Rochester Avenue, Crown Heights..146

Petrikower Anshe Sfard of Brownsville, 493 Herzl Street, Brownsville..148

Prospect Park Jewish Center and Yeshiva, 153 Ocean Avenue, Flatbush..149

Rishon L'Zion, 409 East 95th Street, East Flatbush 150

Shaare Torah, 305 East 21st Street at Albemarle Road, Flatbush... 151

Shaari Israel, 810 East 49th Street, East Flatbush 152

Shaari Zedek, then Ahavath Achim, 765–767 Putnam Avenue, Bedford-Stuyvesant...............................153

Shaari Zedek, 221 Kingston Avenue, Bedford-Stuyvesant...155

Sheveth Achim (?), 276 Buffalo Avenue, Brownsville and The Little Temple Beth Jacob,
    285 Buffalo Avenue, Brownsville..156

Sons of Abraham, 157 Leonard Street at Stagg Street, East Williamsburg................................157
Congregation Sons of Isaac, 300 East 37th Street, East Flatbush...158
Congregation Sons of Judah, 864 Sutter Avenue, East New York 159
Talmud Torah Atereth Eliezer Glovinsky, 747 Hendrix Street, East New York 160
Talmud Torah Atereth Israel, 85–87 Fountain Avenue, East New York 161
Talmud Torah Beth Jacob Joseph, 368 Atlantic Avenue, Boerum Hill 162
Talmud Torah Tifereth Hagro (originally Talmud Torah Tifereth Zion), 425 Howard Avenue,
    Weeksville 163
Talmud Torah Tifereth Israel of West Flatbush, 1913–1915 West 7th Street, Gravesend 164
Temple Beth Ohr, 1010 Ocean Avenue, Flatbush...165
Temple Isaac (aka Ohel Yitzhok), 554 Prospect Place, Prospect Heights...........................166
Temple Sinai, 24 Arlington Avenue, Highland Park...167
Tifereth Israel, 656–8 Willoughby Avenue, Bedford-Stuyvesant 168
Tifereth Yehuda Nusach Sfard, 347 East 49th Street, East Flatbush 169
Tomchai Torah, 1320 Sutter Avenue, East New York...170
Mystery Jewish establishment on Varet Street, 101 Varet Street, East Williamsburg...............171
Congregation Vezras Achim, 341 Pennsylvania Avenue, East New York 172
Woodruff Avenue Temple, 151 Woodruff Avenue at East 21st, Flatbush 173
Yeshivat Rabbi Meyer Simcha HaCohen, 309 East 53rd Street, East Flatbush 174
Yeshivath Torath Chaim of Greater New York (also Young Israel of East New York),
    631 Belmont Avenue, East New York 175
Young Israel of Brownsville and East Flatbush, 1091 Winthrop Street at East 94th Street,
    East Flatbush-Brownsville 176
Young Israel of Prospect Park, 2170 Bedford Avenue, Flatbush 177

Appendix A: Known Architects for Brooklyn's Former Synagogues........................... 178

Appendix B: Using This Book as a Teaching Tool for Various Grade Levels........................... 179

Appendix C: Non-English Words Used in Synagogue Names................................... 182

Bibliography.. 183

Acknowledgements

Many people helped shape this book through interviews, information informally passed along to me, moral support and more. This book grew out of a photography exhibit I displayed at the Brooklyn Historical Society from November 2006 through February 2007. My exhibit was part of their "Public Perspectives" series, and I was thrilled to be part of this program. I had the opportunity to exhibit my work (artistic and research/writing) and to deliver a lecture on my topic. I owe debts to the caring, knowledgeable staff that worked with me and gave me encouragement and an exciting forum. Particular thanks to Janice Monger, Kate Fermoile, Erin (a student assistant) and Deborah Schwartz, museum director.

Thanks to Frank Jump who had owned the Fading Ad art gallery which now exists only as an Internet site at fadingad.com. Frank created a webpage displaying a few of my ex-*shul* photographs with some text; the page has become a reference source that has helped other people.

I am a member of two Jewish congregations, the East Midwood Jewish Center (EMJC) and Flatbush Women's Davening Group (FWDG). Both are important to my life as a Jew, as a Brooklynite, and as an artist. Several people in both congregations helped me in this project by offering information, allowing me to interview them, and listening to me as I bounced around ideas. At the FWDG, I thank Sarah Katz and Freda and Perri Rosenfeld for their information about ex-*shuls*, Shulamith Berger for her archival expertise and suggestions, and all the other members who inspired me and encouraged me to work harder.

There are many people at the East Midwood Jewish Center who deserve to be acknowledged for their help and inspiration. My family joined EMJC when I was not quite seven; as an adult I still call this *shul* my second home. I sing in its choir. Among the people I interviewed here were Rochelle Eckstein, Frank Rosenblum, Stan Hopard and Rabbi Aaron Pomerantz; their insights were worthy. Toby Sanchez, our *shul* historian, shared with me ideas and archival information of great value. I owe a debt to Rabbi Abraham Feldbin for his knowledge and for providing our whole community with the life story of his previous pulpit in Brooklyn, Congregation Shaari Israel of East Flatbush. Thanks also to Rabbi Alvin Kass and many other congregants.

Many of my friends have helped me along the way and made their mark upon my research including Mindy (Braunstein) Weinblatt, Debbie Weingarten, the Goldsmith family, Joshua Sayer and Charlie Endelman, Jen and Kevin Leopold, and Randi Lee Jablin. Thanks to them and to my many other friends.

Thank you to the research librarians and archivists at the Brooklyn Historical Society; the Jewish Theological Seminary, especially Ellen Kastel; the helpful staff of the New York City Municipal Archives and research stacks; the Brooklyn Collection at the main branch of the Brooklyn Public Library at Grand Army Plaza; and the Ratner Library of Judaica at the Main Library on East 42nd Street.

I appreciate the kindness of the many people I met at Christian congregations that were once *shuls,* especially Deacon Herbert Gandy, Pastor N. Samuel, and the congregants of the House of David on Dumont Avenue.

I thank my family for their support, for giving me valuable information on this and related subjects, and for proofreading and helping to select photographs along the way. My husband, Howard Dankowitz, told me about the Brooklyn Historical Society's competition and became the co-curator of the exhibit. I also appreciate the times he watched our two daughters, Jessica and

Michelle, so that I could go take photographs and conduct interviews. His parents, Janet and Robert Dankowitz, also helped me out with various things and attended the lecture at BHS.

My father, Edward Levitt, helped do some research and occasionally accompanied me on research jaunts. I also thank my brother Benjamin, his wife Lauren, his in-laws Sandra and Joel Rotman, as well as my sister-in-law Beverly and her husband Dean Plotnick. Hello to Josh and Robbie, Dani and Ariel. Special thanks to my cousins Willie and Robert DeVries and to Shirley Gerb for their memories of certain old synagogues. And a tip of the hat to my late mother Leah Levitt and her late sister Miriam DeVries.

Finally, I thank Avotaynu for having faith in this book and helping "give birth" to it.

Introduction

Brooklyn has many houses of worship; it has been dubbed "the borough of churches." These buildings serve various Christian, Jewish, Muslim, and other religious groups. A number of these buildings have had more than one divine affiliation. There are a few dozen churches here that were once synagogues.

In some cases, this is quite obvious: there is a church on Arlington Avenue in the Highland Park section that, in 2006, still looked more like a synagogue than a church. There were a few signs to tout the name of the Missionario Cristiano, but they were dwarfed by large Hebrew lettering and the English name "Temple Sinai." As well, the front of the building displayed a number of Jewish symbols, including the Ten Commandment tablets. The cornerstone showed the Hebrew date and secular date of consecration, 1920.

Some churches exhibit a few subtle symbols that reveal their Hebraic past. A church on Woodruff Avenue across from East 21st Street in Flatbush has a series of sculpted Jewish stars that run vertically on the front. They are not so easy to see because they are of a murky color, but they are evidence of the former *shul*.

And there are some churches that have very little or no evidence of their past. Two churches on one block of Malta Street in East New York were both synagogues, but now there are no Jewish stars, no Hebrew writing, no stained glass windows left with Judaica prominent on the outside. They do feature a type of outdoor staircase that was common to many older *shuls*. Through archival research, I was able to uncover their former names, the years these buildings were consecrated, and more.

✡ ✡ ✡ ✡ ✡ ✡

I have been photographing "ex-*shuls*," as I call them, for a few years. It began informally in 1999, when I snapped pictures of former synagogues in the Flatbush region. One was Kesser Torah on Cortelyou Road near the Depression-era Sears Flatbush store. My mother and her sister, my aunt, had attended this *shul* as well as the Hebrew school there. The building became a church, and its appearance has changed over the past several years. Nearby, on East 21st Street at Albemarle Road, was Shaare Torah which is now Salem Missionary Baptist Church. This church still sports some Judaica: the building's front shows the words "Shaare Torah" written in Hebrew and sculpted in metal along with a burning bush symbol, as well as metal railings around the front steps that incorporate menorahs.

I began to search out and photograph more and more of these buildings. As I found them, I realized that I had stumbled upon one of Brooklyn's worst-kept secrets. I began to ask lots of questions about these buildings, some of which are in excellent condition, others in depressing, shabby states.

As I would show my growing collection of ex-*shul* photos to people, from their reactions (much bittersweet nostalgia or bewilderment, but also mild anger, "this is so New York" mirth, and more) I realized that I had to document this further. I also wanted to learn more about these buildings, about the people who had populated these buildings in the past and present, and about greater trends that have shaped Brooklyn over the past few generations.

✡ ✡ ✡ ✡ ✡ ✡

Brooklyn, New York, in 2008 is full of synagogues. There is a seemingly endless number of Orthodox *shuls*, many quite small, in neighborhoods such as Borough Park, Crown Heights, Williamsburg, and Midwood. There are several large Conservative and Reform synagogues throughout the borough. The large majority of these are vibrant sites, where praying and learning, as well as other community activities, take place on a regular basis. I belong to the East Midwood Jewish Center, now more than eighty years old and one of the biggest Conservative synagogues, not only in Kings County but in New York City as a whole.

There are also many former synagogues in Brooklyn (as well as in the other boroughs of New York City). These ex-*shuls* are sometimes easy to spot, sometimes not. Judaism does not hold to the belief in ghosts, in specters, but these old synagogues are ghost-like presences that can easily be found in certain neighborhoods in Brooklyn. Perhaps some might consider them to be quaint or even embarrassing reminders of an earlier time in Jewish life. For many, especially those of us who were born in the 1960s and later, these are baffling creatures, surprising artifacts that we rarely bump up against unless we make an effort to visit particular areas of Brooklyn.

For people who are older, these ex-*shuls* can command memories, often hazy but at times quite specific. They are catalysts of nostalgia, but they can also be bitter reminders of demographic changes in Brooklyn over time. Perhaps some older people feel they have failed these ex-*shuls* because they have become abandoned and because the vast majority of them have become churches.

There are many reasons why I have become so invested in the examination of these ex-*shuls*, and I admit that there is quite a bit of the autobiographic in my approach to these buildings, these memories. As a little girl I attended an ex-*shul* that later morphed into a church. Until I was nearly seven, I occasionally attended Shaare Torah, mentioned earlier, a Conservative synagogue in Flatbush, at East 21st Street and Albemarle Road. I have but vague memories of my times there. When my family moved, we joined the afore-mentioned East Midwood Jewish Center, further south in Brooklyn than Shaare Torah.

I had not crossed paths with Shaare Torah for many years although I heard it was no longer a synagogue. In fact, it had merged with East Midwood (as did two other congregations in the greater area of Flatbush), and I had also heard that it became a church. I do not think I actually surveyed the ex-*shul* until that day in 1999 when I borrowed my parents' car and toured my old Flatbush stomping grounds. I brought along my 1981 Minolta XG-M camera, loaded with black-and-white film, and set out to photograph sights in Flatbush.

So I snapped shots of the old Shaare Torah, now known as Salem Missionary Baptist Church. I noticed very quickly that remnants remained of the old days, especially to the observant Jew. The metal railings leading up to the entrance from the time of the synagogue remained, with the menorahs still incorporated in the design. I chuckled at that and then saw the artistic rendering of the *shul* name in Hebrew letters with a burning bush motif still above the main doors. I took several pictures, and later told people that they had to check out this building, to see it and believe it for themselves. I could not, at the time, understand why the church group that assumed this building had left these Jewish symbols for all the world to see and ponder.

I also went to see the synagogue my mother and my aunt Miriam, her older sister, had attended in their youth. Then known as Kesser Torah (Crown of the Torah), this building, tucked away on Cortelyou Road, not far from the still-classy art deco Sears flagship store on Bedford Avenue, appeared to me as more a hidden surprise than Shaare Torah. On its narrow side street, Kesser Torah had some evidence of its Jewish past: a circle with a Jewish star and "1926" in its center, above the big windows; and a cornerstone, somewhat scratched out, that read "Cong. Kesser Torah" in English.

Somehow, gazing at this building, I felt sad whereas I had not when lingering in front of Shaare Torah. I had never been inside the building when it was a synagogue and would not in the future. Mom had said little about the synagogue, and all I had was a thin, white-covered prayer book with her name in it that she received from the synagogue upon her Hebrew school graduation. She was already starting to fade mentally at this point in her life, and she could not provide me with great detail about Kesser Torah. My aunt tried gamely to remember a bit more and told me about how she and my mother, when they were young girls, would go up in the balcony during services. She recalled going to *shul* with their grandfather, a bearded fellow who walked with a cane and spoke mostly Yiddish.

A few years later I stopped by Kesser Torah, now known as Pentecostal Church of God, and shuddered upon noticing that the Kesser Torah cornerstone had been spackled over. The Jewish star and 1926 designation had been covered over too. A car pulled up and an African American woman asked me if she could help me. When I told her that this had been my mother's old synagogue, and I had seen Jewish reminders of it in the past, the woman told me, "Oh, we removed those years ago." I was sure this was not in the distant past, and with a sigh I left and drove onward.

These experiences, rooted in my childhood and my family's past, were the earliest motivations for an expanded study of ex-*shuls*. But there is much more. Over the years I had noticed a few more curious buildings that I realized had to be former synagogues. The most obvious one was on Ocean Avenue, across the street from Prospect Park on its east side. I asked around and found out that the John Hus Moravian Church had, indeed, been Prospect Park Jewish Center and a yeshiva, a Jewish day school. At some point, I realized that any noticeable Jewish symbols on the building's exterior were now gone.

Then there was the peculiar little building encountered in late 1987-early 1988 when I drove to the Interboro Parkway (later renamed the Jackie Robinson Parkway) on my way to graduate courses and substitute teaching work in Queens. The identity of the building was not obvious, because there were Jewish stars on the entrance railing and a few others, and it resembled a synagogue, but it had no name. Years later, I again encountered this building at the northern tip of the Kings Highway extension, where it meets Howard Avenue and Tapscott Street, now the Grace Church of God. That was an "aha" moment for me. There were a few other curious buildings I noticed in eastern Brooklyn neighborhoods on the rare times I drove through there. Eventually I wanted to learn more about them.

While on childcare leave for a few years, taking time off from teaching high school to be at home for my two young daughters, I had time occasionally to tuck them into the car with me and go on rides to explore Brooklyn. At times it was done to lull them to sleep for naptime. Going into areas I was less familiar with such as East Flatbush and Brownsville, I encountered some of these old synagogues that had become churches. I viewed this as an interesting photographic subject, and after having taken pictures of a handful of these old buildings, I got in contact with the owner of a northern Brooklyn art gallery I read about.

Frank Jump, who in 2004 opened Fading Ad Gallery in Clinton Hill, was interested in my subject. I visited his gallery, at Myrtle and Bedford Avenues, and brought around photographic samples. He gave me criticism on how to improve the shots and told me he was interested in displaying them, but was not sure when and with what other artists' work he would pair it. Sadly,

Frank and his partner Vincenzo closed the gallery, too-short lived, due to the rising rent. However, Frank did create a virtual gallery and made a photographic essay with eight of my photographs (you can still visit it at www.fadingad.com).

When my younger daughter was in nursery school each weekday morning, I was really bitten with the history detective bug. I had to find more, learn more, synthesize more. I decided to delve into research on Brooklyn's ex-*shuls* and tell a story that was hidden from view, but not quite. It was there, some Jews knew about it, some Christians had inklings about it, but there was no book about it, no comprehensive photographic exploration about it. I chose to work on it.

Thus, this study of ex-*shuls* is my attempt at historical research and writing, with religious, sociological and architectural emphasis. Fascinating primary sources were utilized as well as valuable secondary sources. I also learned more about the borough of Brooklyn; I determined that I often liked the design of old *shuls* better than modern ones; and I expanded my knowledge of Judaism and especially ritual. Truth be told, this was also a project that enabled me to utilize skills and techniques learned while in graduate school, first working on my master's degree in history, and then two years toward a doctorate degree.

How I Conducted My Research

The ways in which I researched my study of ex-shuls have been myriad. Once I became serious about delving into this topic and wished to go beyond following a few leads, I strived to be methodical yet flexible. Hints and suggestions floated my way and I latched onto them. It was irresistible to find, in passing, anything that led me to major sources of information. After a while, I engaged in more rigorous research, using both a variety of primary and secondary sources.

I began by asking around casually. My dad told me of a few sites he could recall. One day I decided to look through old Brooklyn phone books to find names and addresses of synagogues. I went to the Central Branch of the Brooklyn Public Library at Grand Army Plaza and asked for the microfilm rolls of the 1927–1928 and the 1947–1948 telephone directories. My father came along, because he was vaguely intrigued by the idea and wanted to see if he remembered any of these places by name.

Sure enough, I found names of old shuls. I was unsure which would still be around, but targeted those with addresses in certain areas such as the Brownsville and East Flatbush areas, and sought names that began with Bnai, Congregation, Beth, Torah, Young, and other indicative words. Looking at "Congregation" particularly helped me.

After one or two car excursions into these areas, I became familiar with certain styles of architecture and architectural features that were prominent on many old shuls. This helped me to spot possible subjects, even if the buildings did not display overt Judaica such as Jewish stars, Decalogues, or Hebrew writing. The windows often had semi-circular tops; big circles out front indicated former windows; there were certain common details near the roofing; these and more I would find as I cruised streets in Brownsville, East New York, Flatbush, East Flatbush, and Weeksville. I started to hear about more ex-shuls from older congregants at our synagogue. I found out about an artist, Jeremy Nadel, who had painted a few of these ex-shuls, and when I e-mailed him, he provided me with a few sites I was unfamiliar with. A short article in the free paper, the New York Press, provided me with the address of yet another former shul by Interfaith Hospital.

I was still poking around. I longed for a directory of old shuls, perhaps a database, but my web searches were sketchy. Then a woman from North Carolina, Ellen Grove, e-mailed me because she found out about my project from a website. (I checked that website soon after and could not locate the information.) She told me about an ex-shul where her brother was bar mitzvahed and, most important, she told me about the WPA (Works Progress Administration) Depression-era survey of all the houses of worship in New York City.

I found out that this material was housed at the New York City Municipal Archives at 31 Chambers Street. I had gone there a number of times when I was in graduate school to find primary sources for research papers. The dozen or so times that I sat and worked with the microfilm containing the WPA survey information on the synagogues were fascinating, if exhausting. Suddenly, I was able to identify most of the ex-shuls I had already found, and I culled addresses for several more old shuls.

These WPA surveys were almost maddeningly thorough. Writers were employed by the WPA to garner information on every house of worship in the five boroughs, and there were an immense number of synagogues represented. I had to comb through three rolls of microfilm (and the print quality of the lettering was not always good, which tired my eyes) to find out the names of synagogues, their founding dates, key people involved in them, and so on.

Just before I began my WPA studies, I also borrowed a library book that helped me greatly. It was *Brownsville: The Birth, Development and Passing of a Jewish Community in New York*, by Alter Landesman. Although this book, a combination of monograph and memoir, had drawbacks (see my essay about it), it was very helpful to me.

I also paid visits to the Dorot research division of the New York Public Library, where I found a few items (not as many as I had hoped) that furthered my knowledge. The Brooklyn collection stored at the Central Branch of the Brooklyn Public Library (BPL) was of help too. The website of the BPL also has a database of old Brooklyn Eagle articles that I used for more primary sources. (I typed in "Brooklyn synagogues" as my keywords and found many articles from 1902 and earlier, many of which pertained to old synagogues I was researching.) Certainly, the Jewish Theological Seminary archives and the publications section of the library were also of great help to me. As well, the New York Landmarks Conservancy, which I decided to get in contact with after studying a New York Times article, was a valuable resource—and they benefited from some of the research that I had conducted. We also provided each other with links to further research and personal contacts with other people who were documenting related topics.

I also accumulated a collection of newspaper and magazine articles during the past few years that had proven valuable to my research. I am indebted in particular to the New York Daily News Sunday paper, which carries the "Faith in the City" column; this has featured stories about some of the ex-shuls in Brooklyn. The New York Times has published a few articles about the old synagogues in Brooklyn, Queens and Newark, New Jersey, so these were good sources too.

A good number of books have provided me with rich sources of information about the ex-synagogues of Brooklyn, as well as information about architecture, crafts, the history of the synagogue, and much more. The bibliography spells out all this, but a few books besides the Alter Landesman volume have been inspirational. I adore the slender Identifying American Architecture, by John J. G. Blumenson, with its many photographs and clear explanations of architectural features. This book gave me a strong appreciation of the major styles of the ex-shuls I would encounter.

Speaking with people who went to these ex-*shuls* long ago, as well as people who go to the present churches, provided a wonderful set of experiences. In general, the fieldwork I have engaged in has been heartening, interesting, and enjoyable, but at times frustrating. Some of my fieldwork was ongoing; I had driven by a number of these ex-*shuls* many times on the way to work or to visit various neighborhoods and places in Brooklyn. I would see them at different times of the year, at different times of the day, in varying weather, and make observations—not just on a one-time only basis.

I examined a few artifacts from the days of the former synagogues, but not many, and this may be more due the passage of time than anything else. In general, I strove to find as many primary sources as possible, to make this all more credible and genuine. The secondary sources, including books, articles in publications and material found on the web, were also important and helped me to organize the material better.

What Else Is Gone?

Studying Brooklyn's bygone shuls can make us nostalgic, and we each have our own brand of nostalgia. Certainly there are a number of Jewish Brooklynites and ex-Brooklynites who have memories attached to particular old synagogues, as well as to customs and celebrations, catch-phrases and people, and favorite restaurants (especially a fabled deli or two). Although many of these ex-shuls live on in some form, other aspects of them are gone, most of all the Jewish people who used them.

These "alumni" of ex-shuls may, and often do recreate various aspects of their old shul customs elsewhere, but other things drift away into the farthest reaches of memory, virtually lost. They could be the murals that once graced the walls of a shul that have since been painted white. They could be the European- or Levantine-bred tunes of prayers that were previously popular but have now been shelved for others. They could be the type of foods prepared for an end-of-service kiddush (prayer over wine, as well as communal snack or meal). Some of these are gone; much of it has morphed; and more of it, even if still utilized, has origins obscured by time.

A major part of Jewish life that has changed is the language, especially the vernacular and the pronunciation. The vast majority of Jews at the ex-shuls in Brownsville, East New York and East Flatbush were of Eastern European backgrounds, and for years most spoke Yiddish. While there are still fluent Yiddish speakers, most are either old and/or live in strictly Orthodox enclaves. Yiddish is not as common in Brooklyn as it once was, despite the efforts of such organizations as the National Yiddish Book Center, tucked away on a college campus in Massachusetts. Many Jews and non-Jews know Yiddish words such as bagel, chutzpah and oy vey (and some still know zetz and kugel[1]), but fewer people speak fluent Yiddish here, and that is a cold fact. Those that do are not always aware of the different pronunciations, which can be quite confusing. (Torah vs. Teyre, kugel vs. kigl, anyone?)

So I wonder about the voices that previously echoed in the Brooklyn ex-shuls, that ring or kvetch (complain) no more, and how about the lesser-known Jewish hybrid languages, such as Ladino (Jewish-Spanish) or Jewish-Greek or Jewish-Italian or Jewish-Persian?

Many people forget or are unaware of the fact that there were non-Yiddish-speaking Jews whose Brooklyn shuls have closed. Alter Landesman briefly discusses the Sephardic synagogues, with Jews of Greek, Turkish or even Spanish backgrounds. What were their tunes, their pronunciations, their customs? They are, perhaps, even more ethereal and lost in the haze of Brooklyn memory. I wonder what a service and kiddush was like for the synagogue at 71 Malta Street, Chesed V'emeth Castorialis. It had to be somewhat different from the more typical Brownsville shul.

How about the word "shul" itself, which is the Yiddish word for "synagogue?" It has become so common among many Jews, but not all Jewish immigrants to Brooklyn would even use that word— some might have said *sinagoga* or used some other term for Jewish house of worship. I apologize to all readers for blithely using the word "shul" all the time. While most of the Jews at ex-shuls would have used that word, others utilized different Jewish-language words. Some, at the more Americanized sites, would have used the word "temple" (and now the Latino Pentecostals will say templo).

So we see that the buildings have changed, the voices have changed, and much of everyday Jewish life in Brooklyn has changed over time. It may sadden some, and it saddens me in many ways—but my response is that you should document things as much as possible so that those in the future can learn and compare.

---

[1] *Chutzpah*–arrogance, nerve. *Oy vey*–oh woe. *Zetz*–slap. *Kugel*–a type of baked casserole

Scholarly Note

The photographs and research that went into this book constitute a labor of love. It is my deep hope that it will meet a variety of intellectual and social goals for readers, and I strived to deal skillfully and sincerely with two important fields. These are urban religious history (at times in the guise of a tour guide) and interfaith relations and understanding. At first I delved into this field because of my love of and great interest in Judaism and affection for my hometown of Brooklyn, New York. As I started to write the text of the book and conducted some of the final research on religious issues pertaining to *The Lost Synagogues of Brooklyn*, I had a scare which sparked an epiphany.

My fear was that some Jews might view my book and aspects of my research methods as wrongful. To some there are religious restrictions regarding visiting non-Jewish houses of worship which would make my topic controversial. Then I realized my photographs and research, and now my writing, are engaged in the field of interfaith relations, even dialogue.

The religious ramifications will be explored later, but it is my sincere desire to build bridges with non-Jews in Brooklyn and elsewhere, and especially focus on furthering the understanding and learning between the Christian and Jewish communities of Brooklyn. I have met with a good number of African American and Latino Christians whose congregations now meet in what were once Jewish synagogues. Bonds of friendship have been forged with members of these churches, and I have taught them things about the Jewish religion and attendant culture. In return, they made me aware of their religious practices and culture.

Interfaith relations, Jewish-Christian bonds, have been especially prominent in recent decades, especially since the devastation wrought by the Holocaust and World War II. How these two religious groups have dealt with each other in the past has many sad and disappointing chapters, around the world and even in the United States. But in recent times there have been many efforts at easing the tensions and working toward understanding and peace. I hope in my small way that I am furthering the progress of this field.

One prominent group working on interfaith relations is the International Council of Christians and Jews (ICCJ), which "serves as the umbrella organization of 38 national Jewish-Christian dialogue organizations world-wide."[2] As well, there are many American groups, on the national and local levels, that promote interfaith discussion.

Many rabbis from the non-Orthodox Jewish movements (Conservative, Reform, Reconstructionist, Humanist) have been involved in this field. Some Modern Orthodox rabbis have too. Typically Orthodox rabbis have been less involved; but the greatly revered Rabbi Joseph Soloveitchik stated that not theological dialogue but non-theological discussion was "desirable and even essential."[3] There has even been a scholarly exploration by Jews and Christians on this topic—the Council of Centers on Jewish-Christian Relations has worked on this with its reassessment of the Rabbi's 1964 article on this topic.[4]

I also hope this book will be a worthy addition to the fields of urban studies and religious studies, as well as a fond tribute to people and places of Brooklyn. I have lived all my life in Brooklyn and have seen so much good and bad, hope, and disappointment in this most heavily populated borough of New York City. Brooklyn is full of surprises, of intriguing things. Much of Brooklyn

---

[2] http://iccj.org/en/index.php
[3] http://en.wikipedia.org/wiki/Joseph_B._Soloveitchik
[4] http://www.bc.edu/research/cjl/meta-elements/sites/partners/ccjr/Intro.htm

that may at first seem mundane is actually quite interesting and stimulating. People in Brooklyn may not always realize this, nor do people who lived here and moved away, or those who have only visited or read about the borough. We can all take the time to realize that Brooklyn, a large and colorful urban landscape, has much to offer us. Sometimes things will cause us to scratch our collective heads in wonder at the ever-evolving story of Brooklyn, Kings County. May you learn and ponder and be entertained!

The Rise and Fall of Jewish Life in Brownsville and Area Neighborhoods

Jewish life in Brownsville, East New York, Flatbush-East Flatbush, Bedford-Stuyvesant and other nearby areas through the 1950s was a lively, rich and varied environment; over the next few decades it dissipated greatly. Brooklyn, in the early 2000s, still had a very large Jewish population, and a significant percentage of the world's Jewish population resided within its boundaries. Now there are almost no Jews left in Brownsville, East New York and Bedford-Stuyvesant. Flatbush has a few, some of whom are younger and have moved from other Brooklyn neighborhoods or from elsewhere. While Williamsburg is home to a great many Satmar Chasidic Jews, as well as some young secular Jews in the hipster sections, the East Williamsburg region is no longer heavily Jewish. Now Jews live in many other parts of Brooklyn, especially Borough Park, Midwood, Gravesend, Park Slope, Sheepshead Bay, Marine Park, Ditmas Park, and so on. The shifts of Jewish population have left their mark on the physical plant of New York City and most certainly Brooklyn.

What became of the legacy of the older Jewish areas in Brooklyn? What physically remains? There is quite a lot of Jewish history that can be easily accessed if one is willing to look for it.

First, some thoughts from two authors in books that are not solely about the Brooklyn Jewish experience but are worthwhile for their exploration of the nostalgic bonds to New York City and the passing of time:

> "Sadly, too many third- and fourth-generation children of the old European migration don't know much about the city that helped make their lives possible."

Pete Hamill assesses the situation precisely. A lot of people today, including Jews, only know the basics about the experiences of their ancestors in New York City (and this could be said of people in other American cities). The factoids they know are often vague, the knowledge of their own families is typically fleeting. The scraps of Judaic legacy are often in great-grandma's handed-down matzah ball recipe or at the plot location of grandfather's grave.

> "But true students, driven by simple curiosity, can still find the places where their grandparents or great-grandparents once struggled..."

Again, Hamill makes a worthy point. Many Jews who had relatives who lived in Brooklyn can make some inquiries or visit the gravesites of their ancestors, and perhaps find out where they worshiped and lived long ago. Many of the old synagogues and communal institutions of the Jewish community still stand today, although we shall see that many of them have been altered, some greatly, some slightly.

> We're all pleading with history, begging not to be forgotten...

Fred Goodman writes this in his book, *The Secret City*, about Woodlawn Cemetery in the Bronx. Does everyone really plead with history and beg not to be forgotten? (Anyone who has read Theodore Dreiser's *Sister Carrie* could certainly wonder about that!) At least in the Jewish tradition, however, there is an emphasis on not forgetting your relatives, and it is carried out in specific ways. We are expected to commemorate the death anniversaries of our close relatives through the chanting of the *kaddish* (memorial prayers) and the lighting of *yahrzeit* candles on the death anniversaries and on the eves of certain holidays. Many of us conduct research on the genealogies of our families and their communities in the Old World. Some Jews still belong to burial societies and *landsmanschaftn*, fraternal groups stemming from towns outside of the United States (typically in Eastern Europe).

Some Jews are fortunate to have physical items passed down within their families. In my own family we have several tokens from my father's side of the family, such as a passport from Europe, photographs, religious ritual items and even some of my grandfather's carpentry tools. My husband's mother has *kiddush* cups, other religious keepsakes from her family, and a good number of photographs. These things, faded and frayed and dented, provide glimpses into a world we cannot really know but want to understand. Occasionally they are even used today and offer a bridge between generations.

Another way for Jews and other groups to learn about the Jewish experience in Brooklyn (and in other urban areas of the United States and Canada) is to venture into the old neighborhood, the areas that once were heavily Jewish, but which are now home to other ethnic groups for the most part. In Brooklyn, which in some ways was (and still is) the way-station for a large percentage of American Jewry, there are many fading reminders of what once was. Often they are not difficult to visit, and I hope that besides reading this book for such information the reader will be inspired to visit sites and learn about the past.

✿ ✿ ✿ ✿ ✿ ✿

The American Jewish pageant is varied and people often forget this. But one of the most enduring and dominant tropes is of the Lower East Side/Manhattan Jewish experience. There were so many Jews from Eastern Europe (and to a lesser extent Central European and Levantine nations) who made their way to Manhattan's Lower East Side district. That has been explored famously in Irving Howe's *The World of Our Fathers*, as well as other books and a number of movies.

Jews stayed there for years, but many then moved on to Brooklyn, the Bronx and other parts of Manhattan (especially Harlem) as well as other American cities, and then the suburbs. Earlier generations of Jews, including those who came during colonial times, had migrated not only to the towns on the east coast of the United States but also westward. There are many worthwhile books that study this history: I recommend starting with Max I. Dimont's classic and well-written *Jews, God and History* as well as Marc Lee Raphael's *Judaism in America*.

The life of Brooklyn Jewry has been documented in a number of books, movies, and television. There has not been much written, especially in recent years, about the remaining presence of Jews in what are now mostly African American and Latino neighborhoods. My research brings together scholarly and more casual works from the 1960s and 1970s, as well as some academic material written in the 1990s and onward which did not focus primarily on Jews of these areas. I also mined a number of primary and contemporary sources for this book.

We start our examination of this place and time with an enjoyable and brief book. Alfred Kazin's *A Walker in the City* is an intriguing, delightful read. Kazin, the prolific literary critic, steeps this book with his mixed feelings, but overall appreciation, for the Brownsville of his youth. His highly detailed portrayals of people and places in Brownsville bring to life a neighborhood that was once one of the most densely Jewish places on earth, let alone in the United States.

> We were the children of the immigrants who had camped at the city's back door, in New York's rawest, remotest, cheapest ghetto... They were New York, the Gentiles, America; we were Brownsville— Brunzvil, as the old folks said—the dust of the earth to all Jews with money and notoriously a place that measured all success by our skill in getting away from it." (p. 12)

Kazin shows the yearning for a better life and the underlying stigmatization of life in Brownsville. He writes of his love and comfort, as well as disgust and confusion, at living in this area before and during the Great Depression. Readers learn about young Alfred's feelings for his *shul* on Chester Street and other aspects of Jewish life here: the markets, businesses and holidays, the cooking and the reminisces about European hometowns, the local socialist and communist meetings to which he and a number of Jews flocked, the interactions between the Jewish community and the outside world.

(In mid-August 2007 the New York Times devoted a front-page article in its "The City" section, along with satellite essays, to modern-day renditions of walking life, somewhat inspired by Kazin's book. Apparently Kazin's joy of strolling the town still had its adherents in a more technologically advanced and addicted age.)

An important fictionalization of Jewish ghetto life, encompassing Brownsville and later the Lower East Side of Manhattan, is found in the celebrated novel *Call It Sleep,* by Henry Roth. (Kazin himself dubbed it "a classic of psychological fiction.") Whereas Kazin's memoir readily conjures up a great swathe of his community, Roth's novel is a more intense portrayal of the inner workings of a family, alongside its interactions with the community at large. Here is a telling comment from Roth, as internalized by the youthful protagonist, David Schearl:

> ...it was a new and violent world, as different from Brownsville as quiet from turmoil. Here in 9th Street it wasn't the sun that swamped one as one left the doorway, it was sound—an avalanche of sound." (p. 143)

We learn of how David regarded Brownsville when he leaves it for the Lower East Side. For all its poverty and dust, a boy could feel the warmth of the sun in Brownsville. Young David's family makes a move that was the reverse for many Jews: the Schearls decamp to the Lower East Side, while many more Jews left the cramped, noisy and dirty Lower East Side for the relative healthfulness and open spaces of Brownsville.

This sense of open space and opportunity for Jews is found in *Brownsville: The Birth, Development and Passing of a Jewish Community in New York*, by Alter F. Landesman. This is a history of Brownsville's Jewish era, written by a man who played a key role for part of the time (he was a rabbi, an educator, and an administrator for the Hebrew Educational Society—more on that later). Written at the end of the 1960s, when Jewish Brownsville was nearing its end in a mournful fashion, this book at times is a heartfelt and scholarly tribute, at other times a semi-dry listing of people, places and things. (Landesman made a point of quoting several lines of Henry Roth's *Call It Sleep* in this book's introduction.)

> Brownsville witnessed the developed of one of the largest communities of East European Jewish immigrants during the last decade of the nineteenth century and the first two decades of the twentieth." (p. 1)

This large influx and settlement of Jews, over time, developed a community that reflected its religion and culture in a multitude of ways. This area was unmistakably Jewish.

> Brownsville became known as the 'Jerusalem of America.' Synagogues did not have to seek a 'tenth man' for a *minyan,* (a quorum required for a full religious service to be carried out); large numbers of Jews attended them for worship and study. Many of the synagogues engaged rabbis, among whom were great Talmudic scholars who contributed to Jewish learning through their publication of *responsa* and rabbinic works.

> (Synagogues and fraternal organizations) became not only the primary social agencies of the neighbor-

hood, but also havens to thousands of the first generation of immigrants who affiliated with them. They provided not only a place to worship and study, but met the immigrant's needs for comradeship, friendship, and fellowship. " (p. 208)

In its heyday, Brownsville's synagogues were among the district's most important institutions, taken as a whole. They served several functions in the religious and social domains, but they were not the only Jewish institutions fulfilling the needs of the Jews here:

> The arrival of the East European immigrants... spurred the growth of a strong radical trade-union movement..." (p. 207) "...a Society for the Aid for the Indigent Sick was organized in 1895...the Brownsville Relief Hebrew Charity was established a little later. Thus sprang up various aid societies which in subsequent years became important institutions." (p. 71)

Brownsville's Jews, as well as greater Brooklyn's and New York City's Jewish community, would establish and support many Jewish institutions of charity, education, health and recreation. The Hebrew Educational Society (H.E.S.) was founded in Brownsville and served young and old, religiously observant and thoroughly secular Jews for many years (it moved to southern Brooklyn, the edge of Canarsie, in the 1960s). There were many Jewish schools, ranging from full-time Jewish studies centers to part-time Hebrew schools to less observant but culturally rich Yiddish schools. There were the Young Men's and Women's Hebrew Associations of Brownsville and East New York. The Dispensary and especially Beth- El Hospital (known now as Brookdale Hospital and still active) maintained the health of Jews and others, with the bonus of kosher food and other sensitivities to the Jewish community. Yiddish theater and newspapers flourished here, kosher food and eateries were typically in abundance.

Even in 1896, the *Brooklyn Eagle* noted how the pulse of Brownsville was so Jewish:

> Brownsville, the home of 16,000 Hebrews, is today observing the day of atonement, or Yom Kippur, which is given up to fasting and prayer. Many of the Brownsville residents will spend the whole time within the walls of the synagogues praying. ...This is the quietest day of the year in Brownsville." (Eagle, September 17, 1896)

Imagine how much stronger this trend would be when Brownsville would house not just 16,000 Jews, but many thousands more. Saturdays, the Jewish Sabbath, would also take on a particular air as the dominant ethnicity influenced the activities of the day.

Carole Bell Ford wrote two books about female experiences in Brownsville. Her observations and interviews with women who grew up in Brownsville illustrate general mores of the area as a greatly Jewish entity:

> Almost every Brownsville home had its *mezuzah* (protective casing which enclosed a piece of parchment with the important Prayer of 'Shemah' written upon it) in the doorway... There was always a *pushke* (charity coin box)... Even those of us who were not observant got dressed up on Saturday." (p. 129 *Nice*)
>
> Although most of their families were not observant, orthodox Jews, Brownsville girls lived amongst the orthodox culture and religious traditions. Our mothers kept kosher homes. Our fathers went to *shul* on occasional Saturdays or to say *kaddish* (the memorial prayers for the dead)... and for other, particular occasions. They always went to *shul* on the high holy days... (*The Girls*, p. 49)

The society in which they lived set standards that many young people adhered to. However, we can already see that a number of Brownsville Jews, especially younger ones, were moving away from strict observance of the many Jewish rules. Regular attendance at *shul* was one of the first things to fade; this is one of many things that set the stage for the demise of Brownsville as a

Jewish stronghold. Yet the social niceties were kept up by many, for tribal and sentimental reasons. These people for the most part identified with their culture, and it was a great part of their daily rituals.

This was not new to Jewish America. The Jewish synagogue ritual was originally what would be called Orthodox, or traditional, in nature. As Jews became more Americanized and secularized, Reform Judaism became more popular in several urban areas, experiencing great growth beginning in the 1800s. The Jewish community before the great East European migration began in the 1880s had already seen the establishment of Reform synagogues. In Brooklyn as well, what is now known as Temple Beth Elohim (the Garfield Temple) in Park Slope was at the forefront of Reform Judaism. Within a few decades, Conservative Judaism would also grow in prominence, especially with the synagogue familiarly called the Kane Street Synagogue in Cobble Hill, Brooklyn.

Most of the synagogues of Brownsville and East New York, Flatbush and Bedford-Stuyvesant were Orthodox in nature, even if not all the congregants followed rituals strictly outside of the sanctuary. Alfred Kazin and his family were examples of this trend. Some Conservative *shuls* were organized in areas near Brownsville, especially in Flatbush. Petach Tikvah on Rochester Avenue, west of the heart of Brownsville, was prominent and large. Shaari Zedek was a huge *shul* north of Crown Heights. Flatbush had Shaare Torah and Shaari Israel, among others. There was also the growth of the Young Israel, a modern Orthodox movement in Brownsville and the Prospect Park areas, as well as elsewhere. (Landesman discusses this also.)

Jewish Brooklyn had (and still has) its individuals who were staunchly observant, who resisted many of the secular aspects of life, but more and more Jews found themselves becoming further Americanized and less religious. Still, one of the most hallowed of Jewish rituals was and is the bar mitzvah, and Jewish Brooklyn reveled in these rites of passage. A light-hearted, yet very revealing rendition of a World War II-era Brooklyn bar mitzvah can be found in Richard Rosenblum's picture book, *My Bar Mitzvah*, about his own experience.

> My whole gang went to Hebrew school... None of us liked to go to another class after regular school every day, so we got into as much trouble as possible. Somehow I learned to read and write Hebrew and to prepare for my bar mitzvah." (pp. 10–11)
>
> The synagogue was filled. My friends from the block sat in the second row and made crazy faces as I read from the Torah scroll. I'd get even at their bar mitzvahs, just as some of them were already getting even with me." (p. 15)

In this book, we see Richard steeped in a life that reflected the tensions between contemporary American and older Jewish traditions. In the picture accompanying the Hebrew school classroom scene, someone wrote "N.Y. Yankees," but the team name is scratched out and "Giants" is written underneath. The boys are goofing off at (and away from) their desks. The scene is meant to be humorous, but the underlying message is clear: Judaic studies were not highly regarded by all young Jews, certainly in Brooklyn. The two-page spread illustrating Richard's bar mitzvah ceremony in the sanctuary of the synagogue shows boys making faces and several other people not paying attention to Richard's chanting of the Torah portion. (Incidentally, seating in this Brooklyn synagogue is depicted as mixed gender.) Most of the rest of the book is concerned with the party afterward, getting gifts, eating and socializing.

I do not mean to minimize the social aspects of a bar mitzvah and do not care to tar a Brooklyn bar mitzvah in particular. But the pictures and text of *My Bar Mitzvah* handily show that, for many American Jews, religion and religious tradition were big parts of life, but did not garner the utmost respect. The lures of the secular life were often greater.

With all the modern threats to Jewish religiosity, in 1941 there were "approximately 450 synagogues... distributed throughout the borough" as documented by Samuel Abelow, a New York City public high school teacher and the author of *History of Brooklyn Jewry*. Eastern Brooklyn (Brownsville and East New York) had 161 synagogues by Abelow's count, the largest concentration in Brooklyn. (Borough Park and the rest of central-southwestern Brooklyn had 93, the second largest amount.) Central Brooklyn in two areas had 76 synagogues, and Williamsburg had 63. It is important to note these numbers because they would change within a few decades. The number in eastern and central Brooklyn would plummet to a handful, while southern Brooklyn would see a rise in the amount of synagogues.

✧ ✧ ✧ ✧ ✧ ✧

The march of time would see the dissolution of Jewish Brownsville arrive for a host of reasons. For "at its height, Jewish Brownsville harbored a vibrant and diverse community, with a full complement of institutions and organizations..." (*Jews of Brooklyn,* p. 41)

"Having moved earlier to neighborhoods of Brooklyn to escape the crowding of their first American habitations, many Jews in the post World Ward II period found themselves prosperous enough to contemplate larger accommodations... and the optimism of fresh habitations." (*Jews of Brooklyn,* p. 14)

Jews who had more money typically wanted to move to more spacious and prestigious housing in less cramped neighborhoods, as well as the burgeoning nearby suburbs. These Jews were not alone in their desires for nicer living conditions. The story of the United States features a stream of people who moved or wanted to move, for their many reasons.

"The Jewish movement out of the neighborhood, which had begun as early as the 1930s accelerated in the 1950s and, especially, the 1960s as Jews fled an influx of African Americans. By 1968, only 5000 Jews remained in (Brownsville), most of them elderly." (*Jews of Brooklyn,* p. 43)

This is the more discomforting factor in the discussion of why Jews left Brownsville, East New York, Bedford-Stuyvesant and a bit later Flatbush and East Flatbush (and later on in the 1980s and 1990s, many who left Canarsie). Yes, many Jews wanted out of their "ghetto" tenements. They wished to graduate to private homes with gardens and better schools, but many left because of fear, prejudice, group pressure, and such. Many Jews were afraid of the growing number of African Americans who moved into Brownsville and environs because of the large housing projects that the government had built. This is despite the fact that African Americans had lived in certain parts of Brownsville and Bedford-Stuyvesant for years, and Alfred Kazin writes of this in *A Walker in the City*. The Jews overall feared the "otherness" of blacks, their seeming poverty, and ingrained prejudices of many. By the early 1970s, most Jews had moved away from the people they often put down as *shvartzes*, a Yiddish word (derived from German) that literally means "blacks," but which nearly came to have the weight of "nigger" in usage.

African Americans moved in great numbers to Brownsville, East New York and Crown Heights to live in public housing as well as private. As a result, the price of the housing stock there began to change. (In some areas, especially Flatbush, blacks with more money began to buy the one- and two-family private homes, in their quest for upward mobility.) The Jewish hold on the neighborhoods waned greatly and manifested itself in several ways.

While Brownsville's black churches expanded, Brownsville synagogues continued to dwindle during the 1950s as their congregants passed on or moved out.

Urban renewal also disrupted Brownsville's religious life. The NYCHA (New York City Housing Authority) demolished two of the neighborhood's largest and most venerable synagogues, Beth Hamedrash Hagadol and Thilim Kesher Israel, to make way for public housing projects." (Pritchett, p. 39)

Synagogue closures accelerated during the late 1950s and early 1960s. Several old congregations were demolished in the expansion of the city's public housing program, while others sold their buildings to the burgeoning Baptist and other Christian congregations in the area.

When they closed, they sold their torahs and other religious materials, and their history died with their last members. Only a few of Brownsville's congregations owned their buildings. (Pritchett, p. 67)

The Jewish people could move themselves and their households away to other places, but they could not pick up and relocate their *shuls*. Most of the toteable things went elsewhere—Torah scrolls and prayer books, prayer shawls and *mezuzot*, some plaques and works of art, but much stayed in the neighborhood. The buildings that still stood were not carted off for historical preservation, as have a handful of old farm houses throughout Brooklyn such as the Lefferts Homestead that now resides in Prospect Park. The old *shuls* were not turned into museums. Many were sold; some were basically abandoned and left to deteriorate.

Friction between Jews and non-white groups was not the only reason for many Jews to move. Walter Thabit, in his study *How East New York Became a Ghetto*, documents the problems with the housing stock in East New York in particular:

Building maintenance had been neglected since the beginning of World War II; landlords continued their neglect after the war's end, complaining bitterly about New York City's rent control laws all the while.

...dissatisfied younger families began to move out of the tenements, not only to housing east of Pennsylvania Avenue but also to residences south of Linden Boulevard, to Canarsie, to Queens, and even to Long Island.

...landlords began renting to blacks and Puerto Ricans at the higher rents permitted when apartments became vacant. Some even harassed their old white tenants, getting them to move so that they could rent to blacks at higher rates. (Thabit, pp. 12–13)

Perhaps this comes as a surprise to learn that non-whites were being charged more rent for inferior housing, while whites including Jews were leaving in droves, buying houses and renting apartments elsewhere.

The Jewish community panicked; many moved south of Linden Boulevard, leaving behind abandoned synagogues and community centers. (Thabit, p. 13)

Panic is an apt description that combines the fears of violence and poverty, the fears of losing businesses and housing stock, as well as synagogues, to riots and crime that vexed Brownsville and East New York in the 1960s. These trends would show themselves somewhat later in much of Flatbush and East Flatbush, but the ethnic changes in these areas were also dramatic: almost all the Jewish people had left greater Flatbush for other areas, and many left due to "blockbusting" in which realtors played up the fears of arriving African Americans so that Jews and the other ethnic whites living there would sell their homes at lower prices just to get out. The practice was like a virus that spread so that only the older, less mobile Jewish people were to remain in greater Flatbush.

A *New York Times* article from October 1976 portrays this melancholy scene:

Like many other inner city houses of worship, the Congregation of Temple B'nai Abraham of East Flat-bush, which a decade ago attracted some 700 Jews for Yom Kippur, yesterday drew 30 devout men and women, all elderly. Their children and their friends, fearful of a changing neighborhood, have fled...

...white homeowners fled, succumbing to intense block-busting tactics.

Temple B'nai Abraham, which opened its doors in 1939, is one of a dozen moribund or dead syna-gogues in the northern part of East Flatbush, an area that was once almost exclusively Jewish. (*NYT* 10-4-76)

(Starting in the early 2000s, this building was being used by Chabad Lubavitch Jews as a site for an early childhood school.)

This departure pained many in the Jewish community. So much time and money had been invested in creating a "new Jerusalem." There were not enough remaining Jews, and not enough motivation within the greater Jewish community as a whole, to preserve the synagogues. The community went elsewhere, and it would have been very difficult to hold onto the buildings that housed the scarcely attended *shuls*.

Alter Landesman wrote at some length about this abandonment. His descriptions at times are aloof, at others deeply saddened.

Today (the late 1960s), practically all synagogues alluded to have been razed to make room for housing projects or have been converted for other uses." (Landesman, p. 211)

At another point, he refers to the mass exodus of Jews as "neighborhood changes." (p. 236) Landesman's cooler words are perhaps an attempt at being polite, or perhaps at holding at arm's length his disappointment at the vast changes he witnessed. Landesman had worked in the Jew-ish community, held important positions, and was thus also emotionally involved in this demise. He documented this not only in *Brownsville*, but in other works. He came over to the newer in-carnation of the Hebrew Educational Society in Canarsie, but he was already older and likely bit-ter about the changes and the abandonment of various synagogues.

The growing prosperity and the change in the ethnic complexion of the area prompted a wholesale exo-dus, beginning about 1960, of the remaining Jews, with the result that the Brownsville Jewish commu-nity has practically disappeared." (Landesman, p. 371)

The changes brought with them a number of problems and imposed hardships on many.... There was the vexing question of what disposition to make of the many synagogues and public institutions, the symbolic reminders of the continuity of the Jewish community. ...In some cases no effort was made to erase the religious symbols and insignia before surrendering ownership.

There was the problem of disposing of the assets of these institutions. Without an overall communal body authorized to submit and enforce suggestions in such situations, each group was left to its own devices in arriving at a decision." (Landesman, p. 372)

In a hurry to leave, there were many leftover loose ends, a sizable mess with economic and re-ligious implications. The less fortunate were left with very little, and others inherited headaches of a legal nature.

Years later it is hard to know which synagogues of Brownsville, East New York, and surround-ing precincts were flat-out abandoned. Determining which were dissolved neatly is also a Hercu-lean task. I have found records and documentation for a few of the old *shuls*. It should be noted that many of the smaller *shuls*, in particular, did not generate a great deal of archival material. This could reflect their more modest aspirations and budgets. Perhaps some of the larger syna-gogues that had more money and more Americanized and better educated congregants gener-ated more archival material, such as *shul* Bulletins, minutes for various committees, and such. It is also difficult to know who may have inherited any surviving materials, although the Internet makes it easier for people to let others know of their archival, nostalgic holdings.

Wendell Pritchett writes of how "Shomrei Emanuei and Anshe Dokshitz (an alternate spelling for Alfred Kazin's *shul*) each sold their buildings to local agents for $10,000 in the early 1960s." (Pritchett, p. 168) This occurred in many cases; the leaders of many *shuls* sold their buildings, if they owned them, to real estate agents. In at least one case, a former *shul* and Talmud Torah were absorbed into the Board of Education system and became a school. As Landesman discusses, the issue of closing up shop for a *shul* was a complicated one.

> The sale of synagogues to Christian churches violated Jewish doctrines and was criticized by many religious Jews. Brownsville was not the only area witnessing racial transition in the early 1960s, and the Union of Orthodox Rabbis made a formal statement condemning the transfer of Jewish religious institutions. But these critics offered no alternatives." (Pritchett, p 168)
>
> But Brownsville Jews realized that what one rabbi called the 'transparent subterfuge' of selling to an agent did not resolve the moral issue." (Pritchett, p. 169)

It was no secret that many of the former *shuls* were being turned into churches. While a few became day care centers, community centers, a psychiatric center, and such (one former *shul* and Talmud Torah, in a different Brooklyn neighborhood, became an antiques store and then years later a wine bar) most that still stood became churches. Pritchett points out that despite the criticism that synagogue leaders faced, they typically had little recourse. If they abandoned their buildings, they could become churches anyway, bought at city auction.

There were congregations that went to court to formally dissolve. The 73 pages of the 1968 New York Supreme Court Appellate Division Record on Appeal booklet for the Congregation House of Abraham, which met at 113 Bristol Street in Brownsville spell out the legalities of dividing up the assets of the *shul*, many pertaining to burial plots and funds in general. It stated that after dispersing assets to remaining members and their families, whatever was left over would be given to charity. Amidst the requisite dry legalese, one gets little sense of whatever vitality the congregation once had, but at least this was a clean way to deal with a dormant *shul*. According to Robert Hammer, who was the Assistant Attorney General who worked on the Congregation House of Abraham case, such dissolutions were not atypical.

Closing the doors on a *shul* in Brooklyn was a mournful task, and some even performed religious rituals for closing down.

Thus, with a sigh, Alter Landesman concludes his volume on Brownsville with this:

> For legions of Jews who have spent some time of their lives here, Brownsville is still a fresh and vibrant memory. For other it is a palpitating, heroic story of intrepid (mostly) East-European Jewish immigrants and their children..." (Landesman, p. 375)

This could be stated about Brownsville and East New York, as well as the greater Flatbush region, Jewish Bedford-Stuyvesant, and other nearby areas. This memory is bound to fade even though it has been documented by a number of writers and artists.

✡ ✡ ✡ ✡ ✡ ✡

What happened in various neighborhoods in Brooklyn also occurred, and still occurs, in a number of other parts of New York City, the United States, and around the world. Parts of the Bronx, Manhattan, Queens and Brooklyn had *shuls* that died out and became converted houses of worship. Certainly many East and Central European synagogues closed down and were even vandalized, in Russia, Germany, Romania, Poland, and elsewhere. In the Middle East, synagogues were abandoned when Jews left *en masse*. Even in South America and the Caribbean, synagogues have closed down and been turned into other entities. In some cases, the congregations sell their buildings and move elsewhere.

Among recent examples of this phenomenon are:

> The leaders of a faltering Conservative synagogue in Minnesota have been considering a proposal to sell their sanctuary to a messianic congregation that promotes Jewish worship of Jesus. The synagogue, Shaarei Chesed Congregation, an aging religious community with 110 families, is weighing a $2 million offer from the Seed of Abraham Messianic Congregation." (*Forward,* October 2004)
>
> With membership fading and revenue dwindling, leaders of the Rego Park Jewish Center view a pending deal to sell their property to a developer for more than $8 million—while allowing the congregation to continue—as the best hope for the future. But a contingent of opponents is working to scuttle the deal..." (*Jewish Week,* June 2004)
>
> Synagogue for sale down South: Congregation Beth Israel in Clarksdale, Mississippi—once home to the largest Jewish congregation in the state—is up for sale. More than 100 former congregants and their families came to pay their respects to the Reform Synagogue." (*Kesher Talk,* September 2003)

There was a newspaper article about an Egyptian synagogue that had so few members that it was weighing its options for closing, and a documentary, *Synagogue For Sale*, about a Koszeg, Hungarian *shul* that was nearing its end. (Geller-Varga)

✧ ✧ ✧ ✧ ✧ ✧

To botch an addled adage, you can take the congregation out of the neighborhood, but you can not take the neighborhood away. In Brooklyn, as in other places, Jews can remove themselves *en masse*, and take the portable pieces of religious life with them to the next desirable sites. But something lingers and waits to be discovered by another generation.

At the end of January 2007, I was assigned to teach at a middle school in Bedford-Stuyvesant, on Gates Avenue at Stuyvesant Avenue. As I drove to and from work each day, using a few different routes, I would pass several ex-*shuls* in East Flatbush, Brownsville, and other neighborhoods. I came to view them as "old friends," old by age and friends by religious and geographical ties. They were on Rochester Avenue, Saratoga Avenue, Howard Avenue, East 49th Street, Kings Highway, Blake Avenue....

Near the end of the term, I asked some students if they went to churches that had once been Jewish synagogues. Two boys, Branden and Marcus, thought so. It turned out that Branden went to a large church, Upper Room, on Vernon Avenue that had been a synagogue many years earlier—and it had originally been a church!

In late August 2007, I took a teaching assignment for a few months at a new alternative learning center (suspension school) in an elementary school on Christopher Avenue, between Glenmore and Liberty Avenues. Again, my route to work took me past a number of ex-*shuls* as well as the ghosts of old *shuls* torn down. The school building at 51 Christopher Avenue was near an old and gone *shul* at 65 Christopher Avenue, as well as another at 135 Glenmore. Where both once were situated now stood a large public housing project. Later on when I taught at a public high school on Broadway, at the border between Bedford-Stuyvesant and Bushwick, I passed certain ex-*shuls* that I had become quite familiar with.

That is perhaps the saddest aspect of this project—going to the location of an ex-*shul* and realizing that it is completely gone. Sometimes even the address is gone, swallowed by a bigger construction that absorbed its plot number. Too often that happens in cities, especially in New York City; one day we realize that a building we once knew of is gone, and there is virtually nothing there to recall it. Unless we find archival photographs or peruse an old telephone directory, there may little to pin a memory on. When you are in the midst of a historical search, this becomes ever more bittersweet, even frustrating. There are businesses in New York City that salvage bits and pieces of torn-down buildings; I have looked inside some of their showrooms over the years. I certainly wish that more could have been salvaged from these ex-*shuls* and other Jewish institutions. Or was there much of anything to be salvaged from some of them, if they were already in such poor shape?

In the end, only God knows.

The Synagogue—Its Historical Development, Evolution in America and Especially Brooklyn

What is a synagogue? A Jewish house of worship and study. The evolution of the synagogue throughout history and the American imprints on this hallowed institution are crucial to the discussion about Brooklyn ex-*shuls*. To provide background, I will focus on the development of synagogues, their roles in the community and how they have expanded, and touch upon the architecture and decoration as well.

The New York City Municipal Archives houses many sources pertinent for research on Brooklyn's ex-*shuls*. Among them is the *Desk Atlas for the Borough of Brooklyn*. Within the 1929 *Atlas,* there is mapped evidence of the ex-*shuls*. There were a few, alongside designations for schools, parks, hospitals, large churches, factories, and dairies. With lists of Brooklyn synagogues in hand, I located a few sizable synagogues such as Shaare Torah of Flatbush (at the time on Bedford Avenue) and the Elton Street *shul* in East New York.

There was a time before Brooklyn *shuls*, indeed, before the establishment of any synagogues. Preceding the invention of the synagogue, there were the holy Temples of Jerusalem that are commemorated in various Jewish prayers and on holidays. A prominent example of this is read during the daytime on Yom Kippur: the Order of the Service of the High Priest in the Temple. Jews read about such things as the water of purification, the incense, the special linen garments, and the always remarkable account of the scapegoat. (I consulted my grandparents' 1928 printing by the Hebrew Publishing Co. for this English translation.)

As to the exalted Temple itself:

> The greatest of all temples was the one King Solomon built in Jerusalem ca. 955. B.C. In ca. 620 B.C., it became the central sanctuary of Judaism... In 586 B.C., the Babylonians invaded Jerusalem, destroyed Solomon's Temple, and carried away many of the city's inhabitants to the Euphrates Valley." (Krinsky, p. 5)
>
> When the Jews were allowed to return to their homeland in the late sixth century B.C., they built a more modest Temple in Jerusalem. (Soon came the) time of priestly ascendancy when there was little room for religious institutions to develop in competition with the Temple.
>
> Whatever the date of its origins, the synagogue developed markedly after A.D. 70. In that year, the Romans destroyed the Temple of Jerusalem which had been reconstructed under Herod the Great beginning in 20 B.C." (Krinsky, p. 6)

The temples had been central sites to which Jews would make pilgrimages. The many styles of prayer services that would develop later on were not present yet in the formats known today. There were many types of offerings, entailing the presentation and sacrifice of livestock and plants. There is debate about what songs or chants or musical instruments may have been involved, and the services were very different from those conducted now, or even hundreds of years ago. It was a very different atmosphere, a set of rituals that are for the most part only read about and imagined today.

So what did the earliest synagogues look like? When did Jews start to designate such buildings? And why do we use the Greek word "synagogue" or the Spanish word "sinagoga"? Simply, the Torah does not have a word for it. Synagogue is derived "from the Greek *synagein*, to bring together." (Krinsky, p. 5)

> Basically both Jewish and Christian scholars have taken one of three positions: that the synagogue originated in the (1) exilic (i.e., during the Babylonian captivity in the sixth century B.C.), (2) pre-exilic,

or (3) post-exilic period. The place of origin ranges from ancient Judaea to Babylonia, Egypt, and Palestine." (Gutmann, p. 72)

There is also a rabbinic viewpoint that the creation of the synagogue many stem from the time of Moses or even before. (Gutmann, p. 72)

The mystery that shrouds the origins of the synagogue may seem in line with the ever-present custom for Jews to debate and speculate, based upon many sources, and come up with no definite date and place, but several possibilities. It is certain that after the destruction of the Temples, Jews still had the Torah and the desire to pray and convene with each other for prayer and study.

> Wherever (Jews) went, the Torah went with them and made a holy place of whatever room the congregation met in.
> According to the Talmud, wherever ten adult male Jews live—a *minyan*—a synagogue must be founded. It can be a private dwelling. (Mirsky, p. 105)

Private prayer is a positive experience, but group prayer is a wider goal. For study and communal prayer reasons, spaces must be designated as synagogues, be they grand or modest. Even in modern times there are congregations that are very small and housed in simple sites, even homes. The traditional requirement is to have a group of ten males with which to conduct prayers, especially to recite the *kaddish* prayer and certain other benedictions.

> The choices made in building synagogues can reveal much about the realities and the aspirations of Jewish communities at different times and in different places... (Gruber, p. 13)
> In the post-Temple period, however, Jews have lavished attention on synagogues when opportunity allowed. The size and architecture of many synagogues are intended to suggest permanence, even though the facts of Jewish history have instead made most synagogues temporary. Centuries of oppression in Europe and prosperity in the United States have both led to the abandonment and destruction of thousands of synagogues. (Gruber, p. 17)

The above statement sums up the fate of many a synagogue I have seen as both a tourist overseas and as a resident of Brooklyn. In Europe I have seen a number of older synagogues, in Amsterdam, Berlin, Prague and elsewhere that may not feature religious services anymore, but are still used by the Jewish community as museums and historical sites. In Brooklyn (and the Bronx, Detroit, and elsewhere in the United States), you will find a number of synagogues no longer used for Jewish prayers nor used as Jewish museums, but for Christian congregations—or for no prayerful purpose at all.

> A synagogue in ruins may be used only for certain secular purposes, because some sanctity remains associated with it. Ideally, the ruins would be left untouched, with wild grass and weeds growing to arouse compassion in the viewer. (Krinsky, p. 10)

There are European and Middle Eastern synagogues that, in the 1800s and 1900s, were bombed and vandalized and desecrated in other ways during pogroms and riots, wartime battles, and through sheer neglect. In their unrestored states, these ex-*shuls* evoke melancholic feelings in Jews and non-Jewish sympathizers. In Brooklyn the ex-*shuls* of several neighborhoods were plagued by vandalism at times, but more frequently by poor maintenance and a lack of funding for repairs.

Synagogues, whether bare-bones or lavish in style, have an ark (which could be a simple wardrobe or a skillfully crafted structure) for the Torah or multiple Torahs. Often there is a landing with which to approach the ark. Depending upon the denomination of the congregation, as well as the ethnic identity of the group, the seating arrangements may vary as well as the stage set-up for Torah readers, the cantor, the rabbi, the honorees of the service, the congregational leaders. It is important to note that due to the nomadic background of the earliest Jews, "they never developed an architectural style" (Mirsky, p. 105) that was specifically Jewish in designation. Certainly there have been trends in *shul* fashions, but more typically the identifying markers of a synagogue have been decorative symbols and place-signs.

> Religious symbols are among the objects that produce emotional reactions in their observers (make them feel secure, hopeful, etc.) (Smith in Gutmann, p. 194)

The obvious and usual symbolic markers for a Jewish synagogue include the Magen David, the six-pointed Jewish star; the Decalogue/Ten Commandments tablets (with Hebrew letters or without, or with numbers); menorahs; lions (the Lions of Judah); and of course Hebrew writing. The Hebrew letters can be on a painted sign; chiseled into stone; on metal carved pieces that are attached to a wall, entrance, gate, or door. Also quite common are cornerstones that reveal a Jewish time-frame: the number of the secular year and the Hebrew year as well (in Latin numerals or in Hebrew letters, which do have numerical value). An example of this type of decorative marker can be seen at the former Temple Sinai, which is now a church, on Arlington Avenue near Highland Park—"1920" and "5760" (as well as the Hebrew letter equivalents) are on the cornerstone.

Of course, for many Jews, especially past congregants and rabbis, it now seems strange, jarring, and more than bittersweet to see these religious symbols and to feel their emotional tug, when realizing that a particular synagogue is moribund and the building is instead a church or a day care center. Its identity has been blurred, it causes confusion; but it can also lead to a history lesson, a religious discussion.

✿ ✿ ✿ ✿ ✿ ✿

Synagogues (and to some extent ex-synagogues) can be found throughout the United States. The earliest synagogue was founded in New Amsterdam. Shearith Israel, the Spanish and Portuguese Synagogue, is no longer on downtown Mill Street (and Mill Street in Manhattan is no longer with us either), but has for a long time resided on Central Park West in the Upper West Side neighborhood. It is not only a working synagogue, but also a landmark of Jewish history, not just American Jewish history. (In 1996, while working on a doctorate degree in history, I visited the archives at Shearith Israel. I donned gloves and handled colonial-era real estate documents about New Amsterdam and New York Jewish life.)

The number of synagogues throughout the United States was small but grew during the later 1800s. The trend would soon change in the later decades of that century:

> With the rapid increase in immigration, synagogues on New York's Lower East Side proliferated, and the competition between them became keen. It expressed itself in ever 'grander' synagogues and ever more costly imported 'star *hazzonim*'(cantors)...
> Moshe Weinberger, in his *Jews and Judaism in New York*, estimates that there were 130 Orthodox congregations on the Lower East Side in 1887." (Karp, pp. 14–15 in the American Synagogue)

A book about Brooklyn synagogues must offer substantial acknowledgement of Manhattan Jewish life, especially that of the fabled Lower East Side. The growth and changes in both areas have many similarities; many old synagogues on the Lower East Side are now ex-*shuls* that have become churches, community centers, or art institutions. A couple of very old synagogues have been or are in the process of being restored. The Eldridge Street Synagogue is the most famous;

it still hosted religious services as well as lectures, tours and the like while being structurally shored up, painted, and polished and is now also a communal center which hosts lectures and concerts.

A number of Jews who had lived on the Lower East Side migrated to Brownsville, Flatbush and other parts of Brooklyn especially after World War One and built or joined synagogues there. Jews were heavily concentrated in these and other urban areas for a number of reasons.

> In many northern cities in the United States, but primarily among them New York, voluntary Jewish ghettoes were established. These were urban areas where an observant Jewish life could be lived." (Zucker, p. 3)

Thus, on the Lower East Side, Brownsville, then Flatbush and Borough Park and later the Five Towns region of Long Island's Nassau County, many Jews could opt to live amongst their brethren so as to feel more comfortable and make ready use of the accoutrements of Jewish life, from synagogues to kosher butchers, from Jewish-run hospitals to Jewish places of culture and entertainment. Jews did move to small towns even in the 1800s, but many tended to gravitate toward urban areas (and later, the adjacent suburbs).

The functions of a synagogue and the people who constituted the congregation therein certainly focused on prayer, marking the weekly Sabbath and holidays, daily prayers, and life-cycle ceremonies such as births, bar and bat mitzvahs, weddings and memorial services (although not the actual funeral services). In Brooklyn as in other areas, the *shuls* either helped set up cemeteries (as did Shearith Israel—its three earliest cemeteries can easily be found in lower Manhattan) or purchased plots of grave sites for their members. (Fraternal and benevolent groups known usually as *landsmanshaftn* also were involved in this.) In Brooklyn and nearby Queens and Staten Island (as well as the Long Island suburbs and nearby New Jersey) there are a number of Jewish cemeteries with sections that had been bought by such groups.

In the older ones especially (or the older sections), one finds gates that identify various *shuls* and fraternal groups that have their members buried in that section. At Washington Cemetery near Gravesend (Brooklyn) or Acacia near Jamaica, Queens, or Montefiore in Springfield Gardens, Queens, or certainly Beth David in Elmont, Nassau County, you will find the gates and pillars erected by many congregations—and many of those no longer exist as such. You can learn many things about the old *shuls*, including where they were located (addresses are sometimes engraved on the pillars or wrought in ironwork on the actual gates), the names of founding members of these old *shuls*, and more.

Synagogues have not just focused on the afterlife. Many *shuls,* including the ones in Brooklyn, had schools for children (especially after-school and weekend programs), informal learning for the adults, lectures and appeals for charitable causes. Brooklyn had many a Talmud Torah for the youth that contained a synagogue within its walls. One of the most acclaimed (and long gone) was the Stone Avenue Talmud Torah. Stone Avenue too is gone—it has been known for years as Mother Gaston Boulevard.

As to the actual buildings themselves, there were some larger *shuls* in these parts of Brooklyn as well as many smaller ones. A handful were remarkable, even opulent sites; some were fairly large and had notable decoration; many others were modest and by the time of the Great Depression some were pretty weathered. A few were tiny and could easily be overlooked, as if they were but summer cottages gussied up for religious rites.

There were many aspects of these old synagogues to assess. Among these were plot and building size; height of building; the color of brick, stone or wood (although in some cases this has been changed from the original design); Judaic symbols and writing on the front and sides; the designs, symbols and the placement of such upon staircases, gates, doors and doorways; attached buildings (typically school buildings or catering halls); placement on streets (corner or midblock, attached, detached or semi-detached, with or without a driveway, gardens); side street or avenue or larger (boulevard or parkway); and if possible, the layout and decoration of the interior. I also became interested in the recent tax assessments of the buildings, to learn various things about the ex-*shuls*—and especially the recently declared values of the buildings. The New York City Department of Finance website makes this information available through the "building, block and lot" designations.

These different aspects of a *shul* can reveal, to some extent, how wealthy the congregants were then, compared to other nearby congregations. There were trends in building styles and decoration to scrutinize. Perhaps competition existed amongst congregations in how they presented their *shuls*, because there were so many in certain neighborhoods. Many Jews who wished to pray regularly, or who had to fulfill a *kaddish* requirement for a deceased relative, would just go to the closest *shul*, or the one where they knew their kin or neighbors from the old country; but as time wore on, more and more Jews gravitated to other *shuls* in order to go to fancier sites or to hear a celebrated cantor or rabbi, or opt for a variance on the service (Conservative, Young Israel). Of course, as years went by and attendance began to slip in most of these *shuls*, some would have tried to attract congregants in more overt ways, with certain features. (Bingo Night ended up being one of these ways...)

Who designed these old *shuls*? I have been curious to learn this and at first had difficulty with this task. Initially I found the names of architects for only a small fraction of the buildings, and these were among the more opulent. I hoped to find out about synagogue architects in a few ways: *From Abyssinian to Zion*, by David Dunlap, discusses every house of worship in Manhattan, including those which no longer exist but had some kind of documentation. Dunlap lists the architects for some Manhattan *shuls* and ex-*shuls*, so I garnered names from there. After Googling the names of the architects of Manhattan *shuls*, I found very few listed, official connections for Brooklyn *shuls*. The WPA study on houses of worship did not include more than a few architects for synagogues. There were a small number of notable Jewish architects working in the late 1800s and early 1900s (there are more now), but I had been stymied in my search for the architects of the vast majority of these buildings—until I met with Ann Friedman of the New York Landmarks Conservancy. Workers at the Conservancy were able to unearth the names of more architects by combing through construction records and also matching up the plans for a few *shuls*.

There certainly are stylistic similarities between many of these ex-*shuls* in Brooklyn. I will discuss generalities among these below and with individual entries describing them.

Size is an obvious factor in discussing the many ex-*shuls*. Sizes vary quite a bit from those little bigger than bungalows to large buildings that take up almost a whole side of a city block. The largest of the Brooklyn synagogues, even dating from the 1920s, could be categorized as "synagogue-centers." A catchy phrase describing these was "*shul* with a pool." (It is also the title of an interesting study by David Kaufman. His book explores the historical development of these *shuls* which also function(ed) as community centers.) Indeed, some of these institutions had the niceties that are often associated with suburban synagogues—pools and gyms with locker rooms and showers, large catering halls with dance floors, libraries and several classrooms, rooms for musical rehearsal, board rooms and separate cloakrooms.

> Most of these large complexes were created in the economic boom years of the 1920s. With the coming of hard times, many hardly functioned before they were forced to close. Changing demographics and Jewish settlement patterns meant that many of these expensive centers were not revived when times got better, but were sold for non-Jewish use. (p. 81 Gruber)

A prime example of this in the heart of Brooklyn was the enormous Shaari Zedek. Even today, inside and out, it is an awe-inspiring structure. The sanctuary is cavernous. There are so many rooms in the building. Many of the founders of the synagogue, who had built another impressive synagogue previous to this one, were well-off and devised a quite Americanized Conservative *shul*, but its heyday was short and it is now a church. In contrast, another very large synagogue complex built in Brooklyn around the same time, the East Midwood Jewish Center, is still a vibrant Conservative synagogue. The difference is their neighborhoods. East Midwood along with its surrounding neighborhoods is still heavily Jewish, whereas the Shaari Zedek neighborhood has hardly any Jews living close by. It almost seems cruel that the fate of such a large *shul*, with its sizable investment in money and time, was determined not by what it offered but where it was offered.

Another celebrated Brooklyn synagogue-center was the Brooklyn Jewish Center, situated in a beautiful, spacious building on Eastern Parkway in Crown Heights. It was one of Brooklyn's premier Conservative Jewish synagogues of the early to middle 1900s. It still stands, with some modifications, but now serves the Chabad Lubavitch Hasidic Jewish community. Thus it is not an ex-*shul*, but a somewhat changed *shul*. Several blocks west and on the same side of Eastern Parkway is the Union Temple, one of the most important Reform synagogue-centers in Brooklyn and of New York City in general. Designed by the architect Arnold Brunner and built in the early 1920s, it sold off its parking lot and now its next-door-neighbor is a luxury apartment building designed by the architect Richard Meier.

What do the Brooklyn ex-*shuls* look like, as well as still-extant older *shuls*? Pre-World War II buildings do have different styles than those from the 1950s onward. (There are even a couple of post-World War II synagogues that have become ex-*shuls*.)

> American synagogue architecture until World War II mostly followed American Christian architecture, but specific influences from European synagogues have also been felt. (Gruber, p. 24)

> Architectural history is an ideal demonstration of the difficulty—if not impossibility—of separating Jewish worship from osmotic influences. (Whitfield in Biale, p. 1117)

There was no particular standard for synagogues in Brooklyn nor for anywhere else in the United States, at any point in American history, however, certain trends can be detected, beyond the use of Jewish stars and Ten Commandment plaques out front. For the most part, the styles of the buildings reflected society at large. American synagogues run the gamut in styles, as do Brooklyn *shuls*.

Due to the nomadic nature of Jewry, historically, synagogue fashions have been varied and reflect the larger society. In Brooklyn, physical space was a major determining factor. Many of the synagogues, older and more recent, have a boxy shape, and most are closely flanked by other buildings. The wide-open-spaces feel of suburban and exurban synagogues, typically surrounded by large lawns (even woods), parking lots, playgrounds and fountains, is rarely achieved in Brooklyn or only on a modest scale. Brooklyn's synagogues are for the most part closely hemmed in by other real estate. Even those that are located on corners are limited in their physical scope.

Most *shuls* and ex-*shuls* in Brooklyn are one-, two- or three- story buildings and cover lots that are the near-equivalents of one or two homes.

The Department of Finance of New York City provides an easy way to find out the specifications of buildings, including houses of worship, through its website. The actual lot sizes and building sizes of the ex-*shuls* vary quite a bit. Many of the buildings have irregular sizes, with fractional measurements. I have included a special section later in the book in which I examine these figures more closely; here I will offer some generalities. I found a few ex-*shuls* that were on small lots, 25x100 feet or 20x100 feet in lot size. Others were over 150x100 feet in lot size. (Among the largest were 100x194 feet and 150.33x130 feet.)

While there were general groupings in lot size, building size varied dramatically. No two former synagogues had the same building sizes, although some were near each other. There were tiny ex-*shuls* that were 20x38 feet or 20x45 feet; mid-sized ex-*shuls* that were 50x86 feet, 40x100 feet, or 65x97 feet; and large ex-*shuls* standing at 150x94 feet and 88x182.42 feet. Compared to many suburban synagogues these buildings are small. Builders of ex-*shuls* made do with what they could find and afford. If they wanted to build in congested areas such as Brownsville, they may not have had all that much choice, especially with modest budgets. As with most urban settings, builders aimed upward to generate more space, and many ex-*shuls* were just renovated homes, especially two-family abodes.

As far as architectural detail and general style, there were ex-*shuls* that resembled little more than the modified two-story detached houses they started as, but many congregations did build synagogue buildings from scratch. Others took over older synagogue buildings or vacant church buildings. These buildings often utilized one or more identifiable categories of architecture.

An invaluable and enjoyable book that helped me with this research pursuit is *Identifying American Architecture, A Pictorial Guide to Styles and Terms 1600–1945*, by John J.-G. Blumenson. As illustrated in Blumenson's book, the two styles that are most clearly identified with many of the old and ex-*shuls* of Brooklyn are Romanesque Revival and Neo-Classicism. The highlight of buildings in this style is "the semi-circular arch for window and door openings." (Blumenson) Many of the older *shuls* and ex-*shuls* I have identified in Brooklyn have these windows, and some have doors decorated in this style, as well as arched decorations of varying heights and widths on the fronts and sides. Often these buildings show a blend of stylistic components, because many were built after the heyday of Romanesque Revival. There are also some churches in Brooklyn that have this appearance: St. Brendan's, a Roman Catholic church in the Midwood section, has many examples of the semi-circular arch.

The neo-classical style, "based on primarily the Greek and to a lesser extent the Roman architectural orders" (Blumenson) is easily characterized by pillars and porticos in the front of the buildings. There are a good number of ex-*shuls* in Brooklyn that have these features. As well, there are several pre-World War II churches in Brooklyn that could be described as Neo-classical.

I could boil it down to two most recognizable non-religious features: the old synagogues with semi-circular arches and the old synagogues with the porticos, the stately triangles at the entrances of the old synagogues. Then of course, many of the ex-shuls have been modified when converted into churches, so these features (especially the semi-circular arches) have been changed—for instance, bricked over, or a large sign hung in front of the features so that they are difficult to spot. A number of ex-shuls were just boxy, fairly plain buildings with minor adornments, such as some stained glass windows, small Hebrew symbols, or types of trim and brick patterns. These buildings do not reflect a major architectural style other than Basic Urban Dwelling, early 1900s. I do not state this to be snide, but rather to be frank. The Neo-Classical style is found on a number of the bigger (and biggest) of the ex-shuls. That was the trend, especially during the 1910s and 1920s, when most of these ex-shuls were constructed. Some ex-shuls look like banks, serious and weighty in overall feel.

Many of Brooklyn's old synagogues have been preserved by being recycled; however, in this process, all the buildings have undergone changes to some extent. From the outside, some still look like synagogues for the most part, with signs discretely posted heralding the different religion now on the premises. Some of these ex-shuls are an odd mixture of both Judaic and Christian decoration. Some retain virtually no reminders of the Jewish past, or the few that remain are difficult to find and only detectable by those who are acutely aware of Jewish culture and signifiers.

Sadly, there is only one synagogue in all of Brooklyn that has been landmarked by the New York City Landmarks Preservation Commission, the Magen David Synagogue at 2017 67th Street in Bensonhurst. There are at least ten Manhattan synagogues that have been landmarked, including several from the Lower East Side. One old synagogue in Manhattan had its status revoked and the building, the Mt. Neboh Synagogue (earlier known as the Unity Synagogue) of the Upper West Side, was knocked down. Many people protested this unfortunate series of events.

There are more than a dozen Brooklyn churches that have been landmarked, and they are located in several neighborhoods around the borough. I am puzzled as to why more synagogues have not been landmarked in Brooklyn, although there is often controversy surrounding the campaigns to landmark any buildings, including houses of worship. The landmark designation places limits on how to modernize and change buildings. Typically there are factions in favor of and against the process of landmarking. and many old, handsome buildings do not qualify for various reasons.

While I researched and visited several of the ex-shuls, some current parishioners asked me about landmarking and grants to restore and repair their buildings. It was pleasing to hear that there are people who want to fix up these buildings for historical and community reasons, however, many of these buildings, because they have been altered so greatly, no longer qualify for landmarking at the very least. While there are charitable foundations that are working to restore old shuls and even ex-shuls in Central and Eastern Europe, there is less interest in the United States. The Sacred Sites program of the New York Landmarks Conservancy, a non-sectarian group, is working toward certain restorations, however. Churches often have their individual buildings fund campaigns, but there is no major Jewish group now or yet that has earmarked funds toward restoring these old synagogues or working with Christian groups and congregations to do this. Obviously there are many old (and not so old) functioning synagogues that need money for fixing up their buildings, and economic concerns and the vagaries of the financial markets also affect how much money can be offered for their refurbishing. Quite bluntly, tough choices have to be made. Who gets funds and who deserves funding is a troubling issue.

Brooklyn's ex-shuls, as viewed today, can be utilitarian or lavish, in very nice condition or pathetic shape, retain a great deal of their past appearance or are severely changed. I will describe many of them in this book, along with pictures. This book is your armchair guide. Perhaps later you will pass by and see for yourself the rich history that can still be experienced.

Shaari Israel:
An In-Depth Study of an Ex-Shul of Brooklyn

Most of the synagogues described in this book have not left significant paper trails. We will never know how many minutes from meetings are lost; how many congregational bulletins are gone; or even the whereabouts of all the prayer books and *tallisim* (prayer shawls), nor the various decorative items such as the curtains on the Holy Ark, the frayed fabric Torah covers, the doorway *mezuzot*. The list of lost is endless; this is something that the Jewish people have dealt with for so long, when we consider how many lives and items, both mundane and important, have been lost to us through war and anti-Semitic acts, and also through neglect and conditions of poverty and the inevitable process of aging.

On occasion I found the locations for selected items from a few of ex-*shuls*. One transplanted Brooklynite in Arizona e-mailed me and wrote that he has a ceremonial loving cup from his grandmother, which she received from her (ex)*shul*. My mother had an abridged pocket-sized *siddur* (prayer book) with a white cover that she received from Kesser Torah, her childhood *shul*. These and similar items that people possess now can bring these ex-*shuls* to life, ever so briefly, by triggering memories, or at least offering glimpses of an older time.

Shaari Israel is an ex-*shul* with wonderful, brimming archives—boxes of documents of various types, photographs and mementoes. They can be accessed at the Jewish Theological Seminary in

Manhattan simply by making an appointment to view them. Samples of this archive can be seen on the Internet. This treasure trove helps Shaari Israel and its story stand out in a way that few other ex-*shuls* of Brooklyn will ever be able to.

Shaari Israel was a Conservative synagogue in East Flatbush, on East 49th Street and Avenue D. It is now a Pentecostal church, with a sizable yard adjacent to it. It is one block away from a vibrant commercial strip on Utica Avenue. It was, and still is, a smart-looking and well-maintained building of brick and sandstone accents, with pretty windows.

The reason that there is even an archive to turn to is because of careful planning by the final rabbi of the *shul*, Rabbi Abraham Feldbin. Rabbi Feldbin had been the rabbi during two different periods of the *shul*'s duration, including the decline. After it closed the Rabbi pooled together many items ranging from the regularly published Bulletins, architectural plans, the Golden Book, sisterhood meeting minutes, a junior congregation felt patch, photographs of a parade, and much more. He did a thorough job of arranging the material and then donated it all to the Jewish Theological Seminary (JTS) making it available for viewing in a section of their research library.

Briefly, this congregation was founded in May 1929. For nearly two years they met in storefronts. The building was finished and dedicated in May 1931. In 1932 Shaari Israel joined the United Synagogue of America, the Conservative movement in the United States. The heyday of the *shul* was in the early 1960s as far as membership and Hebrew School registration, but for a number of reasons, this *shul* would soon experience trouble, much of it due to demographic changes. Eventually the congregation closed down and the building was sold in 1991, however, Rabbi Feldbin arranged for a Masorti, or Israeli-Conservative synagogue, to become its sister congregation in Jerusalem. The memorial tablets and other important religious ritual items were transferred to the Holy Land. This was the rare occasion of a dormant Brooklyn synagogue being reborn in another, Israeli congregation. (There is at least one other, and it will be described in a later chapter.)

In July 2007, I visited the synagogue's archive at the Jewish Theological Seminary. I will describe several of the items and documents I found not in any particular order. The dates will jump around somewhat, but one still gets quite a feel for the life of the synagogue and its congregants, on different levels.

Document 1

> 806–810 East 49th Street
> between Avenue D - Foster Avenue
> Dear Friend:
> You are most cordially invited to attend
> THE CORNERSTONE CEREMONY
> to be held at
> Our New Synagogue Building
> at the above address on
> Sunday, September Seventh, 1930
> at 2 P.M.
> We promise you a most interesting time
> Sincerely yours,
> Congregation Shaari Israel of Brooklyn
> Prominent Speakers will be present
> Music by the Pride of Judea Orphan Asylum
>   Band"

This program was signed by 15 people; I assume they were all members of the *shul*. They include the treasurer, the recording secretary, the vice president, and the publications director.

Shaari Israel had been started not long before and had met locally while the building was constructed. Here was the proud, momentous opening ceremony. The hard work and sacrifice paid off and here was their new home for worship, however, this ceremony had to be overshadowed by the murky economic time during which it took place. The stock market crash had occurred less than a year earlier. Each member must have been affected by the turn of events.

I am struck by the phrase "We promise you a most interesting time," because that sounds like an awkward attempt at humor, opting for an off-hand comment. Why not a more impressive phrase, a more inspiring or religiously oriented sentence, even a famous quote from scripture or a well-known Jewish scholar? I have wondered if this was typical of the time, just as mock-ironic commentary has been so common in the 1990s and early 2000s.

The Pride of Judea Orphan Asylum was located in Brownsville-East New York. It was a well-regarded institution, and alumni have banded together over the years for reunions. They even maintain a website.

Document 2

> No. 111
> Bond (6% interest)
> 10 Dollars
> (August 28, 1929)
> No. 112" (and a handful others)

These bonds were of the same issue and a consecutive run of numbers. It was a way for the congregation to raise money for the building of their *shul*. These bonds were issued a little more than a year before the Cornerstone Ceremony described above.

Document 3

> GOLDEN BOOK
> Congregation Shaari Israel
> of
> Brooklyn
> May 24, 1931
> Dedication of Synagogue
> In Honor Of
> (about thirty families and individuals listed)
> Purchaser of the Key
> (with a hand-drawn skeleton key)
> A. Levey
> 738 East 32 Street, Brooklyn
> (Phone Number BU4-8804)"

This large, heavy book became the depository of much of Shaari Israel's history, some of it crucial, much of it unextraordinary. It holds congregational information and names for the duration of the *shul*'s existence.

I noted the hand-drawn illustration of the key. It was a light-hearted, cute touch. I wonder if A. Levey noted in the document drew it, but Levey did not live too close to Shaari Israel; his address is somewhat south of the congregation, near Brooklyn College. I do not know, obviously, how often Levey went to Shaari Israel or why Levey went here instead of a nearer Conservative *shul*, such as the East Midwood Jewish Center (perhaps relatives or friends attended Shaari Israel). People who attend Orthodox *shuls* tend to live close to their chosen *shuls*, as they often did in Brownsville (for convenience sake, but also due to certain religious restrictions about how far one can travel on the Sabbath); but people who attend Conservative *shuls* (as well as Reform, Reconstructionist, and others) take upon fewer religious restraints and often come from a distance to attend their *shul*. They may travel by car or public transportation to be at a particular synagogue.

Note the phone number with its two-letter exchange. "BU" stood for Buckminster. When I was a little girl in the 1960s and my family attended Shaare Torah (another area ex-*shul*), our phone number was BU4-8029. Some things you cannot forget.

Document 4

p. 133

(1951–1952)

Dear Friend:

We urge, for the sake of your family and the dignity of the religious services, that all of the men who are to be called to the Torah on the day of your son's Bar Mitzvah, "brush up" on the blessings beforehand. Otherwise, ignorance and errors cause embarrassment to all concerned and is a reflection on the family of the Bar Mitzvah.

Enclosed are several copies of instructions and the Torah blessings. Please see that the members of your family who may need "brushing up," get copies. The undersigned will be happy to give any further assistance necessary.

Sincerely yours,

Abraham I. Feldbin

Rabbi

This letter is poignant, although at the time and even now some people would find it to be an affront and a scold. Although this might not occur often in an Orthodox *shul*, in Conservative and Reform synagogues I have seen people given an *aliyah*—the calling up to read from the Torah—and make mistakes during the recitation. Even in the 1950s, this must have been a problem as more and more Jews became Americanized and less familiar with regular rituals of the synagogue service. Rabbi Feldbin had to tread a fine line in urging men to be fluent with the Hebrew blessings, and he stressed the social aspects of such a *faux pas*.

Mispronunciation would not be merely a social gaffe, but also a religious error. So the Rabbi's suggestions and tutorial would be common sense moves, as well as indicative of how mid-century American Jews had to be reached so that they would comply with religious instructions.

Document 5

Dear Member,

You are cordially invited to attend our annual Jewish National Fund Breakfast on November 28, 1971, at which time Shaari Israel will honor our own Rabbi and Betty Feldbin with a forest of 10,000 trees to be planted in Israel and which will be known as the
'Rabbi and Mrs. Abraham I. Feldbin' Forest.

It was 25 years ago that Rabbi Feldbin and Betty first came to Shaari Israel, so in a way we will be celebrating their silver anniversary...

Sincerely yours,

Sol Laurentz, President

Shuls in Brooklyn and everywhere have often involved themselves in raising funds for various Jewish causes, and certainly the State of Israel and its many needs are of paramount concern to many congregations in the Diaspora. The Jewish National Fund, or JNF, has been and still is a particular favorite cause for many Jews. Shaari Israel joined the crowd by participating in buying trees and in making bulk tree-purchases in commemoration of a person or persons.

Israel figured highly to this congregation (and not just by dint of its name) because the Rabbi also led congregational excursions to Israel in 1974 and 1977; the notices for these tours are also in the Golden Book of Shaari Israel.

It should be noted that by the 1970s many other Brooklyn *shuls* in Brownsville, East New York, and elsewhere had already folded or were in the process of doing so; therefore, they would not have been able to be involved in such things as group pilgrimages to Israel. Many of these *shuls* were starting their declines as the modern state of Israel, established in 1948, was just starting to flourish. The growth of suburbs and Jews in American suburbia, as well as the modern incarnation of Israel, took off around the same time; while the reshuffling of urban Jewry and the rise of Hebrew to greater prominence, as opposed to the Eastern European Yiddish, was also set in motion. Sunrise, sunset.

Document 6

The account book shows its last few dues entries, in 1991, for members William Bogatz, Marvin Fishman, and a few others. Shaari Israel managed to stay alive longer than most of the other surrounding *shuls*. Nearby B'nai Abraham had gone under in the late 1970s; Shaare Torah on Albemarle Road had merged with the East Midwood Jewish Center in 1979; but Shaari Israel soldiered on. Other documents will reveal some of the issues pertinent to this. These last members showed their loyalty, their respect.

What motivated them to stay around? Where were they planning to go next?

Document 7

Yorke Construction Corporation
200 West 34th Street
New York, NY
LO3-1231

November 4, 1963
re: Alteration and addition to Building

810 East 49th Street, Brooklyn"
(Several pieces of correspondence in the early-mid 1960s about the proposed addition, renovation, air conditioning, heat, and other mechanicals)

The congregation had big plans to build an addition to their site. A lot of time and effort was put into the groundwork, but it came to naught. Instead of an expansion they undertook renovations and upgrading.

These technical documents may be mundane, but there is something melancholic about how the congregation dreamt of bigger things and then did not go through with them. Did it just cost too much, or were congregants looking around at other Brooklyn neighborhoods to realize that the Jewish population of Flatbush and East Flatbush would soon go the way of Brownsville? We know now that this was to be, but at the time perhaps the Jews living comfortably in Flatbush thought that their congregation would be okay, that enough people would not flee to the suburbs or other parts of the borough, and hasten the decline of even this *shul*. In retrospect, they probably did the right thing by not expanding; also, they had just started constructing their building when the Great Depression hit. Sadly, this *shul* did not always have the best of timing as far as large societal changes.

Document 8

A black-and-white photograph, 8"x10", showing boys in a color guard marching south on East 49th Street, past Shaari Israel. The view is looking northwest, across and slightly south of the *shul* building.

This shows part of the groundbreaking ceremony in 1963 and the attendant fanfare arranged for the day. The building at the time had a large Jewish star, a Magen David on the front of the building, and Hebrew writing paired with Ten Commandments tablets chiseled in the stone. These decorations are now gone from the building.

Document 9

Ground-Breaking Ceremonies
for the
NEW BUILDING OF
Congregation Shaari Israel

The program, which goes along with the above photograph as artifacts of this auspicious day in Shaari Israel's history, is dated April 21, 1963. Edna Kelly spoke. Representative Emmanuel Celler was supposed to speak, but took ill.

Document 10

Progress Shaari Israel 1963
(booklet with drawing of proposed original building and expansion)

Handwritten on the cover: "This was projected but never materialized beyond groundbreaking ceremonies." No name is attached to this pithy statement which coolly deflates the potential, the dream that this congregation had of increasing its physical plant. I wonder how the congregants felt about the cancellation of this major project. Sadness? Disappointment? Embarrassment about making a fuss but not seeing it through? Relief that the money would not be spent? What factors influenced this decision not to build again?

On page 7 of this booklet it says, "Shaari Israel now offers you the opportunity to enlarge your circle with a new building in which you will be able to take justifiable and memorable pride. This new edifice, looking to your comfort, will give new meaning to your prayers while attending services..." There was no indication how much money was pledged and for which particulars. This situation reminds me not of a divorce but of a broken engagement. There was a match made, a plan on the drawing board (literally), but then it was cut short. How many other ex-*shuls* of Brooklyn were ever in situations such as this, where the congregation had big plans which never materialized. Or were many of the ex-*shuls* so much more modest in their dreaming and planning? Was this more the thinking of the middle-class neighborhood of East Flatbush rather than the poorer people who tended to be in Brownsville and East New York?

Document 11

The Sisterhood
Second Annual Dinner-Dance
De Luxe Palace
December 31st, 1930
Officers 1930

Bessie Meiselas
President
Suzette Berman
First Vice President
Estelle Bauer
Second Vice President"
(etc.)

This is printed on the cover (silver with blue writing) and on the second page of the booklet that was distributed at the Sisterhood Dance, a New Year's Eve soiree. Here is Shaari Israel on the cusp of both its young life as a congregation as well as one reckoning with the effects of the Great Depression. How many other synagogues in Brooklyn, both gone and still in existence, were devastated by the Depression? Undoubtedly many were, some to a greater extent than others.

The dinner-dance booklet has several advertisement pages, for Ebingers, Lundy Brothers, Tobias Goldstone—"our architect"—and more. Brooklynites of a certain age (myself included) remember Ebingers with glee, with sighs. They were a chain of local bakeries featuring sweet standbys such as the Blackout Cake, Ladyfingers (spongy pastries which I adored as a young child), and more. I am friendly with a woman who grew up in the "Ebingers House," a beautiful and slightly unusual home in the Ditmas Park area, which was once owned by someone in the Ebinger clan.

Lundy Brothers: Lundy's was an institution as a seafood restaurant, on Emmons Avenue in Sheepshead Bay, which had a successful run for many years, then floundered, then made a comeback and then stalled again. Incidentally, Lundy's was not a kosher restaurant, but I suppose that some Shaari Israel congregants went there and ate, perhaps avoiding the outright non-kosher foods such as lobster and shrimp. Still, someone sold them a Lundy's ad for this journal and it is printed here. I was grateful for the ad about Mr. Goldstone, as this is how I found out who designed this building.

Document 12

The following was typed, with handwritten notes in red ink, and deposited in the Golden Book.
"1968–69" was written in ink atop the page, but it seems incomplete, as judged by the language:

> (to us) against all the other inducements offered to them (by other organizations). It takes money: And in the only way we can (continue to) keep open is to run a Bingo game. Or would you be happier to (see our) Temple (closed) or close the Talmud Torah where we have less students all the time, because our people are getting older. (or cut out other important Jewish activities) Remember we do not operate in a community (with) only one Temple, (there's another one across the street.) Even our membership dues have to be kept to a minimum to keep and not to lose (our) members.
>
> (We hope) you get our point of view. I believe you may see our position in a different light. It is bingo that keeps this Temple open and provides all the best services to keep ours an honest to goodness Jewish community.
>
> Our membership believes wholeheartedly in the conservative Jewish movement, in the Liberal Jewish ideas as developed (by) your organization, but there must be exceptions provided for, when the situation warrants it.
> Sincerely yours,"

This has to be one of the most touching documents I encountered in this archive. The tone of desperation, the sense of frustration, the assessment of the financial problems facing Shaari Torah, the sense of competition with another *shul* (Jewish Center of Hyde Park) are laid bare. I could not decipher who wrote this, and the first page was missing. Who penned this? To whom was it addressed—the rabbi, the *shul* president, more than a few people? Would bingo really help the congregation limp along, if not thrive, for a few more years? The *shul* stayed open a little more than twenty years after this letter was written.

The writer lays out some of the issues facing Shaari Israel at this crucial time: fewer young people, more older people (reflecting the changing demographics of the neighborhood—this was the time of real estate "block-busting," of low-bidding and racially motivated fear-mongering to make sales), competition from the *shul* across the street (which today operates as a special education facility for Orthodox Jewish children), how much to charge for dues without driving away members. In hindsight it is easy to see that this congregation was starting to decline. What were the congregants, active and less so, to do? Pump more money and effort into maintainance? Face harsh realities and jump ship to a more vibrant *shul* and community? Many *shuls* faced this, others still do, and throughout New York City as well as the greater United States: how to deal with economic difficulties and shrinking populations? Some congregations may have gone out with a whimper, but this group put up some fights.

✿ ✿ ✿ ✿ ✿ ✿

The next few documents are excerpted from the Bulletins published by the congregation. Regular bulletins which list events, issue community announcements, and provide a forum for the rabbi and other notables in the congregation are a fine source of information when researching a house of worship. Sadly, I do not know how many other ex-*shuls* of Brooklyn have left such a written legacy. Many of them may not have even printed and distributed such written materials.

Shaari Israel regularly mailed out their Bulletin—at times it was monthly, sometimes more frequent, toward the end less so.

Document 13

> p. 2
> September 1945
> Elul-Tishri 5705
> Meet Rabbi Englander...
> Library

> "We have installed a lending library in our reception room, and solicit contributions of books of general Jewish interests as donations to this library..." p. 4
> "As of March 1st, 1945, it has been revealed that more than 8,200 American Jewish men have received citations and decorations for valor in combat and meritorious service against their foe. Among these are 78 Jewish men who each have to their credit, ten or more awards for heroism."

Among the carefully dated and classified things we can learn about Shaari Torah is that there was a meet-and-greet with Rabbi Harold Englander, that establishing an on-site library was a project engaging some members, and that everyone still thought about World War II. The patriotic, straight-forward tone of this page 4 announcement would be meant to bolster support for the War and especially for the Jewish contribution to the war effort.

Document 14

> October 1945
> Tishri-Heshvan 5706
> Talmud Torah
> Release Time Classes
> Release time classes will be held in our synagogue building this year as in the past...

"Release Time" basically covers off-site religious instruction for public school students, who are permitted to leave school early once a week for this education. I had only known it to apply to Roman Catholic students in my own grades, while the Jewish children who went to Hebrew School or Talmud Torah would get instruction on Sundays and after the public school day ended. Release Time was on Wednesdays in my part of Brooklyn for the children to go to Our Lady Help of Christians and St. Rose of Lima—and apparently for a basic Jewish education at Shaari Israel. In the 2000s there are other Jewish programs (the Lubavitcher have conducted programs for Release Time in recent years), so it is somewhat more equitable.

Document 15

> November 1945
> Heshvan-Kislev 5706
> LATE
> FRIDAY NIGHT SERVICES
> OUR ANNUAL
> ARMISTICE DAY services will be the opening service of our season. This will be held jointly with the Kings County Council Jewish War Veterans of America.
> All are welcome
> November 9, 1945
> 8:30 PM

Orthodox synagogues have their Friday night, Erev Shabbat services without fanfare (and as long as the legal quorum of ten men, a *minyan*, is met). Many Conservative and Reform synagogues do not hold regular Friday night services, and when they do there is often a theme or special event that acts as a focal point for the occasion. Thus Shaari Israel made their special late Friday night service a patriotic event in this post-World War II time. Perhaps that night (or other Friday nights) there were regular, lower-key services, but this was a special event linked with an organization, and they made a point of announcing it as "the opening service of our season."

Document 16

> February 1947
> Shevat-Adar 5707 page 3
> That Lynne Kaufman, daughter of Mr. and Mrs. Nathan Gelfer, became a mother with the arrival of baby Caryn Beth. Would like to see Nat pushing the baby carriage along Clarendon Road some sunny afternoon. Mazel Tov.

This was one of several listings in that month's "Did You Know" column, the social announcements installment of the regular Bulletin. The style of this offering, as well as others, has a chummy, humorous tone, with a bit of sticking-it-to-you ("pushing the baby carriage"). Instantly, I conjured up an image of some middle-aged Jewish man pushing a baby carriage on this street in East Flatbush, with a look of mingled pride and sheepish obligation.

In general, the Bulletins of synagogues are forums for *kvelling*, for offering congratulations to members and joining together in good cheer for the births of children and grandchildren (and great-grandchildren) as well as graduations, bar and bat mitzvah ceremonies, weddings, and various honors of a professional and social nature.

For all we know, Lynne Kaufman herself may be a grandmother now! Perhaps she still has a copy of this Bulletin to refer back to.

Document 17

> September 1962
> Elul 5722
> CALLING ALL GIRLS! (with drawing of a girl)
> Well, not all girls, really. We're primarily calling those of 8 and 9 years of age with no previous religious schooling. Our Girls' Session (Bas Mitzvah) department is ready and willing to serve them.
> Bas Mitzvah girls in Shaari Israel have a 4-year curriculum. ...Upon graduation, they take part in a most beautiful Bas Mitzvah service.
> ...Register her now for our Girls' Session department!"

I have admiration for Shaari Israel and this endeavor. This was a progressive move on their part, to reach out to girls without Hebrew schooling and entice them (or their parents, at the very least) to enroll the girls in a specially designed program. I do not know how it differed from the regular Hebrew school package, in comparison to what the boys were learning.

I went to an afterschool/Sunday Hebrew school program (called the Talmud Torah at the East Midwood Jewish Center) from second grade through the end of twelfth, but knew that several of my girlfriends did not go to Hebrew school, even when their brothers did so. I was glad that my parents considered it worthwhile for me to go to Hebrew school, and when I petitioned for a bat mitzvah ceremony, my folks agreed to it. As well, my mother and her older sister went to Hebrew school, but they were even more the exception to the rule in their time.

Shaari Israel showed that it was a forward-thinking congregation. This was more typical of Conservative synagogues, but a number of the Brooklyn afterschool programs (Hebrew, Yiddish, and others) at the time did include girls.

Document 18

> June 1963
> Sivan-Tammuz 5723
> Please check your home for skull caps which you are not using and return them to the synagogue."

A touching, pithy reminder that synagogues need their *kipot* returned to them. This typically happened by accident, where a culprit would exit with the borrowed cap still atop his head. The cost of replenishing the stock of spare *kipot* may not be the most obvious expense of a *shul*, but it exists.

Document 19

> June 1968
> Sivan-Tammuz 5728
> From the Rabbi's Study (a four-paragraph essay from Rabbi Fenichel)
> There is no doubt that the young people of today are in a state of revolt against what they term the
> establishment. It has been found that many of these young 'revolutionists' are students attending col-
> lege far away from home...

Rabbi Fenichel was warning parents and grandparents about the perils of letting kids go away to college. They might buck the system, including organized religion. Perhaps he preferred to see a Jewish college-aged child attend nearby Brooklyn College rather than UC Berkeley or Kent State. (Would he quibble with Harvard or Princeton?)

This essay was written when there were many changes, often quite frightening, happening in American society. Many Brooklyn *shuls* were closing or had recently closed; issues of race, generational mores, poverty, the Vietnam War, and other foreign affairs all presented a challenge for an urban synagogue that was just trying to survive, and even thrive, beyond thirty-plus years. Likely enticements for young Jews at this time (and a threat to synagogue attendance) typically were Eastern religions and meditation, which seemed so much more hip to many young Jews (although the Havurah movement and Jewish meditation, among other trends, were also then becoming popular with some young Jews). I think that many "establishment" Jews who were frightened by and angered by Eastern religions and cults tended to forget that in years past, a number of Jews instead opted for Christian dominations, especially to get ahead economically and socially.

This was the final glossy, large-size Bulletin issued by Shaari Israel. After this they downsized, and switched from slick magazine stock to off-set printing and smaller pages. This had to be an economizing move. Undoubtedly finances and congregational size were already starting to diminish, and the Bulletin manifested these woebegone trends. No wonder Rabbi Fenichel railed against out-of-town colleges and revolutionary youth, but what about the middle-aged parents who were flocking to the suburbs or other Brooklyn neighborhoods, thus changing the sizes of these congregations? "White flight" was a bigger factor in the slow demise of Shaari Israel and so many other Brooklyn *shuls*.

Document 20

> September 1, 1977
> 18 Elul 5737
> School for Converts
> The first session of the Onkelos School for Judaism, the Brooklyn Rabbinical Assembly School for
> Converts will be held on Tuesday evening, October 11th.
> For details call Rabbi Feldbin.

Who was to attend this School for Converts—people engaged to marry Jews, who wished to convert before the wedding? People who just wandered by and became interested in Shaari Israel? African American Christians in the neighborhood? Brooklyn College or Pratt Institute students? In any event, the school had a tie to Shaari Israel. The synagogue thus had some interest in being inclusive—perhaps it would keep the congregation going a little longer.

Document 21

May-June 1990
Iyar-Sivan 5750 page 2
Sharing a Thought
Rabbi Abraham I. Feldbin
(final paragraph) This Bulletin, dated May-June is the last of the current Jewish year. What or where we will be next year, or even tomorrow, only God knows. May we enjoy the privilege and opportunity to perform *mitzvot* and be blessed with the means, time and energy to do so much good that we will be pleased with ourselves and 'find favor in the eyes of God and Man.' page 3
President's Message
We're approaching the summer and, as with any Congregation, certain activities slow down. But we're still planning for the future. You've received enough mail to know that we have problems and are working on solutions. But we will go on as best we can."

This final Bulletin of Shaari Israel dealt frankly but politely with the coming of the end. Rabbi Feldbin wrote an essay that filled up most of page 2, which I excerpted. He is bidding farewell in a calm fashion. Even if they could eke out a few more months, everyone knew that the congregation was going to close, the building would be sold, the congregants would be moving on to other synagogues. Certainly, this is a sad set of circumstances; demographics, economics, and various other practicalities are sounding the death knell for a place that many of the congregants were certainly fond of. Routines would be disrupted; friendships would wane; questions would abound regarding how to deal with the building, the holy items within it, any debts and other issues. Might as well as go out in a positive way, while crying inside.

Warren Parbus was the *shul* president at the time. I excerpted his final message also. He strikes a somewhat different note from the Rabbi. He dares to mention "future" in the same paragraph as "problems." Was he more optimistic? Did he feel he needed to say this in print, while privately realizing the futility of doing so?

This collection of documents helps to make vivid the life of this congregation, from its earliest days brimming with promise to the uncertainty and defeat of the end. It is difficult to find a way to tell the story of a congregation without such materials as those in this archive. It is hard to tell how typical or mundane was the Shaari Israel experience, compared to the many other Brooklyn ex-*shuls*. I selected only a few documents. I particularly enjoyed reading through the Bulletins, comparing their entries to the Bulletin from my own synagogue and other contemporary *shuls*. If only the walls and floors of these former *shuls* could talk; if only there were more people who held onto items from these ex-*shuls*; if only more active documentation had taken place at the time. Certainly the WPA (Works Progress Administration) survey acts as one of the most important documents of Brooklyn *shuls,* but this only whets the appetite for more primary sources, more true memorabilia.

Rabbi Feldbin wrote a book, *Reflections Are Not Shadows*, and part of his book deals with Shaari Israel. Thank you again, Rabbi Feldbin, for having the foresight to amass these items for the JTS archive and for donating them to this esteemed facility. If only more old congregations had leaders or members who had thought to do this, this book would be even richer with insights. Perhaps the stories of ex-*shuls* would have been even more varied. We would have all benefitted from these sources. A note to all active congregations: maintain your archives, so that future generations may learn from them.

Pleading With History:
Memories of Brooklyn's Ex-*Shuls*

In Fred Gorman's book, *The Secret City*, which features "Woodlawn Cemetery and the Buried History of New York" he writes, "We're all pleading with history, begging not to be forgotten." (Gorman, p. 157). This is debatable; there are people who wish to be forgotten, overlooked, who do not actively pursue a route toward immortality, but most people hope to be remembered, by family and friends, by professional colleagues, by fans and neighbors.

Jews stress this desire and need to be remembered; it is proscribed in commandments and customs. Many Jews want their names and accomplishments to be remembered through the yearly *yahrzeit* traditions, by having their names inscribed upon tombstones and synagogue plaques and metal plates in synagogues.

What happens to the long-gone Jews who attended Brooklyn's ex-*shuls*? How are they remembered? Is this now the sole responsibility of the extended families? (Pity the bachelor and spinster.) Who will drop by an ex-*shul* on Elton Street in East New York, now a Seventh Day Adventist church, and spy their great-uncle's name? Who will visit a former synagogue on Newport Street in Brownsville and recognize their grandmother's name on a plaque commemorating the Women's Auxiliary? How many people do not remember exactly which *shul* they went to as youngsters, other than that it was *zayde's shul* (grandpa's synagogue) and that's what they called it? How many young adults even know where their great-grandparents *davened* (prayed) in Brooklyn?

I thought about this throughout explorations in these neighborhoods, my actual visits inside several ex-*shuls*, and cemetery visits where I was able to locate the burial plots and gates of certain ex-*shuls*. The Christians who attend the churches that are now housed in the ex-*shuls* rarely can read Hebrew, and for the most part they have little idea of what they can glean from the plaques and inscriptions found in these buildings. Some may surmise these are lists of names, honors of some sort, dates and events described, but it is largely untapped information for the Christian congregants. Likewise, very few knowledgeable Jews enter these buildings, for their many reasons, and thus cannot let the world know of the information to be found, the history that is still present within the walls.

Many people may have begged not to be forgotten, but they are overlooked, their essence in a dormant state. I assume that many Christian congregants realize that significant keys to the past are held within these walls, a past that is quite different from their own, but they notice it only in passing while they are walking to their seats, or to a committee meeting, or to a book shelf. Just as people often overlook the ads in the subway cars as they take seats or overlook street vendors on the city sidewalks unless necessary, these congregants often have only a passing interest in the Hebrew writing and symbols gracing the ex-*shuls*. Perhaps they think about it here and there, during a lull in their Sunday morning service or Thursday evening Bible study session. I don't fault them; the Hebrew letters have become a familiar part of their landscape; they're used to them. But sometimes the Christians do become curious about their surroundings, and they may trace with their fingers the carved-out lettering or peer at the orphaned *Ner Tamid*, eternal light, or an oft-painted-over *mezuzah* that still guards a doorway.

These are compelling reasons to explore these ex-*shuls*, and for some Jews to see them and take pictures, outside and inside. This is a way to attempt a reconnection with these pasts, to be reacquainted with some old names, to explain a few things to the Adventist or Baptist or Church of God faithful who have an interest in their surroundings.

The initial reason for my interest in photographing and then conducting research about Brooklyn's ex-*shuls* is, as I mentioned earlier, because I attended one as a child. Shaare Torah, on East 21st Street at Albemarle Road (the southeast corner) was my first synagogue. My earliest memory dates from preschool. My father and I were at a morning service in the *bet hamidrash*, not the main sanctuary. I recall shelves of books around us. I would stand up when the other congregants would stand up, sit down when they did. I held a prayer book in my hands; I felt mature. Then a man (not my father) took the book from my hands, then put it back in them right side up. I was a bit surprised or embarrassed, but it is a fond memory. I do recall going to services with my father at other times.

One time when I was older, I was at Shaare Torah with my mother and my brother. I wore a pretty checked jacket with a black velvet collar. In retrospect, this must have been the holiday of *Simhat Torah*, Rejoicing in the Torah, the holiday when Jews finish reading the Torah and start all over again for the year. We were outside the *shul*, standing on the corner and even in the road, waving paper flags and eating apples (typical rituals for children on *Simhat Torah*). There was singing and many people milled about. I was excited about standing in the road with no cars chasing us out of the way.

I have other, vaguer memories of Shaare Torah. I think I was there once for a Hanukah candle lighting ceremony. I recall the red carpeting on the floors. My father has more detailed, extensive memories of this synagogue:

> We *davened* (prayed) in the basement—that's where the *bais midrash* was. I only went upstairs for the Friday *mincha-maariv* (afternoon-evening) service. I went for saying *kaddish* (memorial prayer for a deceased close member of the family). I started saying *kaddish* for my father." (My grandfather Louis, or Eliezer in Hebrew, died November 1963, when President John F. Kennedy was assassinated.)
>
> Saturdays and Sundays I went to the *bais midrash* for the early *minyan*. After (the period of time for saying) *kaddish* was over we'd go on Sunday mornings. I took you (meaning me) a couple times. One time I gave you scotch (whiskey) and told you it was ginger ale.
>
> I even remember some black people coming in, to give *tzedakah* (money for charity). I remember this guy Meyer Pike who opened up the *shul,* and I remember this guy Levine. He was a butcher; he had a store somewhere on (nearby) Nostrand Avenue. He was a very nice man, he *davened* nicely, an exceptionally nice person.

I had heard that Levine helped give me my Hebrew name (arguably a Yiddish name) of Elka. He had asked my father what my English name was when I was a newborn. "Then he asked me what my father's name was in Hebrew, and that was it." Eliezer, who had died just a few months prior to my birth, inspired my name of Elka. This is an Ashkenazic, or Eastern-Central European custom, to name a child after a deceased relative.

My dad also remembered "a guy named Wagner. He was a lawyer and a book publisher; he was a nice guy. He called me 'Didi' after my Hebrew name, Yedidyah."

Going on, my father mentioned that the rabbi officiating at Shaare Torah when we first started was "Rabbi Miller, but he passed away before we moved. Then Rabbi Kreitman came from Brooklyn Jewish Center on Eastern Parkway."

I find it interesting that my father remembered specific people, and not just events, when speaking of Shaare Torah. It really is the people, the congregants, who make a synagogue come alive, not just the building. Probably someone could recall the major physical aspects of a *shul*, and major events that he or she attended at the *shul*, as well as the rabbi or *hazzan* (cantor) who officiated. Would congregants also remember their fellow congregants? I am glad that my father could also recall some of the personalities there.

At Shaare Torah, my father started his pattern of attending early services, typically more intimate settings because fewer people want to get up early. But some congregants are devotees of the early *minyan* service because they also get out earlier, and like my father, they are early risers.

Rabbi Joseph Miller was the rabbi at Shaare Torah for over forty years. The Jewish Theological Seminary has a collection of his papers in its archives; a set of his sermons in English, Hebrew and Yiddish; as well as notes for his sermons and lectures; and a few letters. He was ordained at the JTS. He died in 1967, and a family member gave these materials to the JTS collection.

Other people mentioned Rabbi Kreitman to me, in relation to Shaare Torah, and they have fond memories of him at the pulpit. Rabbi Benjamin Kreitman is a well-known rabbi (and his daughter is also a rabbi) who had been at the Brooklyn Jewish Center, which was a major Conservative synagogue in Crown Heights on Eastern Parkway. He then officiated at Shaare Torah. I have not focused much attention on the Brooklyn Jewish Center even though it has great importance in the Conservative movement and in Brooklyn Conservative Judaism: it is not an ex-*shul*. As I noted earlier, this beautiful building changed hands and became not a church, but a Chabad Lubavitch school and synagogue. Although there have been stylistic changes made, it still stands as a Jewish house of worship and not a Christian church.

Another person who recalled Shaare Torah is Lester S., a retiree who attended activities at the Kings Bay YM-YWHA in Sheepshead Bay. He had fond memories of Shaare Torah, but they were on somewhat different features of the *shul*:

> I was not that active; my wife was more active there. I remember Rabbi Kreitman. The *shul* had a beautiful catering facility, nice affairs. On Rosh Hashanah they had a ballroom, and they'd sell tickets for seats to people who were not members. That service was lead by Rabbi Trainin who was active in the bikur cholim (a type of group devoted to caring for sick and infirm Jews).
>
> It was a beautiful facility. My cousin had a catered affair there. There were beautiful apartments in that area. We were there for the service on Yom Kippur when Rabbi Kreitman made an announcement, that Israel was being attacked—in 1973. Everybody gasped when they heard.

The catered affair held a particular place in Lester's memory; some *shuls* are esteemed for their halls and food. Small *shuls* might have had just a small social space and not much of a kitchen, if any. (Although *shuls* that were originally homes, converted into houses of worship, would probably have functioning *kitchens* on site.) Shaari Israel also had a well-regarded hall for affairs.

The memory of the Yom Kippur War is poignant and specific. Memories of catered affairs can blend into one another; but news of the outbreak of a war, especially one in Israel, are especially timely and chilling for the congregation at a *shul*. People often remember where they were when they heard about central events in history. The Yom Kippur War is tied to that holiday always, for many Jews.

✿ ✿ ✿ ✿ ✿ ✿

In January 1971, my family and I moved to a house a few miles southward, and we no longer attended Shaare Torah. We attended the East Midwood Jewish Center, less than two blocks away. The Hebrew School entrance was even closer, because it was on the side street. East Midwood would play a very large role in my childhood: I went there for Hebrew school, religious services, Girl Scouting, Young Judaea youth group, swimming in the pool, sports in the gym, and various special events. Regrettably, we never revisited Shaare Torah, as far as I can recall. Occasionally, we did drive by if we went to shop in certain Flatbush area stores (especially Macy's Flatbush and later Sears) or if we went to Prospect Park or the Brooklyn Botanic Gardens. It was just a block away from our usual Ocean Avenue northbound route. I would quickly glimpse it from the car window. It looked the same from the outside.

I realized in the late 1990s that I had not seen Shaare Torah for some time. I asked my parents what had become of it; one of them said, "I think it became a church." Back then I was not so familiar with this changing of the religious guard, except for two other *shul*-to-church switches I had noticed. On my birthday in 1999, I took that fateful drive (with my parents' car) through my old neighborhood of Flatbush. Little did I know at the time that I was embarking upon the first leg of a fascinating, lengthy mission of research. This journey would last for years, as I became more interested and further devoted to the cause of documenting the many ex-*shuls* in Kings County, New York.

✿ ✿ ✿ ✿ ✿ ✿

On that day, I also took pictures of the former Kesser Torah, the ex-*shul* that my mother and aunt had attended. Unfortunately, I have not come across other people besides them who have memories of this congregation. Whereas some people knew Shaare Torah quite well (I even spoke with a woman my age, Molly, who had gone there as a child and had pleasant memories of going there for services) and could provide me with commentary on that site, only my mother and aunt seemed to have experienced Kesser Torah at any length, and I did make a point of asking many of the people I interviewed if they had familiarity with this *shul*.

Both Mom and my aunt Miriam went for Hebrew School classes at Kesser Torah. They also went to a Jewish summer sleep-away camp, Shomria, part of the HaShomer HaTzair movement. We never went into Kesser Torah when I was young, and I do not recall driving by and having my mother point it out. I think she knew that it had become a church (in the late 1960s) and didn't have the stomach to go look at it in its different state. I had to ask her, when I was an adult, where it was. She was reluctant to tell me and not interested in driving there, even though it was not far from our home in Midwood and was a block away from Sears Flatbush.

✿ ✿ ✿ ✿ ✿ ✿

Another case was that of Prospect Park Jewish Center on Ocean Avenue. I have passed that building hundreds of times in my life, because it is on the way to places I have frequented: the Brooklyn Botanic Garden, the Brooklyn Museum of Art, Prospect Park itself, and various other attractions and northward neighborhoods. I distinctly remember this building as a synagogue. I realized at some point that it had become a church known as the Jan Hus Church, but I still saw a few relics of its Jewish past including a Jewish star high above the entrance. In the mid-late 1990s, I looked, blinked, and realized that the Judaica had been removed or covered over. Several people I know were familiar with the synagogue and then its change, because of its easily seen location. As I conducted more and more interviews and widened my pool of interviewees, I found several people who had connections to this old congregation.

✿ ✿ ✿ ✿ ✿ ✿

Thus these ex-*shuls* and a handful of others constituted the first group that drove my interest in the topic. I have found so many more, and this chapter features the memories many people have of these old, long-gone congregations of Brooklyn.

Most people I interviewed in this capacity have been in their 50s through their 90s, however, I have found younger people who do remember a few ex-*shuls*, especially one located in Canarsie on East 96th Street. This particular ex-*shul*, known popularly as Kevelson's, became a church in the early 2000s. There are people who were born in the 1960s and 1970s who attended this *shul*. Canarsie still had a large Jewish population in the 1980s; many of these families had relocated earlier from Brownsville and other areas, migrating southward. Many of these families, in turn, moved out of Canarsie, and some of the synagogues closed and changed religious hands. Canarsie, however, still has a Jewish community, though reduced in size, and there are a few active synagogues (a few Sephardic synagogues, a Reform congregation on Rockaway Parkway, and others).

In the fall of 2006, I worked at a secondary school in Park Slope and spoke with one of the paraprofessionals, a man named Ivan who grew up in Canarsie and had gone for many years to Kevelson's. He told me that he was very fond of the *shul* and had sung in a choir there. My friend Jen who is ten years my junior, grew up in Canarsie; although she usually went to a different synagogue in the East 80s, she knew of Kevelson's because of its presence in the neighborhood and had gone a few times.

My friend Mindy knew Kevelson's very well. Here are her memories of it:

> That was my grandparents' *shul*, my father's parents—my Grandma Nettie and Grandpa Nat, before the whole *mishpachah* (family) moved from Canarsie to Brighton Beach. I have fond memories of going to Kevelson's (that's what we called the *shul*) on Rosh Hashanah when we would go to my grandparents for the holiday meal. I'm also proud to say that my Grandpa Nat designed the signs that were used in the *shul*. He was very artistic, so he painted their signs.
>
> It was a traditional Orthodox *shul* in Canarsie. My grandparents lived on East 93rd Street near Avenue K in Canarsie, so Kevelson's was only a couple of blocks away. I also remember my Cousin Steven's Bar Mitzvah was there. Most sentimental for our family is my grandparents' 50th wedding anniversary celebration that was held there. I was in high school at the time, and I remember I had just started playing the flute a year or two before their party, so in honor of their anniversary I played '*Sim Shalom*' (a common prayer) on the flute at the party. It was quite a celebration—a catered affair with a live band and my grandparents surrounded by family and friends, including their *chevra* (community) from Kevelson's.

Mindy has very fond memories of this ex-*shul*, and it was significant to her family. Many people I have talked to about their old, ex-shuls for the most part have positive memories of their experiences there. Time may make things seem rosier than they really were, but I have been struck by the positive feedback many people have had about these ex-*shuls* because in the American Jewish literary and cinematic worlds there has often been tension, even downright hostility, toward the experience of being in the synagogue, with rabbis and cantors, the prayers and rituals.

Is it that the Jews who have fond memories of these ex-*shuls* tend to be engaged in their religion and their culture, whereas those Jews who had negative memories just drop any level of observance and do not bother to send even a bitter reminiscence about their ex-*shul*?

When the ex-*shuls* get turned into churches or other institutions, some changes are usually made, and sometimes many changes are made, inside and out. There have been instances when an old *shul* in Brooklyn originally was designed to resemble a European *shul*, in furnishings or decoration. So when the ex-*shul* building is altered, a fragment of history is erased. Soon it becomes just a memory (unless someone photographed and documented it).

I interviewed two people who attended an East Flatbush *shul* that had part of the interior painted to resemble that of a European *shul*. This *shul*, Rishon L'Zion (the First of Zion, which is the name of a city in modern Israel), was located in the northeast corner of East Flatbush, minutes away from Brownsville. Today it is a church, the East Flatbush Church of God. I wrote to this congregation, as well as others in the spring of 2006, and this was one of two churches that extended a formal invitation to me. In a later chapter I will describe in greater detail my visit there, but I wish to point out now that while the Christian congregation has retained a good deal of the Judaic detail inside and outside this building, one feature they deleted was the painted interior, which they painted white.

Charlie is a life-long resident of Brooklyn who grew up in East Flatbush but now resides in Gravesend. A retired public school teacher, he provided me with interesting details about his childhood synagogue:

> It was one of the most beautiful *shuls* I had ever been in. We had another *shul* in the basement for Rosh Hashanah and Yom Kippur overflow services. During the year it was used by the Junior congregation.
>
> I had lived in East Flatbush for the first 17 years of my life. It was like the Garden of Eden. I still remember my mom, may she rest in peace, walking down to Church (Avenue) and Remsen (Avenue) to see the last lettuce and cabbage farm in Brooklyn. About ten blocks south of us, there was a poultry farm. Three blocks away there was a stable with livery horses. Along the five-mile length of Church Avenue, from Rockaway Parkway all the way to Ocean Parkway, you had every store you could think of. High class shops, restaurants, you name it. You could walk around there any time of the day or night and no one would bother you.
>
> We were the last whites in our apartment building and left only when the next door neighbor, an elderly Panamanian man with what was probably Alzheimer's, broke through my parents' bedroom wall with a hammer and was staring at them at 2:30 a.m.
>
> I had attended High Holy Day services with my father at the Rishon L'Zion, had my bar mitzvah there, and had a few close friends there. A truly beautiful synagogue. For many years, Chaskele Ritter, one of the foremost cantors, sang with his choir on the High Holy Days. In 1962 we had to move away.
>
> Years later I got married and Blanche and I moved to Bensonhurst. One Saturday morning in the fall of 1974 or 1975, I got this funny feeling in my gut that said, "Charlie, go back and get a look at that synagogue." Blanche asked me where I was going, and when I told her she said I was nuts for going there.... I ignored her, took the half-hour drive, parked the car in front of the synagogue, and went in. Most of the men whom I had known had died. It was the last day the synagogue would be in use. It was sold to a church. It is customary that when a synagogue is being shuttered to take the Torahs out of the Holy Ark and walk them around the synagogue seven times.... The men were too old and frail to carry the Torahs.
>
> They were so happy to see me come in, and I was so sad to be there on the last day. A chapter of my life closing, forever. They asked me to walk a Torah around seven times, and believe me that was one of the few times I cried in my life... Had I ignored that gut feeling or instinct, I would not have had the honor to do the final *hakafah*, walk around, with the Torah. All the Torahs were later transferred to other synagogues."

Rishon L'Zion, like Shaari Israel, was located in the largely working- and middle-class neighborhood of East Flatbush. Some sections had very nice private houses, and others had pleasant two family dwellings, as well as well-appointed apartment buildings. It was considered a step up from the grittier precincts of Brownsville and East Flatbush. The synagogues also tended to be a bit more spacious and better detailed than many of the *shuls* in eastern and northern Brooklyn, however, most of the East New York synagogues were on their way out by the 1970s, with only a few plodding along some more years.

Charlie engaged in a mournful ritual when he made the circuit with the Torahs. Ordinarily such a *hakafah* or circuit is a joyous event—as on the fall holiday of *Sukkot* (Tabernacles) when Jews march around with *lulav* and *etrog* (palm branches and citrus), and on *Simhat Torah*, one of the most joyous days of the Jewish calendar, when all the Torahs in a *shul* are taken out and marched and danced around. A similar ritual is seen at Jewish weddings when the bride (and sometimes other relatives) circles around the groom (typically) seven times (and sometimes the groom circles the bride too). There are other examples of this marching, encircling, and usually they are positive rituals. In this case, Charlie helped carry the Torahs on their final forlorn journey at this particular *shul*.

Another former congregant of Rishon L'Zion is Rochelle, whose memories are less dramatic but still rich in detail:

> When you walked in the *shul* office was on the left, the social room was in the basement, the entrance to the main sanctuary was on the first floor. Women sat in the balcony. The Talmud Torah classes were in the balcony; three or four classrooms were up there. The ceiling was painted a beautiful sky blue with clouds in it, as if you were approaching *shamayim* (heaven).
>
> Rabbi Gilbert Steinberg was there and a Hebrew teacher was Esther Z. (couldn't recall the spelling). If you went to the school you learned how to *daven* (pray) and a little bit of Hebrew conversation. There was a *seder* for the Talmud Torah children for *Pesach* (Passover).
>
> Guest *hazzanim* (cantors) came—Chaskele Ritter and other High Holy Days *hazzanim*. The *hazzan* would walk in from the back, his eyes closed—this was the biggest thing. My father loved this.
>
> I had a friend there, an émigré from Castro's Cuba. There were a lot of (Holocaust) survivors there.

Rochelle also mentioned that another nearby *shul*, now ex-*shul*, was called B'nai Israel. It was located on the west side of Kings Highway. Now it is a public elementary school, but back then "that was the fancy *shul*."

Ritter certainly made an impression on both Charlie and Rochelle (who, incidentally, do not know each other although they are close in age). People would "*shul* hop" or come from other congregations to see certain celebrated cantors.

I was impressed by this description of the *shul* having a ceiling painted to resemble the sky. That must have been impressive and cheery, especially to children. This detail is gone, and the ceiling is painted a plain white. Some synagogues and a few ex-*shuls* have notable ceilings (for example, Shaare Zedek on Albany Avenue had a marvelous ceiling, and the church that meets there now has retained this) and more commonly some synagogues have (or had) lovely stained glass panels and windows. More modest *shuls* did not have this.

Unlike Charlie, who paid a fateful final visit to this *shul*, Rochelle said she felt uncomfortable going back to see the current state of the building. Some people feel conflicted about going to see their old *shuls* in Brooklyn; they are curious, but they do not want to see how the *shuls* became churches. It is too painful for some of them.

Other people have been willing to see their old *shuls* and sometimes even visit inside. I visited Shaare Torah by myself and later my father accompanied me; another time my father was willing to look at the former *shul* (now a medical center) on East 53rd Street where he had his bar mitzvah ceremony. Some people are scared to go in a neighborhood where they feel they will stand out (a white among so many blacks and/or Latinos) and some people have expressed a kind of embarrassment; they have the sense that you can't go home again.

My mother-in-law Janet was comfortable with going to see her old *shul* on Lenox Road, and when her extended family (including many cousins) took a bus trip through East Flatbush, she went along and told them about her old *shul*. It is a good thing that they undertook this trip in the early 2000s because the building is now gone. It was knocked down (it had morphed into a day care center, Maple Leaf Academy) and now a sizable modern building stands in its place:

I went to a *shul* on Lenox and East 55th Street. It was an orange building. Men sat in the lower level, and women in the balcony. My grandfather, uncles and father used to go there. I would visit *zayde* (grandpa) and he would say "*Gay avek!*" (Go away!) because I was in the men's section. Men would walk through the streets with their *tallis* (prayer shawl) and bag. *Zayde* would go to the morning *minyan* when he retired.

It was very crowded on holidays. They did have a Hebrew School; (cousin) Bobby went there. It was an Orthodox synagogue. I don't remember the *shul*'s name. All the men in the neighborhood went there. I lived on Lenox Road and East 54th Street, diagonally across from the *shul*. A more Jewish neighborhood you couldn't get, except for the Borellis, who lived next door to the *shul*. (They were Italian-American and Roman Catholic.)

On Saturday you had Arabs riding on bicycles; they would be *Shabbos goys* (non-Jews willing to do a few chores for Jews constrained by Sabbath restrictions), to stoke the furnace, and so on. We just called (our synagogue) 'the *shul*.' When we took the (family bus) tour in late December 2001, there was something on that building that still told you it was once a synagogue.

She also recalled the former *shul* that had been the site of my father's bar mitzvah ceremony. "The rich people went there. It was much bigger, a lot fancier. I think I went in there once. It had a big sanctuary and the women's area was bigger."

✡ ✡ ✡ ✡ ✡ ✡

This interview and others reveal a sadly familiar issue: that of "the *shul*" that has no easily recalled name. A number of people I interviewed about Brooklyn ex-*shuls* did not know the proper names of the *shuls* they attended or lived near. They either just referred to them as "the *shul*" or by the main street location, such as "the *shul* on Sutter Avenue," but Sutter Avenue and which cross street? In a way I am amused by this casual familiarity, that many Jews would just say "the *shul*" (I don't usually hear Christians refer to "the church": they will clearly state something along the line of "St. Brendan's" or "OLHC" or "Pastor Smith's church") but it certainly makes research more difficult.

I found out the formal name of the Lenox synagogue by using the Department of Finance website. There was another *shul* on the next block, according to the WPA survey, at 902 Lenox Road. Was it located within a home or did the people working on the WPA survey make a few mistakes?

Many *shuls* also had similar names, which adds to the confusion over precise names. There were many ex-*shuls* in Brooklyn whose names began with Beth (House of), B'nai (Sons of, as in B'nai Brith—Sons of the Covenant), Ansche or Anshe, Shaare or Shaari, Chevra or Chevre, Kehillath, and other common names. There were several Talmud Torahs. For many people it became more convenient to refer to a *shul* by its main street. These *shul* names often seem more official than anything else, used more for telephone directory listings or real estate purposes or for the WPA survey writer. Although today most Jews in Brooklyn and New York City in general refer to their synagogues by the proper name or a shortened version thereof (people at my synagogue often just call it "East Midwood") or by the initials ("OZ" for Ohab Zedek), there are some *shuls* that are usually referred to by their location as they were in the past. (There is a sizable Orthodox *shul* on Avenue N near McDonald Avenue that certainly has a Hebrew name, but most people just call it "the Avenue N *shul*.")

It is also interesting to find that people compared the various *shuls*. It is not too surprising that some *shuls* were attended by "richer" people, or at least considered to be for richer people, by dint of their size, their more elaborate decoration, the typical clientele. This even occurs today. People are very aware of which synagogues are bigger and fancier now and which are quite modest or hampered by an older, sparser membership and are on the verge of closing or merging. Certainly some ex-*shuls* are in nice shape, or are being renovated extensively, while others are dowdy and look ready to be knocked down. (Incidentally, Janet's ex-*shul* did not look shoddy. Perhaps someone just wanted that prime piece of real estate, and the building she once knew went the way of many other buildings that are bought only for the land they sit upon.)

Janet also recalled that "all the men" in the neighborhood went to this *shul*. In East Flatbush, as in Brownsville especially and to a lesser degree in other neighborhoods, there were many other *shuls* in Brooklyn from the 1920s through the early 1960s. There were lots of choices. People often went to the closest *shul*, but not always. Jewish "consumers" of houses of worship faced an array of choices for fulfilling communal religious requirements. If you became upset at one rabbi or one set of congregants, you could start a new *shul* (there are a number of cases in which a *shul* splintered and several congregants set up shop elsewhere, often not too far from the original synagogue) or just go to another *shul*. Still happens today, certainly. To a child, however, it may seem like every man in the immediate area showed up at yours.

Elsewhere in Flatbush there is an ex-*shul* on Woodruff Avenue, now known as Calvary Baptist. For a while I had difficulty finding the original name of this ex-*shul*; my two cousins, who had lived just a few short blocks away from it when they were children, couldn't remember the name as anything except "the Woodruff Temple." Then I spoke with Lester G., the father of two old friends of mine. Although he didn't attend this synagogue, he did have a reason to go there:

> I fixed the roof there. That was Rabbi Goldberg. I took Hebrew at Brooklyn College and he was teaching it. When (my son) Moshe was born I made a *kiddush* in his class. They had an organ at this *shul* and they played it on *Shabbos*. It was Reform.

Lester G. also spoke about other Brooklyn ex-*shuls* such as the "Park Place" *shul*, between Ralph and Howard (Avenues), near P.S. 210. On Yom Kippur you couldn't get in unless you showed a card. They had a guard, a uniformed guy, and you had to show a ticket. It was a big Orthodox *shul*. There was "Twin Cantors" at Eastern Parkway and Rochester Avenue, a private house with a canopy coming out to the curb. Another *shul* on Stanley Avenue off Linden Boulevard was in the middle of farm land. When Rena (his oldest daughter) was small we went there. A farmer built up the whole neighborhood. There also was the Prospect Park Yeshiva, and boys and girls went there together then."

Some time after interviewing Lester G. I found an old photograph of the Woodruff Avenue building, showing how it looked as a *shul*. It was known by a Hebrew name as well as the Woodruff Avenue Temple. The church that resides there now has changed much of the front of the building (removing or blocking stained glass windows and more), but has retained a Jewish star design that runs vertically on sides of the building. My interviewee fixed the roof because he was a roofer, and had a business for himself (which he has since sold as he is now retired). Although Brooklyn does have Reform synagogues, including a few that are quite old (Park Slope's Beth Elohim, also known as the Garfield Temple, Temple Beth Emeth on Church Avenue in Flatbush, the Union Temple on Eastern Parkway), the Woodruff Avenue Temple was among very few ex-*shuls* I found that someone identified as Reform. However, it was not the only ex-*shul* to have an organ, and in the next interview someone contradicts the Reform designation.

The Park Place *shul*, properly known as Men of Justice, is now Bright Light Baptist Church. It retains much of its outer Judaica and is an attractive, sizable building. Today people still have to present tickets at many synagogues around the borough, as well as the nation, for the Rosh Hashanah and Yom Kippur services. Even those synagogues that do not ask for congregants and guests to flash their seat tickets usually sell these seat tickets as a major fundraiser each year. In fact, it is notable when a synagogue advertises free seats for the High Holidays.

There is still a building on Eastern Parkway that has a sign for "Twin Cantors" Catering. There is no ex-*shul* standing now at Stanley and Linden (there were other *shuls* on Linden Boulevard; some were knocked down, others completely redone as residences or churches). The Prospect Park Yeshiva on Ocean Avenue, across the street from Prospect Park, moved to the Homecrest neighborhood in Brooklyn and became an all-girls' school. This Yeshiva was not the only one to move to a different Brooklyn area but retain the old name: hence the Crown Heights Yeshiva, CHY, which is now several miles south of Crown Heights, in Mill Basin, at the Flatbush Park Jewish Center east of the Kings Plaza shopping mall.

Sarah K. grew up in Flatbush and knew of a few *shuls* there:

> I went to the Judea Center on Bedford Avenue between Clarkson and Lenox. The rabbi was Rabbi Felman, and Cantor Saul Wahrsager was there. What was interesting there was they didn't have separate seating but it was Orthodox. There was no *mehitzah* (physical divider, such as a curtain, between the men's and women's sections of the synagogues). Later on they cordoned off a section for women.
>
> They had a Hebrew school. I got a U in Synagogue Attendance. My brother was bar mitzvahed at the *shul*. When the Seventh Day Adventist church took over later on, they took off the Hebrew writing.
>
> I thought the Woodruff Avenue Temple was Conservative!

It is unclear what the Woodruff Avenue Temple considered itself to be, but they were not Orthodox. Then again, Judea Center seems to have been in flux about its level of observance too.

As for Freda, a life-long Brooklynite:

> I went to school at Prospect Park Yeshiva. When you went up the stairs there was the huge sanctuary, the basement with classrooms, the *bet midrash*. It was a real *shul*-slash-school, in a big building. (The school) bought the synagogue on Bedford between Lenox and Clarkson (Judea Center, described by Sarah K. above) and in the 2nd, 3rd, 5th and 6th grades I went there.

Freda also described the nearby Young Israel of Prospect Park:

> It was a big, cavernous building, like a castle and very beautiful. It had a separate parsonage attached, and *Shabbos* playgroups. Rabbi Rabin was there. There was an L-shaped sanctuary, and the rabbi was at the end of the L. It had a *mehitzah*.

This Young Israel is not the only one in Brooklyn to have become a church later on, but it might be the only Young Israel to have been housed in a former church, and then revert to being a different church. It lasted as a *shul* into the early 1990s.

Norman, who now resides in Arizona, recalled my father's synagogue as well as others:

> I am from East Flatbush and originally went to a *shul* on East 51st Street between Clarkson and Winthrop. I then went to a *shul* on East 53rd Street between Linden Boulevard and Church Avenue. I remember it was Orthodox and the rabbi was Rabbi Hecht. The reason that I remember that is because he and his family lived next door to me on East 53rd Street. I was bar mitzvahed there.
>
> My next venture into a temple other than going to High Holiday services is when I got married on January 16, 1961, at of all places—Shaare Torah. My wife used to go to the East Flatbush Jewish Community Center located on Linden Boulevard and Schenectady Avenue before I met her. The rabbi there was Rabbi Leibowitz, one of the two rabbis that married me....The other rabbi that performed our ceremony was the rabbi of Shaare Torah. I do not recall his name.

Living next door to your rabbi may not be most children's cup of tea—there must be pressure on you to be good and be observant. The East Flatbush JCC is gone. Not to make fun of Norman, but I find it humorous when someone says something along the line of "the rabbi that married me." (Unless you are the spouse of an actual rabbi.) Norman seems to recall the names of some of the rabbis in his Brooklyn past, except for Rabbi Singer of Shaare Torah.

Madeline Israel, the mother of Long Island Congressional Representative Steve Israel, is a former Brooklynite and current Arizonan who also remembered the East Flatbush JCC. She responded to one of my on-line requests for Brooklyn *shul* memories:

> I attended infrequently as a child, and as an adult, moved to Long Island. The rabbi was Jacob Leibowitz, who officiated at my wedding in 1956 at Temple Auditorium. The synagogue was quite Orthodox, women and men seated in different sections. My father, who was an extremely handy person, did all of the sound system work, on a volunteer basis, of course.
>
> I do remember that the High Holy days brought out everyone who didn't go to *shul* the rest of the year, and the women all bought new clothes for the occasion. Children were not permitted to stay in the *shul* for *yizkor* (memorial prayers). How sheltered we were then!

These two memoirs of the East Flatbush *shul* bring it more to light with personal touches. It is still true in many synagogues around the nation and world—certainly to some extent in Brooklyn—that the High Holidays bring out people who only attend for major holidays of the year.

The issue of whether children should be present during the *yizkor* (memorial) prayers is not necessarily an issue of sheltering them. These are memorial prayers for close family members (memorial prayers for the community and Holocaust victims have been added to the liturgy of this section), and most rabbis hold that children who have two living parents need not be present or should not be present. In some synagogues this causes friction, while in others it is understood that if you are fortunate to have two living parents (and none of your siblings has died) then you should leave the *yizkor* prayers to the others who are less fortunate.

✿ ✿ ✿ ✿ ✿ ✿

Onward to Brownsville and East New York to bring light and life to specific synagogues there. The people who recall these areas are somewhat older, because these *shuls* changed hands at earlier dates. I do have a different relationship with synagogues in this region. I am an outsider, an interloper, at these ex-*shuls*. I passed through Brownsville and East New York as a child, on the way to the Interboro (now Jackie Robinson) Parkway, to Queens. I taught in a school in this area, but I did not grow up around here and came to know these ex-*shuls* as a religion tourist-researcher. At least two of my grandparents (my father's parents for sure) did live part of their lives in Brownsville, however, and my father came around here often as a child. My grandparents are gone, but my father has provided me with some of his memories of Jewish life in the greater Brownsville area.

Arnold S. left Brooklyn in 1943, but recalled details about *shuls* in eastern Brownsville and East New York:

> I was brought up in Brooklyn, born in 1929. I lived near Lincoln Terrace Park, in East New York. I went to Yeshiva Toras Chaim at Belmont (Avenue) and Jerome. I left Brooklyn in 1943. I also went to the Ashford Street Talmud Torah; it's row houses on that street now. The *shul* building is gone. It was on Ashford between Blake (Avenue) and Sutter (Avenue). Most of the time I went to the Ashford *shul*. My grandparents lived across the street from the *shul*. Ashford was a big *shul* with a big staircase.
>
> Elton (Street *shul*) was a large *shul* too, but you walked right in. The pews, the *bimah* (stage) at all the *shuls* looked very much alike inside. The ladies sections were (often) on the second floor.

It was not a very rich community, almost a ghetto. Sometimes we went to any *shul* around. My family moved every two, three years. We lived in apartment houses. If the landlord didn't paint, you moved.

"There was a small *shul* on Hegeman and Berriman. In the 1920s there were a lot of farms around there, along Linden Boulevard. There was a *shul* on almost every street. The population was 99% Jewish.

It may have seemed like there was a time when Brownsville was 99% Jewish, although in reality the percentage was lower. The Elton Street *shul* is a smart looking building, but it is now a Seventh Day Adventist church.

Perhaps my oldest interviewee was Frank R., who was 91 1/2 at the time of his interview. He walked without a cane but wore two hearing aids. He regularly attends the East Midwood Jewish Center and has seen Brooklyn, up and down, throughout his many years:

I went to the *shul* on Williams Avenue between Glenmore and Liberty. Can't remember the name. It was a church originally. I only remember it as a *shul*. I went for the holidays and for my bar mitzvah. I went to a storefront to learn Hebrew. I learned the *haftorah* (reading portion from the Prophets). They gave me an *aliyah* (Torah blessing).

There was one (*shul*) on Hinsdale between Pitkin and Glenmore. There were *shuls* all over the place! The one on Glenmore (at Miller Avenue) was for the rich people. Also the one on Arlington (Avenue). Gorgeous buildings. The butcher was the richest guy in the neighborhood. His son went to the (*shul*) on Miller.

Once again we hear about the *shuls* for wealthier people, and these two ex-*shuls* are still impressive structures. Except for a sign on the corner of the building, both still look exactly like synagogues. There are Brooklyn Eagle newspaper clippings about the Glenmore synagogue, B'nai Joseph. Once again, we hear from people who cannot recall the name of their old *shuls*.

Later in this chapter, we will hear from someone who does remember the synagogue's name because his grandmother went there and passed onto him a *shul* memento. The ex-*shul* on Hinsdale was at number 133, Congregation Eliezer of East New York between Pitkin and Glenmore. It became a church. A fence surrounds it, it is weed strewn and looks to be in poor shape. No Judaica is left, but Frank's comment helped to determine that it was a synagogue at some point.

Roslyn is a former Brooklynite who lived in a few different neighborhoods:

I grew up on Powell Street, corner of Liberty Avenue. My address was 66 Powell. The *shul* my mother and I attended was on Glenmore Avenue. It was a small *shul* where the women sat upstairs behind a curtain. If memory serves me correctly, it was a private house converted to a *shul*. There was a very large synagogue on Stone Avenue between Pitkin Avenue and Belmont Avenue. I believe it was called the Talmud Torah.

In 1955 I moved to 1562 Ocean Avenue... In 1962 we moved to Sheepshead Bay and attended a synagogue on Nostrand Avenue. It was located between Avenue W and Avenue X. I left Brooklyn in 1970 for Arizona. I honestly never regretted moving here even with the heat... My children grew up here and have never gone to visit. I had been back several times as I had a sister who lived on Neptune Avenue near Ocean Parkway.

Roslyn moved southward to more upscale neighborhoods. The well-regarded Stone Avenue Talmud Torah is gone, replaced by public housing. Her commentary and lack of regret about leaving Brooklyn is atypical. Certainly Brooklyn is not for everyone, but does she regret that her children have not visited? Would they be interested in seeing their mother's former home? The Nostrand Avenue synagogue she referred to is likely one that is mid-block, one that became a small yeshiva years later. It is on the west side of the street.

Joan, who also resides in Arizona, used to live at the northern edge of East Flatbush, near Brownsville. She had some memories of a lighter kind:

> My family attended services at a synagogue on Remsen Avenue and Avenue A. I went to Hebrew school there. I don't know if it is still a *shul* nor do I remember the name—sorry I can't remember.
>
> Kids always hung outside the *shul* on holidays. The boys would hit the girls on the head with hankies that had rocks or marbles in them. When we would be inside with parents *davening* (praying) and it got noisy, the men on the *bimah* would bang hard (upon it). They would announce the Yom Kippur pledges... amounts were small... at least in the basement part where my parents were... $5, $10, etc.
>
> I went to children's services every Shabbat. The boys did everything even though at that time I knew most of the prayers by heart. I remember lots of people smoking outside on Yom Kippur. Lots of people parked a few blocks away... shame, shame...
>
> I remember it being dark after Hebrew School in the winter and I had a long walk home. I lived on Ralph Avenue and Beverly Road. I used to run all the way home. When I went back about 15 years ago... there were bars on my old windows but the houses were still kept pretty decent.

The details Joan provided give some different color to this topic. The mischievous actions of some kids, the girl's realization that she could do a fine job of leading the service but was restricted by religious convention, the modest pledges congregants made during holiday pledge time, the way some people would hide (or not hide) their less observant habits—all these bring more life, more levels to the typical story of going to *shul* and watching the adults do the rituals. I do wonder if the people were actually smoking not on Yom Kippur but perhaps on other Jewish holidays when smokers are allowed to light up from an existing flame. Would many congregants agree to such an admission?

The *shul* she attended is named by the next set of interviewees. Shoshana and Dave are a married couple from Brooklyn who now live in Arizona. They lived in a few different neighborhoods in the borough:

Shoshana:

> My husband who is from Canarsie/East Flatbush attended a *shul* at Avenue A and Remsen Avenue... After we were married we joined Community Temple Beth Ohr on Ocean Avenue, which I believe is now a church. ...We were married at East Midwood Jewish Center.

Dave:

> Beth Israel (the ex-*shul* on Avenue A and Remsen Avenue)—I went to *cheder* (religious school) there from about age 6 to age 16, post-bar mitzvah. They were Orthodox and very large in the late '50s through the mid '60s. We moved to Midwood in '67. I knew of some smaller *shuls*—(East) 93rd and Church Avenue, and I remember driving through Brownsville as a kid when it was still Jewish— Pennsylvania Avenue, Blake Avenue, Fortunoff—a long time ago in a land far away. I knew of some *shuls* north of Church Avenue but the family went to Beth Israel as did my friends.

Small world isn't it that two different ex-Brooklynites now living in Arizona are alumni of the same East Flatbush synagogue. This ex-*shul* only became a church during the summer of 2006. I passed this building at times while I drove to nearby Brookdale Hospital and was aware that it had previously been a synagogue.

Temple Beth Ohr has an interesting story. It had been a private residence, then a Reform synagogue, then a church, and now it is a private residence with an office. A renowned architect designed this Ocean Avenue building.

Fortunoff is a storied business that began in Brooklyn but moved to Manhattan and Long Island. You can still see a "faded ad" for the Brooklyn branch of the store in Brownsville, a large, outer-wall painted advertisement for the legendary store that stocked jewelry, better grade household goods, and more.

May, a spry octogenarian and lifelong Brooklynite attends the Kings Bay YM-YWHA. She said,

> I knew of a *shul* on Pennsylvania Avenue and New Lots (Avenue). It took in people from East New York and Brownsville. I was brought up mostly in Brownsville. There was a *shul* on Howard Avenue between St. Mark's Place and Prospect Place. All my friends went there after school, boys and girls. It was Orthodox to a degree. I would hang out there, so to speak, on the afternoons. When the parents went to *daven*, all the kids would play in doorways. All that marble (there)—funny how you remember these things.
>
> For *Succos* we went to a *shteibel* (very modest *shul*) on Prospect Place between Hopkinson and Saratoga (Avenues). One of my grandfathers was very Orthodox, and he lived in East Flatbush.
>
> My son went to the H.E.S. (Hebrew Educational Society, now located in Canarsie). When I was registering him for camp, I had an argument with the person there. H.E.S. summer camp—Hopkinson and Sutter (Avenues)—he loved it. Somebody recommended that I take him there. (She was divorcing her first husband then.) My nephew went with him there, but the counselors couldn't handle him because he peed in bed. They asked David (her son) to take care of him there (at sleep-away camp).
>
> You walked from one *shul* to another on the holidays. Lincoln Place (*shul*)—they had some beautiful affairs there.

Another devotee of the H.E.S. was Jay, who had happy athletic memories of the place. He recalled an even earlier site:

> The H.E.S. was (then) on Hendrix Street between Sutter and Blake (Avenues). We had a team in the basketball tournament for about five years.
>
> I have information on a synagogue my grandmother, Sarah Hyman, started in Brooklyn. I also have the silver engraved loving cup that was presented to her as the first president in 1930. It was on Williams Street between Liberty and Atlantic Avenues in East New York. It was known as Talmud Torah Ohr Chodesh. It held at least 500 with the men and women separated by a *mehitzah*. The building was originally a church, and (the grandmother) was instrumental in purchasing the church. Services were conducted by the members except on the High Holidays when a cantor was hired. The rabbi was the school teacher.
>
> There was another small *shul* on either Hinsdale or Williams just south of Glenmore but I don't remember the name.

This was yet another synagogue that earlier housed a church. It is now a school although the building number is different (60 instead of 58). I walked over to this block during my lunch hour one overcast day in mid-October 2007. The block has one- and two-family houses, a big parking lot for school buses, this school and a business. I realized this was the synagogue that Frank R. had discussed in his interview, even though he had confused one of the cross streets. I assume that the "small *shul* on either Hinsdale or Williams" is actually the other synagogue that Frank R. mentioned, because it is indeed located on Hinsdale and is just south of Glenmore Avenue (although Williams certainly had other *shuls* back in the day). When I make these kinds of connections between the various interviews I have conducted, I am grateful for everyone's memories and the way they help to support my research. Perhaps Frank R. knew Jay's grandmother? Was she present at Frank R.'s bar mitzvah?

Mel grew up in the Brownsville-East New York area and spoke about the many *shuls* around, as well as another *shul* that remains a bit elusive to identify:

> In East New York-Brownsville there were more *shteiblach* (plural of *shteibel*) than any other place in

the world. It was noted for that. This one had a tremendous youth congregation. Everyone knew this *shul* as "the Cong." It was unbelievable. My father took me for *Simhat Torah*; they had hundreds of kids.

I had a connection with Shaare Torah when I lived on Ocean Avenue and Albemarle Road. We lived at 645 Ocean Avenue. My aunt Margie was also a member. I played basketball at Shaare Torah.

No one else spoke about "the Cong" so I have had to do guess work. Perhaps this was the *shul* and school at Pennsylvania Avenue and New Lots Avenue. Somehow several people I interviewed have a connection to Shaare Torah, so I truly feel a sense of belonging to a kind of club, the ex-*shul* club, Shaare Torah division, and Shaare Torah did (does) have a nice gym.

Deborah R. mentioned different kinds of Jewish organizations she was involved with:

I am a retiree who grew up in Crown Heights. Although my family never formally belonged to a synagogue, we attended holiday services at a *shteibel* on President Street near Rogers Avenue. I attended their Released Time religious program. I also was a member of the Union Temple Girl Scout troop. We were friendly with a family who were members of the then-Chabad and attended many of their events. I also attended their Talmud Torah on Rogers Avenue. When I brought home too many dicta, my mother switched me to the Arbeiter Ring (Workman's Circle) in a storefront across the street which emphasized Yiddish. I joined Habonim when I was eleven and attended their functions on Kingston Avenue and became a non-religious Labor Zionist."

Even though the majority of the ex-shuls were Orthodox in practice, we can see that like Deborah R. many of the congregants were not that observant in reality. Some ended up going to Conservative shuls later, and some even changed to groups such as Workman's Circle or non-observant Zionist groups.

Some chapters in this book may never truly be complete, and this is one of them. I hope that I can find more people who attended ex-shuls in Brooklyn. I appreciate hearing their memories, however patchy. There is a sense of urgency, to an extent, in that this population is aging. The age factor is also probably a reason why I have not located as many people who attended ex-shuls in Brownsville and East New York, as well as Bedford-Stuyvesant and Bushwick. Many Jews who did live in these areas have already died, or are not able to summon up these memories.

Who knows what mementoes are stored in someone's attic or treasure box? Perhaps readers will be encouraged to plow through the memorabilia of their families and may find some things that add to the history and documentation of the ex-shul phenomenon.

In the Harry Potter books Four through Seven, there is a clever device called a Pensieve. Author J.K. Rowling conjured up this captivating creation which helps characters to view their own or someone else's memories. A memory, which seems to be a liquid or gas stored in a special vial, is poured into a stone basin. The memory swirls around and then a person can slowly dive into the memory and see a full-blown memory, not even a recreation but an actual memory (but not interact with it—this is strictly a means of observation).

What it would be like to have vials full of memories of people who went to ex-shuls in Brooklyn. Ah, to pour them into a Pensieve, dive in and see what actually went on in the shuls, see the people, hear them pray and sing and gossip, examine the buildings in their Jewish forms.

Meeting Amongst the Faithful:
My Visits With Congregants of Converted Ex-Shuls

Most of us do not live in the same home for our whole lives. Who would not be curious to see at least once, briefly, what our former homes looked like years later? How would our memories compare with what others have done to our old abode? What would it be like to visit your old schools, your former favorite neighborhood haunts, your old house of worship?

I have not been inside the apartment I grew up in from infancy through the age of nearly seven years, although I have driven by that apartment building hundreds of times throughout my life. I have not been inside the house I lived in afterward, because my father sold the house in 2000, and the current owners knocked it down. I have been inside my two former elementary schools a few times, as well as my former junior high and high school, and I have been to my old synagogue, although it has changed.

As I wrote earlier, I was rather young when I attended Shaare Torah. I was either in kindergarten or first grade the final time I visited the synagogue. I have vague memories of a smallish room where my father took me for prayers, which was the *bet midrash*. I recall red carpeting in the hallways. I remember being outside the *shul* with a crowd of people and waving a paper flag. (I realized later on that we were celebrating the holiday of *Simhat Torah*.)

When I finally went inside the building, now known as Salem Missionary Baptist Church, in March 2007, the first thing I noticed was red carpeting on the floor. I was shown around the church by a friendly female congregant, and while I appreciated my visit, nothing quite gave me such a sense of return as that red carpet. Then on a midsummer day in 2008, my father and I visited and filmed inside this building with director Charles Bowe and his two-man film and sound crew, who shot footage for his documentary *The Battle of Brooklyn*. We were shown around by the assistant pastor. We were able to see that the old doors that had been in front of the Holy Ark when the building was Jewish were still present, but they had been relocated further up the front wall. As well, the Hebrew Ten Commandments display was still in place, but a large metal cross had been placed upon it—and not one letter of the Hebrew had been covered up.

In the course of my research on the many ex-*shuls* of Brooklyn, I visited the interiors of about a quarter of them. My primary motivations for visiting inside and not just snapping photographs from outdoors are thus: for historical and cultural research, to see what has happened to former synagogues, to see what has been preserved and what has been altered or discarded, to speak with congregants who had knowledge of the conversions of these buildings from Jewish synagogues to Christian churches, to hear about what the congregants and clergy know about the old synagogues, to experience a little bit of their lives inside these buildings.

Thus I played the roles of historian, researcher, cultural emissary, chronicler, curious Brooklynite, translator, and more. I was always welcomed by friendly folk and sometimes by befuddled believers. I made it clear to everyone that I was Jewish and was conducting research in as respectful a fashion as possible. I shared my knowledge of the former synagogues, translated plaques and cornerstones and other spots with Hebrew or Yiddish writing and symbols. In turn, I learned invaluable things about many of these former synagogues, through sharing words with people, and through studying the interiors of the buildings and the various artifacts to be found. I hope these folks learned something about the history of the buildings and something about the Jewish lives of the former congregations.

No one attempted to convert me; no one insulted my religion and culture. I was asked many questions and I asked many questions, and I have to believe that my intentions were good and so were those of the Christians I met. There were a variety of emotions while visiting these ex-*shuls*: wonder, amazement, embarrassment, sadness, bitterness, joy, humor, confusion. I know that some Jews will disagree with my decisions to visit these churches, because by strictest interpretation a Jew should not be inside a different religion's house of worship, certainly not the sanctuary, and there are a number of reasons for this. I made it clear to everyone that I was a Jew, however, and that I was there for research reasons. In a way, I believe that I also acted as a bridge between religions and cultures. I am interested in the field of interfaith relations and hoped and still hope that my visits contributed in a positive sense to harmony amongst the faithful.

Often I stood in the ex-*shuls* and wondered what it would have been like so many years ago to *daven* (pray) in these buildings, to kiss the Torah as it was paraded around, to celebrate a bar mitzvah or wedding, to drink wine or grape juice at the after-service *kiddush*, and to chat with my friends and neighbors.

I thought it would be interesting to visit some of the ex-*shuls*, now churches, on a Sunday, aside from chancing upon an open ex-*shul* or scheduling a meeting. I wanted to experience, however briefly, the Sunday worship service and Sunday schooling while gazing upon whatever was left of an ex-*shul*'s interior Judaica. Certainly, this is exotic to someone like me. I have been to a fairly wide variety of Jewish services, from classic Reform to west coast Chabad, from a traditional service in a famous Budapest synagogue to an Israeli *shteibel* (small synagogue), and several Conservative synagogues in addition. I could not help but wonder about services of other religions, especially African American congregations. Would the people sing continuously? Would they call out "hallelujah" frequently? Would anyone fall to the floor in rapture? Does everyone shake a tambourine?

Would they stare at me so intently that I would blush too much? Would they ignore me or ask me a lot of questions?

I went on a series of such visits in 2006 and 2007. One visit was coordinated in advance, but the others were mere drop-ins on my part, although I had planned in advance which ex-*shuls*/churches I would visit. I was particularly interested in some of the larger, more elaborate buildings, and I also visited others that were nearby, to make fullest use of my limited time.

I dressed modestly for these visits, typically in a skirt, short-sleeve blouse, stockings (even in warm weather) and loafers. I was well aware that at African American churches, many congregants dressed quite well for Sunday service. I knew I would stick out.

The first time I conducted Sunday visits was a warm Sunday in July 2006. I went to four houses of worship. My first stop was to the Pentecostal Church of God, formerly Kesser Torah. The traffic in this area of Flatbush was very heavy for two reasons: the police department had blocked off certain streets for a street fair later that day and church-travel traffic was heavy. With some nervousness, I entered Pentecostal. Their service was going on, and ushers greeted me. One was a middle-aged woman, wearing a full white outfit with gloves; the other was a man in a nice dark suit. I explained quickly that I came because my mother had attended this site when it was a synagogue. "It became a church in 1968," the female usher told me. The male usher spied my cameras and asked me not to take pictures during the service.

The lady showed me to a seat toward the back, on the left side. People turned to me and smiled. I did not feel too embarrassed. I opened my notebook and took notes. The first thing I wrote about was the remaining Judaica inside. The *Aron Kodesh*, the Holy Ark for Torahs was still in front. I could not tell if it was marble or wood painted to look like marble, but the ark was mottled brown with some interesting carved details. There was a red velvet curtain with it. I sketched the ark; it had four columns on each side, with small panels. Above the ark was a large stained glass window, of just a few colored panels. I could make out a faded Jewish star on the glass, its black lines mostly faded or scraped out. I looked up at the balcony, which now was unoccupied.

That was all the Judaica I could find, so then I focused on the experience of a Sunday service in a Pentecostal church. I had been to very few Christian Sunday worship services in my life, and those mostly in passing, peeking in at church services in session. It was a bit entertaining, as well as curious to me, to be seated in a once-*shul*-now-church, taking in the music, the singing, the speech.

"Hallelujah! How do you feel this morning?" someone shouted from the dais. I heard some cheery replies. A woman clad all in bright red stood up and began testifying. "His praise will continually be in my mouth," she started and then told about a visit she had with her extended family, including a female relative who just turned 100. People clapped and cheered at that news. "God is just so good!" she added.

Then they sang a hymn which I assume is called "Our God in Victory," because that was the most oft- repeated phrase. It was in the key of D major, fairly simple in words and tune, but very joyous. I could not help but smile as I watched almost every congregant, young and old, participating in this number. They sang, swayed, clapped, stomped their feet, and shook their many tambourines. There was a band on the side of the dais, a few musicians, and they did not overpower the congregation.

I watched two young girls, dressed nicely, as they toyed with their tambourines and the ribbons hanging from them. I noticed that each tambourine had a cross painted on the skin. At the end of the song, everyone sat and I heard scattered "Praise the Lords" (which I knew enough to abbreviate in my notebook as PTL.)

I stayed for a moment longer and then left. Each person I passed was more than polite to me, greeting me kindly (although some latecomers were too busy running upstairs). On the sidewalk I looked over my shoulder at the building and I felt moved, almost ready to cry. In my car I fought back tears. Was I sentimental about the service itself, which I found so rousing? Was it that I almost imagined my mother and my aunt and their family sitting in a pew so many years earlier, partaking of a very different religious service? Perhaps it was the fact that I had not been inside this building, as far as I knew, when my mother was alive and we were still living in Flatbush. Perhaps also seeing that I was regarded so pleasantly here. The people I spoke to seemed interested in the fact that I knew of the former synagogue, and that I had a familial connection here.

I got stuck in slow-moving traffic on Bedford Avenue. I wanted to get to Flatbush Avenue, but with the police blockages and the buses and more, I decided to switch plans and visit Brownsville to see some churches I had noted previously. I drove quickly on Lenox Road, and soon I was in Brownsville.

I went to visit Grace Church of God, an ex-*shul* that I first noticed in late 1987, when I commuted a few days a week to Queens College for classes, and I would take this route to the Interboro Parkway. Back then I did not notice a sign, and for quite some time I was certain it was either still a synagogue or recently abandoned. The building stands on a corner where three streets meet—Howard Avenue, Kings Highway (which ends here) and Tapscott Street. This church still has the Jewish star railings out front, as well as a few Magen Davids on the Tapscott Street side. I parked across the street and entered. The door was new, not the one I had photographed more than a year earlier. Sunday School was almost done and I spoke with a few people in the lobby.

There were about twenty children inside, mostly of elementary school ages. I noticed that there was an ark up front of light varnished wood, fairly plain. There were stained glass windows, not fancy, and I could not tell if they were original. This building had no balcony, which surprised me. The air conditioning was just right.

Back in the lobby I spoke with a few people. When I asked one woman how the people here felt about the Jewish stars, she said, "It's okay, it doesn't bother people." One man, a bit restlessly, asked me "Should we take it down?" I said no. Then he gave me a sly smile.

The service was just getting started with introductions, so I slipped outside. ("Don't you want to stay a while?" a woman pleaded.) I got into my car and drove a short distance to a red light. Suddenly, a religious Jewish man in the next car rolled down his window. "*Ma shlomech?*" ("How are you?") he called out, in Hebrew. I laughed; how did he know I was Jewish, and why did he assume I knew Hebrew? I answered in Hebrew, "*B'seder*" ("Okay,") and he and his wife nodded. "This is a Jewish neighborhood?" he asked me, his Israeli accent now obvious. "Not now, not since the 1970s maybe," I answered. They moved on when the light turned green. This had to be the funniest part of my trip. Or was it a fated meeting?

There was intermittent light rain around this time, so I decided to go to a nearby church, an ex-*shul* that was once known as Ahavas Achim Anshei D'Brownsville, now called the Peoples Baptist Church. Their service was to begin at 11:30 AM, later than the other churches I had already dropped in on. It was the after-Sunday School, before-service time and people were glad to speak with me. A cheery man told me that there was a Star of David in tile that was covered over by the blue carpet in the vestibule. There were also two stone tablets with many names engraved (I was able to read several names) that were only partially visible; the church had placed wooden panels in front of them, along with a table holding pamphlets and recently made Sunday School crafts adorned with beads. Accidently, I knocked off a bead from one craft, so I rushed to stick it back on the still-damp glue patch.

I was disappointed to see that the Holy Ark had been removed from the front of the sanctuary. There was a mural painted in the space. It was weird to see the vacancy, especially since I knew what had been there and why. In its unused state it reminded me of a pit shoveled open, awaiting a casket. There was no other Judaica in the sanctuary, but there was more in other parts of the church. Also, in the vestibule, I gazed at an impressive chandelier hanging from the middle of a large Jewish star on the ceiling. Right outside the main doors I was shown an interesting sight: hidden behind the church sign was more raised Hebrew writing of the former *shul*'s name. I pointed this out to two early-teen boys, who were relaxing by the outside railing after Sunday school, and they were surprised to see this. They had no idea their building had once been a Jewish site.

The pastor had been helpful in showing me the Judaica and was interested in my translations. I wrote down for him the address of the Municipal Archives where he could find the WPA survey as well the ex-*shul*'s name in phonetic Hebrew and translation. I asked him about leaving the Judaica, and he said, "We would never remove it." Then he went to greet a couple who said they were newcomers to the church.

The rain had let up, but the sun wasn't shining. I checked my watch and decided I had time for one more visit to a nearby site. I drove to Amboy Street, but realized that I was too far south. I doubled back on Boyland Boulevard, formerly known as Hopkinson Street, and spotted a few places I had photographed months ago: a Baptist church whose street number I couldn't make out, the Bethany Chapel that was once known as Hebrew Ladies Day Nursery, and the old HES (Hebrew Educational Society) building. I found the church I was searching for and went in.

St. Timothy's, long ago known as Congregation Chevra Torah Anshei Radishkowitz, was my last visit of that morning. I could hear the service, and there was no one at the door, so I quietly slipped in and admired the vestibule. It was chock full of Jewish mementoes, what with a few stained glass windows, half-moon shaped, featuring Jewish stars, as well as several plaques and even arches featuring Hebrew writing. I read one that listed the "Building Committee" (this written in phonetic Hebrew) along with the names of patrons. I stepped around many bags and boxes strewn around the two stairwells, one on each side. Was this for a clothing drive? I quickly realized that the main sanctuary of the *shul* was not in use, and the two staircases were now for storage. I snapped a few photos and went into the service held in the basement.

This was the only church I encountered that day that had no air conditioning. Fans buzzed loudly as the preacher talked about the joys, the fruits, and scenery of St. Vincent's. Someone cried rapturously "Oh, yes!" The wooden pews must have been from the *shul* days; I saw that one had a hinged wooden shelf attached to it, with faded Hebrew writing. "Let's live together for Christ," the preacher intoned. Ushers then took out the collection plates, and a young woman began to sing a song about "I shall be given." She sang robustly in an unadorned tone. I figured now was the time for me to exit, although an usher implored me to stay a while longer. I got into my car, her plain singing echoing in my ears. I revisited this church a year later, when I realized I had a professional link to the congregation. That visit is described later on.

✿ ✿ ✿ ✿ ✿

Altogether I had enjoyed my maiden "church hopping" venture. Overall, people were very pleasant to me, and many showed genuine interest and curiosity in my research and the information I imparted. I could feel the congregants' enthusiasm, their comfort in their customs.

I thought about my place in this scheme. Was I the nosy anthropologist or sociologist, gathering data? Was I making an odd nostalgia trip that was probably quite rare? A bit of both, especially at the Cortelyou Road church. I also compared their services to what I am used to at my own synagogue and others. I tried to imagine what it was like to sit so many years ago, and see different religious props, hear different religious tunes and liturgy, and sit amongst a very different ethnic crowd. I saw mostly African American worshipers, a few Latinos in the crowd, but today I was the lone Caucasian face. Usually in my synagogue I am part of the majority, although I do know some African American Jews who attend synagogues regularly, including my own.

The next time I had a chance to visit a Sunday worship service was several months later on March 18, 2007, when there was melting snow on the ground and dripping from awnings. I drove over to Salem Missionary Baptist Church, which had been Shaare Torah, my old *shul*. I approached the door, excited but nervous, because this would be the first time since my childhood that I was entering my former synagogue. Parishioners made me feel welcome immediately, especially when I explained that this had been my "temple" when I was a little girl.

I was bowled over by the sight of the red carpet, one long-ago detail that I had recalled. A woman gave me a tour, showing me the chapel, the catering hall downstairs, offices, and other rooms. The building was in very good condition; although everything was not brand new, it was clean and well maintained. My one disappointment was that I did not have the chance to see the main sanctuary and the remaining Judaica inside it, because the service was going on, including a sermon.

I took a copy of their pamphlet, a folded handout that featured a pastor's message and listed their many groups and activities. I was impressed by their music department, which coordinates eight choirs. (My synagogue has an adult choir only. I do not know how many choirs Shaare Torah had.) I thanked everyone for their time and left in a nostalgic mood.

The spring semester of 2007, I taught at Middle School 143 in Bedford-Stuyvesant, a school slated to be closed the following year. A few of my students had told me about churches they attended that they thought had been Jewish synagogues, and I followed up on a few leads. Branden J. told me that he sometimes attended The Upper Room on Van Buren Street, and indeed, I had stopped by and photographed that church the year before. I even went inside the ex-*shul*, because they had a soup kitchen and community center, so I had gone downstairs, then up to the church, and talked to a congregant who showed me around a bit. The building had no Judaica inside that I had seen, but outside on the avenue side I found the Hebrew word "*bet*" (house) and some other letters. They had been carved into stone or some other material and had been painted over numerous times, but I still spotted this and snapped pictures.

Another student, Marcus A., told me that his church had been a synagogue, but he gave a confused address (two streets which I knew were parallel to each other). One day I asked his mother (who worked as the school parental advocate) and she gave me the correct address. In July, a few weeks later, I did find that ex-*shul*/church. Another student or two told me about churches they thought had been Jewish at some point, but they were sketchy about the addresses.

One June day, several seventh grade teachers had taken most of the seventh graders on a field trip. I stayed back with about 15 children and a few teachers, one of whom was Mr. Samuel. I saw him reading a Christian newsletter and asked him if he went to "CCC" (which in Brooklyn refers to the Christian Community Center, a mega-church on Flatlands Avenue). He was a bit surprised that I knew about the CCC, but said no, he was a pastor of his own congregation. Where was it? On Amboy Street. I looked at him, pieced two-and-two together, and asked if it was St. Timothy's. Then he furrowed his brow and asked, "Were you the lady who came to visit us last summer?"

We both realized that we had indeed crossed paths before. Yes, I had stopped by and sat in during the service; yes, he was the pastor who had spoken about St. Vincent's. I guess enough people had remembered me, the white lady with dark hair and glasses who came by and explained why she was interested in the building. I told Pastor Samuel more about my research goals, and he invited me to visit again, so that I could see inside the sanctuary that was usually closed off.

We arranged that I would visit in mid-July before he went on vacation. At first, I thought I would bring my father on the visit, because he seemed somewhat interested in this particular building (as a boy he had known someone who lived on that block of Amboy Street), but he had other plans that day. Instead, I took my daughters with me. I explained to them that we were visiting a church that had been a synagogue a long time before. (My older daughter had accompanied me on another ex-*shul* visit, to Gethsemane Baptist Church the year earlier, but we did not sit in on a service.)

The two girls were a bit bashful, but once we greeted Pastor Samuel they got a bit chatty. He served them cookies and juice; then we looked around. I had gotten a bit confused about something he told me, but then I understood: he was phoning a woman who was a pastor of another congregation that met in this church, but she ran an afternoon service. She was the actual care-taker of the building and had keys to the sanctuary upstairs. Pastor Samuel's congregation, which shares space in the building, is called the Love Tabernacle Fellowship, Intl. Their slogan is "Saving Families, Building Communities."

Soon Pastor Samuel went to give his sermon, so my girls and I went into the hallway, and I showed them Hebrew words and names that had been carved into the marble and then filled in with gold paint. My older one recognized Hebrew letters she knew. Then Ms. Chrysanthius Spann Williams arrived to meet with us.

Her congregation is St. Timothy's Cathedral. She recalled the old H.E.S. building around the corner, but the Catholic Diocese owned the building by then, in the 1950s. Her church moved to Amboy Street from Osborn Street. Her mother bought the building for one dollar. There had been a fire here, in the late 1960s. It was boarded up. (You see the effects of this mostly in the off-limits sanctuary, which I will soon describe.) Ms. Spann-Williams says that it was prophesied that they would have this building.

"There is lots of work to be done," she said frankly. They used to offer space to a day care pro-gram, an after-school program, and a food pantry. She recalled that in the 1960s or 1970s there used to be bus tours that came around. She would see people, perhaps from Israel, coming by to see this synagogue and others in the area. I heard about this from a few other people, but for the most part this happened years ago, and not in any large-scale, organized fashion in recent years.

I snapped two camera-phone photos to remind me of the layout and once-dignified features of the sanctuary, but I can still recall much of the forlorn detail seen here. This had been a large, airy space with two side balconies for female congregants. By the time I visited, the remaining stained glass windows were fading and in poor shape. Many of the wooden pews remained, but several have been pushed around. The wooden floor was warped and worn in many spots. Where the Holy Ark once stood there was now a big empty space. Above that, there must have been a fancy round decoration; what remained were the flourishes around and atop. On the ceiling right above this was a large Jewish star and the original hanging lights.

Pigeons flew about. Parts of the walls were worn away, so you could glimpse the timbers. Pieces of wood and metal and cloth were strewn about in some areas. No one had been up here before us for a very long time. Apparently, in the past there had been paintings depicting biblical scenes, but at some point they were covered over with white paint. There was much water dam-age in the ceiling.

This was a sad, pathetic scene. I felt more than a bit detached as I studied the battered sanctu-ary, slowly walking around it and trying to memorize the forlorn details. Obviously, there are synagogues around the world that have suffered greater blows, that have fallen victim to anti-Semitism and war. For the most part, the Amboy Street ex-*shul* shows vandalism plus a great deal of neglect due to lack of funds for upkeep; this was certainly one of the worst situations I uncovered during my visits to ex-*shuls*. I have read that this was considered a beautiful *shul* in its heyday, full of remarkable details. The outside, especially the front of the building looks fairly decent, and the hallways with their engraved Hebrew names look okay, but the condition of this sanctuary was close to heartbreaking.

Money can work wonders; during the summer of 1984 I held an internship through the Hillel-JACY (Jewish Association for College Youth) program. I was placed at Anshe Chesed on the Up-per West Side of Manhattan. Among my tasks were assisting in fundraising activities. At that time, the main sanctuary was also in poor shape; birds had the upper hand there, and in other ways the place looked rather dire. With the investment of money and time, it is now a beautiful sight. I have been to a few services there in recent years, including a bar mitzvah, and it is a very nice-looking space. The neighborhood people have money, the *shul* now experiences steady use, and support has turned a once-disheveled spot into a notable place. St. Timothy's, once Ansche Radikowicz (one of the variant spellings) has a sanctuary that will not easily regain its former glory.

✿ ✿ ✿ ✿ ✿ ✿

On Sunday, July 29th, 2007, I went to visit three more ex-*shuls* that are now churches. The morning went from drizzly to steady rain, but I still enjoyed my sojourn. The first site I visited was the former Congregation Shaari Zedek. In contrast to the woes of St. Timothy's, this huge former synagogue and current church (First Church of God of Christ of Brooklyn) looked to be in very good shape, inside and out. This building was one of the few that caused my jaw to drop. This is no has-been. It is very well preserved, with lots of original stained glass windows, handsome pews, carefully painted designs in the vestibule, and more. The paintings inside the sanctuary are intricate and still appear to be in fine shape.

To some extent the style is over-the-top; back in the 1920s this was certainly opulent, and now it seems like a sumptuous Hollywood set. It is awe-inspiring, and more so that the place is kept so well. In a few spots in the basement or elsewhere, I did see peeling paint or slight water damage, but someone is taking care of that sanctuary and the main entrance, and the outside is still highly impressive.

One of the few disappointments is that the pipe organ is gone; a female congregant who eagerly showed me around said that "someone Jewish removed the pipe organ." In Hebrew words, painted over a burning bush depiction above the stage, you read "*Ehiyeh Asher Ehiyeh*" (I am what I am). She also said the church had redone one of the main bathrooms to make it bigger and had added the outside gates and sign. Overall, I saw few signs of neglect; for a variety of reasons, this once-glorious synagogue is now a still-glorious church.

The rain did not keep me from making two more stops. I stopped in briefly at the Greater Bibleway Church on Rochester Avenue at Lincoln Place, formerly known as Petach Tikvah. From the outside, this is a handsome building, although the attached building on the avenue shows wear and tear, including cracked windows and peeling paint. I was particularly interested in this building, because it had been one of the few Conservative synagogues, not Orthodox, and was somewhat prominent. A few friends had mentioned this ex-*shul* to me when I first started my research. Outside there are a few Jewish stars, but when I went inside I saw that the Judaica had been removed or covered over. There are original stained glass windows, but they tend to be abstract designs only.

I had to watch my step in the main entrance, because there were many wires on the floor and recording equipment set up; the church tapes its services. The pastor, Huie Rogers, is prominent in his denomination. I couldn't get into the sanctuary although I glanced at it, and it didn't seem to have any Judaica. I asked some congregants, and they said they did not think any remained. One woman said that a rabbi had just recently visited there and that he had a connection to the old Petach Tikvah congregation.

My final destination that day was Eastern Parkway at Lincoln Place, a church known as Universal Temple Church of God, formerly called Adath Yeshurun. This ex-*shul* had been one of the first I had noticed a few years earlier, because it has an unusual shape (the two streets come to a sharp angle). Dodging heavier rain, I parked on the side street and went inside. There is a Jewish star near the roof and another present outside, but inside there was no other visible Judaica. I arrived just when the service music had commenced in what I would call a real old-time pump organ sound.

The congregants I met were, as usual, quite friendly and receptive to my mission. I spoke at length to Mr. Tracey Henderson. Now one of the ministers here, he lived across the street as a child and was the "*Shabbos goy*" (his words) for the *shul*: "I turned off and on the lights." His cousin had told him that the building had become a church, and he had been here since the early 1970s. Upon hearing that this was once a synagogue, a young woman starting up the interior stairs looked surprised. Mr. Henderson, however, knew that several old synagogues around here had become churches, such as Greater Bibleway which I had just been to earlier.

As I glanced over the August calendar of events for Universal Temple, Mr. Henderson also mentioned to me that this building had been a theater before it had been a synagogue. This surprised me, because it doesn't quite have the size and shape for a theater. A few blocks away, also on Eastern Parkway, there is a huge former theater (The Parkway, which featured Jewish programming) which is now a huge church with a soup kitchen and many other programs. (The WPA survey confirms Mr. Henderson's information about the building's origin.)

I shared with the congregants much of the information I had about the former synagogue here, including the name in Hebrew and English, and they were appreciative to learn this. Their service was about to get into full swing (this service had a later start time than the last church I had visited) so I bid them farewell.

On Columbus Day, I paid another trip to an ex-*shul*, and I must have come by just as a service or meeting had broken up, because a handful of congregants spoke with me. This Flatbush-area ex-*shul* was known as the Judea Center, on Bedford Avenue.

In a way I was embarrassed about the fact that I had overlooked this particular site. I am not sure if I came across this one in the WPA survey, but more than one person had informed me of the location. In particular my friend Sarah K., one of the people I interviewed for the previous chapter, as well as another friend of ours, Freda R., had both mentioned it to me at other times. What happened was that I had driven past a different old building, at Bedford and Church Avenues, and saw no sign of Judaica. This decrepit old building, I believe, was at one point a girls' *yeshiva*, a religious day school, and further south on that block had once stood the earlier version of Shaare Torah.

I finally did find this Judea Center on the east side of the street. From the outside it was an attractive building which was boxed in by its neighbors. The doors tipped me off; they had many Jewish stars on the inside and outside. Outside, I found the cornerstone, which immediately reminded me of the nearby Shaari Israel because someone had chiseled out part of the Judaica, and it had been painted over several times. I was still able to make out some of the words in Hebrew, including "Talmud Torah" and "*Yeru- shalyim*" (Jerusalem).

I introduced myself to the congregants inside and told them of my work. One woman seemed a bit defensive, but acted with gentle humor, asking me if I would pay her for the time she took to talk with me. The other people quickly said no; minutes later this was the woman who wanted to see the cornerstone and listen to my translation of what I could decipher from it. She and the others said there was no other Judaica inside that they knew of, but they had been aware of its former life as a synagogue.

Several hours before the New York Giants beat the Green Bay Packers in the third-coldest football game ever played (and in overtime) I braved a cold but not daunting morning and dropped in on three ex-*shuls*, with mixed results of discovery. Initially, I had taken this trip to reshoot pictures of a particular ex-*shul* church in Brownsville. (A man walking by volunteered to me that "This used to be a Jewish synagogue!") Since I had a little time to spare, I stopped into three sites.

The first was at 611 Williams Street. I opened the door and a female parishioner stared at me. I greeted her and told her this had once been a Jewish synagogue. For the first time that I had made these trips I received an awkward reception. "No, it was not," she said dismissively. I told her it was, that I had read this, and she insisted, "No." I gave up on persuading her. She just said, "This is an African church!" and then turned away from me.

Not far from here I stopped in at 71 Malta Street, the former Chesed V'Emeth, now West Baptist Church. I encountered a handful of female congregants clad in choir robes. I told them I was looking in because this had once been a Jewish synagogue. "Oh!" a few said and nodded. They said they did not think there were any more Jewish symbols inside, but I did notice that at the front of the stage, there were red curtains drawn where once may have been the Holy Ark and perhaps other Jewish items. They were polite and asked me if I wanted to stay a while, but I told them I had to get home to take my older daughter to a birthday party (in far-off Sheepshead Bay) so they laughed and bid me a goodbye.

My last stop was at a church that only recently had taken residence in an ex-*shul*, the former Beth Israel on Remsen Avenue at Avenue A. They were in the midst of conducting a Sunday School session (singing an *a capella* rendition of "Come to Sunday School"—the teacher was gamely leading some sleepy children of various ages in this tune). The parishioners were polite and very aware that this had been a synagogue not long ago. I was surrounded by Judaica here— at the end of each wooden pew there was either a carved Jewish star or a carved crown. There were windows adorned with paintings of the Twelve Tribes and a menorah with light bulbs on the stage.

The windows were of an interesting style. They were not stained glass; rather, they had been painted with pictures as well as words in English and Hebrew for a *faux* stained-glass appearance. There were also memorial windows with the names painted on—Eichler, Tabachnik, Konofsky were among the names I read. One woman memorialized here had passed on in 1960. With sunlight streaming in the effect was pleasing. I found it a bit touching; the church crowd can appreciate the Old Testament themes and the English translations, but do the Eichler, Tabachnik and Konofsky families know that they are still being paid tribute today? Most of the windows were in good shape, but in a few cases the paintings were fading.

I also pondered this artistic endeavor. Stained glass is expensive. It is harder to construct, repair, and maintain; water and weather damage are major culprits, as well as accidents and vandalism. So the congregation had commissioned paintings on glass. I am not belittling these efforts; rather, I point out that a fairly modest Jewish congregation had made an effort to beautify their building in a somewhat offbeat way, and it had a different feel to it than that lent by typical stained glass windows. It was more contemporary and even, shall I say, less stuffy. I wonder if it will stand the test of time better than stained glass windows which may break, leaving certain congregations little choice than to remove the remainders and remove the old Jewish themes. Both the typical stained glass windows and the painted windows are vulnerable and are akin to orphans, perhaps cared for by foster parents who may not fully understand their needs, their feelings.

Although I did not sit through a complete service at any of these churches, I do think that I got a taste of the lives of these now-churches. I enjoyed the music and camaraderie, and the act of sharing information and being given tours pleased me greatly. Certainly there is friction (and even bloodshed) at times between various religions and sects of religions around the world. Even in New York City, overflowing melting pot that it was and still is, there are flashpoints between religions, between denominations, between congregations. Often, however, we can find common ground. I could visit several churches and speak with the congregants and clergy and tell them frankly of my research and interest; this was very heartening to me, and I believe to them. Too often people forget that African American churches and Jewish synagogues do have a number of connections. Brooklyn plays host to an astonishing number of such links, and I have been glad to bring people along for a tour.

More Visits with People at Synagogues That Became Churches

For the first several months that I worked seriously on my old *shuls* project, I was literally an outsider looking in. I viewed these buildings only from the street. Just one time, when I drove up to the Jan Hus Moravian Church on Ocean Avenue, did I speak with someone at one of these churches. I knew that building had been the Prospect Park Jewish Center, and as I snapped a few photographs a man approached me, telling me he worked there. He asked me if I wanted to step inside and take a few pictures. I went into the vestibule, but it was dark and I had no flash with me. He also said they had no Judaica. (He did tell me about some other former synagogues, one of which turned out to be the place where my father had his bar mitzvah ceremony.)

For quite a while, I would just go to these buildings, stand outside or sit in my car, and take pictures. I was embarrassed to go up to people and say, "Hi, wasn't this once a synagogue; can I step inside and poke around?" I thought they might find me to be weird, nosy, intrusive. I also thought they might find it odd that I wanted to snoop around inside, perhaps wondering whether or not I was a thief, a real estate appraiser, or an undercover cop, and thus not trust my true motives.

I decided in the spring of 2006 that I should phone a few of these churches and ask if it was all right to visit. I left messages and got no replies. I was a bit put off wondering why no one welcomed my inquiries, but in the course of my visits to the ex-*shuls*, I finally did interact and went inside several.

The first was the New Ammies Chapel at 308 Atkins Street by Sutter Avenue. On June 19, I snapped pictures when I noticed two men sitting and watching me. One asked why I came by and I asked, "Wasn't this once a synagogue?" "Yes, it was—do you want to see some old plaques inside?"

I followed the pleasant caretaker inside, and he showed me the four remaining tablets they had, with names and dates. From what I could read, they appeared to be of donors and then-active members of the old synagogue. The main sanctuary still held the Torah ark topped by a Magen David. There were a few wooden chairs and the pews which were from the days of the synagogue. The pews now held scattered tambourines, hymnals, paper fans with memorial faces. I noted on the wall a Ten Commandments poster made by children. I asked the caretaker, who seemed gratified that I had an interest in the remaining Judaica, if other people had come to photograph the sights. He said they had once or twice, but he couldn't remember exactly when.

I decided to build upon the enjoyable experience of visiting an ex-*shul* by writing to a dozen or so churches that I had full addresses for. I also e-mailed one church that had quite an elaborate website. Two people got in contact with me: Deacon Herbert Gandy of Gethsemane Baptist Church at 144 Newport Street and Clover of Church of God of East Flatbush at 409 East 95th Street.

I brought my daughter Jessica to Gethsemane, because she had finished school, but not started day camp yet. We were welcomed warmly by Deacon Gandy, an elder of the church, as well as two ladies who were setting up a soup kitchen lunch. Deacon Gandy showed us around the building except for the third floor balcony which was blocked off. Drug dealers set the building on fire in 1985 or 1986, and upstairs on the third floor they sustained the most damage. He told us, "Sadly, there had been a huge chandelier up there, as big as one in the Waldorf Astoria; I believe it was crystal. We had to take it out, because it was too expensive for the church congregation to restore it." He said the neighborhood was much better now, but he still felt cautious.

We went into a small office, and I spotted a plaque that had been painted over a number of times. I could still make out some of the Hebrew letters, but only part of the plaque was visible; a desk obscured the rest of it. In the main sanctuary, I saw the wooden doors for the Torah ark. A portrait of the minister covered Hebrew words above the ark; I could only make out part of them. Deacon Gandy tried to move the portrait but it was too heavy. He was interested in finding out the message there, for the only word I could fully read was "Brownsville" written phonetically in Hebrew. Also, there had been a stained glass window with a Jewish star in it on the front of the building, but it broke and the church found the cost to fix it prohibitive. "We didn't want to demolish the whole thing; why take it down?" So they spackled it over instead.

In the lower level where the women were readying the food kitchen, I saw another ark at the back. Deacon Gandy told me, "There was a fellow who came here once, his grandmother belonged here when they came over from Germany, but I didn't see him again." It seemed my daughter and I were the only Jewish persons in a long time who had come to see the old remnants. I promised Deacon Gandy I would find out more information about the old synagogue which had been here and would send him a copy of the photo that I had taken. I did sometime later.

My visit to the Church of God of East Flatbush was shorter, but also gratifying. I had found out about this former synagogue first from Rochelle E., who was older daughter's teacher. She had attended this East Flatbush *shul* as a child, but had not wanted to revisit. That made her uncomfortable, and she had too many site-specific memories. When I gave her a copy of a picture I had taken of the front of the church, which still had Hebrew writing on the gate, she was very grateful and taken aback.

When I visited the church in early July, there was a day care camp group in the basement, preschoolers coloring pictures. Clover, who greeted me, was a church secretary and chaplain. She said the church had been at this location for about thirty years and elsewhere before that. I noted that they had removed the Torah arks, but there was a lot of other Judaica left. There were Jewish stars in the front of the sanctuary and on several stained glass windows, and the ceiling had a big raised Jewish star. Rochelle had told me that when she attended the synagogue, known as Rishon L'Zion, the ceiling had been painted sky blue and was very pretty; now it was plain white. I asked Clover why the church retained so many Jewish symbols and she said, "You buy a building, you're not going to change all the little things." They decided to retain the stars, the pew benches with stars, and more.

I asked if other Jewish people had stopped by to reconnect with their memories of the building, and she told me that "a woman at the office in Somers (Arthur Somers Intermediate School, just a few blocks away) came by and said she came here as a child."

I met with people at other former synagogues-current churches such as Christian Light Baptist Church on Winthrop Street, which had been a Young Israel synagogue; at the First Temple of the House of David on Dumont Avenue, which has an impressive number of items leftover from the previous *shul*; Brooklyn Christian Center on Snediker Avenue, which had been a modestly impressive East New York building; New Gethsemane Church on Rochester Avenue, which has a clothing pantry; and others. These visits were relatively calm and informal compared to my visits to actual Sunday services in these locations.

Overall, people at the churches were particularly intrigued by any Hebrew to English translations of plaques, carvings, and the like that I could offer. Did they feel a deeper connection to their sites after my visits? Did this inspire them to do anything different to their buildings? Would they be more apt to preserve the facilities so that the Judaica would linger longer? Would they be interested in engaging in more interfaith activities? Would they conduct further research on their buildings? Perhaps!

What Does Jewish Law Say About All This?

A Jewish congregation sees its membership fall. Only a few active, interested members remain. The neighborhood seems less hospitable than in the past; Jews are becoming the minority amongst other minority groups in the area. Someone from a church approaches the Jews about buying their *shul* to establish a church there, or the building is falling into disrepair and is vandalized. What do the Jews do? This scenario could have taken place in the 1960s, the 1970s, the early 2000s, and it probably will continue to play out in particular regions.

The Jews in Brooklyn, as in many other urban (and sometimes suburban) areas in the United States and Canada, have faced dilemmas about how to handle their sacred sites and the items held within when the congregation is shutting down or moving elsewhere. Do they abandon the buildings? Sell them outright to a church group? Sell them to a real estate broker who may sell the building to a church? Does the congregation purposely seek a non-religious organization to sell the building to, such as a school or medical center or to the city/town for public use?

What does Jewish law say about this? Civil law may allow for fairly simple transfers. A market economy allows for such transactions, but when Jewish law is involved, the issue is rarely simple. For those who want to do the right thing by *halakhah,* Jewish law, there are a variety of issues regarding how to deal with a synagogue that is dormant or becoming so.

There are particular laws and a gamut of interpretations. The Orthodox, traditional approach handles it a certain way; the Conservative movement has somewhat different opinions regarding this. I could have written this book and ignored the whole topic but I felt that was wrong, disingenuous. It is a topic that has been dealt with for quite some time and is still being dealt with, because synagogues still die out, move to different locations, and so on. We will look at the original sources which analyze the topic and then at derivations and real-life scenarios.

Here are a few situations to show the variety of ways in which this has been handled. A synagogue on East 53rd Street (near the ex-*shul* where my dad had his bar mitzvah ceremony) called B'nai Abraham (Sons of Abraham) was written about in a *New York Times* article in the 1970s which depicted the woebegone state near its end. This building now is being used by an Orthodox Jewish group as an early childhood center. While the people there now are a different group, the building did not face the fate of many other ex-*shuls;* it stayed within the use of the Jewish community. The other ex-*shul* on East 53rd Street was sold to be renovated and used as a medical center. It now looks quite different than it did even in 2006, when it still featured much of its outer Judaica, but it is not a house of worship for another religion, which is a particularly sticky issue in Jewish law.

Many other former shuls, as depicted throughout this book, have become churches representing several Christian denominations. How does this square with Jewish laws and customs? When the particular Brooklyn neighborhoods focused on had large Jewish populations, they were certainly able to adhere to the following: "When ten people pray together," says the Talmud, "the *shechinah* rests amongst them." (Berachot 6a) Judaism, therefore, attaches great importance to public worship (*tefillah betzibur*). (Appel p.16) Certainly these neighborhoods, including Brownsville, East New York, East Flatbush, and others, were home to many synagogues, many sites of public worship. Typically, from the early 1900s through just after World War II, it was not difficult for these many *shuls* to each assemble a *minyan*, a quorum of ten Jewish men, required for many prayers and for Torah reading. Once the Jewish population began to dwindle, *minyans* became scarce if not impossible to form. Would the following instead be an issue?

"Where there is no steady *minyan*, they may compel one another to assemble regularly for a *minyan* so that communal worship may not cease." (Appel p.57) Who would make such an appeal, and who would heed the call? There were cases of Jews who moved from their old neighborhood of Brownsville but still returned (at least for a while) to their old synagogues to help maintain the required *minyan*. These ties eventually eroded, and who was left? In a largely secularized society, how compelling would this be to the majority of Jews who were abandoning areas such as Brownsville?

So the first thing to discuss here are the laws and then the interpretations surrounding the sale of synagogues that are no longer able to function properly. "If Jews have moved out of a neighborhood and the synagogue is left without a *minyan* of worshipers, or if it is not possible for them to maintain it for services, it is permitted to sell the synagogue, if possible through the intermediacy of a third party, such as the bank that holds the mortgage." (Appel, pp.61–62) This interpretation, based upon the Concise Code of Jewish Law (*Kitzur Shulhan Aruch* and other traditional sources), may be seen as common sense, yet it can be heartbreaking for those who had associations with the particular shul. The straight-forward tone of the above obscures the emotions behind the decision and the history of the group, of the building. Rabbi Louis Jacobs wrote in 1995, "The question of selling a synagogue that is no longer used has been much discussed. As stated above, the question is discussed in the *Mishnah* (*Megillah*, Chapter 3) and in the Talmudic elaboration of the Mishnah. The final ruling is that when a synagogue can no longer be used it may be sold, on the grounds that synagogues are sanctified on the condition that they are used as such, so that once a synagogue is no longer used it loses its sanctity and may be sold." (Jacobs, available through www.myjewishlearning.com) Extrapolating from that, Jacobs states that authorities allow for a synagogue to be sold and then turned into a church or mosque, although this is usually achieved through indirect sale to a third party (agent, bank, government, even a non-profit organization).

Who within the congregation gets to make this big decision? This could be a bone of contention among some members while others could be indifferent, disinterested. Some *shuls* chose to go to civil court to finalize their congregational assets. Did some *shuls* dissolve into arguments over how to contend with the assets, including the building? Did some *shuls* simply abandon buildings out of fear of rising violence in the neighborhoods or for indecision over how to handle dissolution? Unfortunately, this has not been systematically documented and easily accessed for research purposes, in most cases. It often became a private matter whose memory has faded with time. A few *shuls* moved elsewhere (even to Israel, where two synagogues became "transplanted") and to the suburbs (this happened a number of times in Chicago—see *Chicago's Forgotten Synagogues,* by Robert A. Packer) and some merged with healthier synagogues (the East Midwood Jewish Center of Brooklyn absorbed the former Shaare Torah, for instance). While there are a few ways in which synagogues have been phased out, there is no central depository for this information, so it is uncovered with luck and intense sleuthing. Some ex-*shuls* took civil legal routes; some dissolved in a member's living room. The Conservative movement as well as the Orthodox community has also studied the topic of selling holy property; this includes *shul* buildings and any sacred items such as Torah scrolls, prayer books, books of study, ornamentation associated with holy items—pulpit covers, Torah covers, the *yad* (pointer used by Torah readers), furniture (especially if it has Judaic ties such as a lectern for the reading of a Torah scroll). Even smaller items such as *tallisim* (prayer shawls), a *ner tamid* ("eternal light" fixture) and ceremonial wine goblets have to be dealt with by a congregation in its sunset (although there are cases of *shul* buildings that were left with many of these items, which were sometimes incorporated into the churches).

The Conservative committee, by examining *Mishnah Megillah* 3:1 stated that "1. Holiness accrues to certain items used for worship and study. 2. If the holy item is sold, the holiness transfers into the funds for which it was sold. 3. Holiness is not uniform, but is distinguished by degrees. (Examples from the *Megillah*: 'If they sell a synagogue, they must buy an ark. If they sell an ark they must buy the dressings for the Torah.') (Rabbi Fine, p.1) Thus there is intrinsic value to various religious objects, and these items cannot just be sold at a garage sale. Care must be taken in selling them and in how money received will be used.

It is easier, therefore, to sell a synagogue than a Torah scroll. Once the building has been stripped of Judaica, it is just a building; however, a Torah scroll's letters cannot just be erased, nor the other elements recycled. It is easier, and more desirable, simply to donate an unused Torah scroll to an active shul or school.

What should a shul nearing its end do with any money earned from the sale of the building and its holy items? According to the *Megillah*, the money cannot just be divided up by remaining members and/or their relatives; a higher purpose must be sought for the pool of money. In many cases, this has actually meant that the money was donated to another synagogue, religious school, or Jewish charity. "One may use the proceeds from the sale of a synagogue for the construction of a Jewish school." (Fine, p.8) Other less holy funds may be derived from any membership fees the congregation had banked as well as burial plots purchased by the group.

Perhaps the easiest way to take care of any of these items from a closing *shul* is to give them to other congregations and schools. Even then, however, such items should be examined for structural problems. This is particularly important with Torah scrolls, which can be considered *pasul* (unfit for use). (A Torah must be mended by a qualified scribe.)

The other *halakhic* consideration I had to make while researching this book regards entering churches. I have photographed over ninety former synagogues from the outside and scouted out about a dozen more from the street, and many of these buildings now house churches. I have been inside almost thirty of these buildings in order to investigate the Judaica inside, as well as to take photographs of their interiors. I spoke with members of the current churches on several occasions. At times I examined former and current social halls, libraries, classrooms, lobbies, rooms used as food pantries and for clothing drives, and many of the sanctuaries.

There are Jewish laws regarding Jews entering non-Jewish houses of worship. There are various interpretations and opinions about the appropriateness of doing this. Jews are offered several options depending upon their level of observance. Certainly, many Jews, especially those who are not very observant, have little or no problem with entering a church. For those who are more observant, there are more issues, restrictions and considerations.

According to the website askMoses.com, "it is forbidden for a Jew to enter the sanctuary of the church, i.e., where the active prayer services are held. This could be misinterpreted as identification with the philosophy (of the church). However, it is permitted to enter other rooms in a church for non-religious purposes." Rabbi Naftali Silberberg posted this in a straight-forward passage, especially targeted to Jews who are less likely to have studied the laws pertaining to this.

Rabbi Jeremy Rosen, a British rabbi, also addressed the *halakhah* of entering churches on his website:

The law banning entry to a house of worship is predicated on the assumption that it is pagan...

The Maharal of Prague (ShoT 24), the Tifferet Yisrael (Avot 3.14), and the Noda Biyehuda (in the introduction to *Hitnatzlut HaMechaber*) all declared that Christianity was not idolatry because it accepted the idea of Divine revelation...

Amongst the answers is that of *eyvah*, a Talmudic principle that requires us to maintain good relations with those we live amongst, regardless of their religion....

In fact, I, personally, have gone into churches to look at art and architecture and to listen to concerts.... (Jeremy Rosen, pp. 1–2)

While I investigated former synagogues which are now churches, I was not praying and made it known that I was there to conduct research. Everyone I met at these houses of worship respected my wishes and seemed to understand my intentions clearly.

Here is another look at the issue:

Entering a house of *avoda zara* is forbidden for four reasons: The first is the prohibition of *mar'ith 'ayin*, making it look as though a Jew would think of worshipping *avoda zara*.... There is the assumption of someone participating in a church service. The second is a more controversial point: a house of *avoda zara* is considered in the category of *meshamshei avoda zara* and is therefore...forbidden to derive any benefit from it, e.g., shelter from the sun....

If there are no statues in the building, (one) prohibition would not apply...." (*Jewish Mailing List*, vol. 17, Number 42, December 1994)

This response was directed to a more scholarly and strictly observant audience, but it is included to show that there is debate about the act of a Jew entering a church. Yes, someone could see me entering a church and assume that I came for the service. The actual reason was to conduct research and people were told of my research project. People at these churches were told that I was Jewish and came for historical and interfaith purposes. Some will disagree with my decisions, but it was necessary to access material that could only be seen in these houses of worship. One of my goals was to bring to life "hidden" Judaica, to make fuller the story of Brooklyn Jewry. Some of these buildings may be gone or significantly altered in a few years or many years down the road, and I wish to relate at least some aspects of them for future generations of Jews, as well as all Brooklynites and anyone else interested in urban Jewish history.

Conclusion

Is there a bond between Brooklyn's ex-*shuls* and ski slopes? Witness NELSAP, the New England Lost Ski Areas Project. It is devoted to telling the stories of ski areas that are gone, some recently, some decades ago. There are trail maps, photographs, testimonies, and more to document the passing of several hundred ski sites throughout New England, as well as the mid-Atlantic states and elsewhere in the United States and Canada.

I am fascinated by this website not only because I ski, but also for the greater themes behind this—displaying affection for a type of fading institution, in this case the passing of ski places (especially smaller ones) and the urge to uncover the hazy histories of such destinations. This website may be concerned with a sport and American culture and may have little to do with religious expression, but it is similar in many ways to the goals of my book and the photography exhibit that preceded it. I have hoped to uncover aspects of religious history and of urban Jewish culture, and I have explored a few synagogues that were part of my life at certain stages. Just as I found out information about and reflected upon my memories of a Berkshires, Massachusetts, ski center that I used to enjoy but has closed (Brodie Mountain in Lanesboro, MA), I have pieced together research on synagogues in the borough of the city that I love most and with which I have had personal interactions.

Writes Jenna Weissman Joselit in "Museum Woe," which appeared in the *Forward*,

> And yet, there's something about a synagogue-turned-museum that saddens, even disturbs. It's an axiom of modern-day life that today's fashions are yesterday's news, that neighborhoods come and go, that most things have a very limited shelf life. When seen from this perspective, the inability of a *shul* to sustain itself over time ought to be par for the course, part of the natural order of things. But somehow it's not. Perhaps that's because the waning, and ultimate disappearance, of a *shul* is no ordinary event, no simple casualty of change. It carries the whiff of disappointment, the sting of failure about itself."
> (Joselit, the Forward, B3, 1/4/08)

She wrote this about the renovation and repositioning of the Eldridge Street Synagogue of Manhattan's Lower East Side into a museum, but this quote and the whole essay speak volumes about the ex-*shuls* of Brooklyn and elsewhere. Yes, Brooklyn's Jewish neighborhoods have shifted to a great extent. Certain neighborhoods such as Brownsville and East New York, East Flatbush, and Flatbush were previously heavily Jewish in population and in tone. That has changed, and the synagogues that proliferated in these areas were indeed casualties of demographic shifts. Although some people have bittersweet emotions about these changes, for the most part, Jews have accepted them—for what else could be done? Jews living there moved or passed away. Who would support over a hundred *shuls* that had become empty? So other people bought the buildings and made them into their own vessels, typically vessels of Christianity.

There is the "whiff of disappointment, the sting of failure" that Jews can sigh about, rail against, uncomfortably chuckle over. Not enough Jewish people wanted to stay in certain neighborhoods; not enough Jewish people wanted to support these synagogues; not enough Jewish people remained to make these buildings viable as synagogues. Jews of a certain age and of a certain place may think back fondly to these neighborhoods, but for the most part they wanted to move on and in the process move up to more prestigious areas, to homes with bigger front and back yards, to houses instead of apartments, and often from very ethnically Hebraic surroundings to a more secular, more homogenized version of their American Dream. Most of the Jewish people in these areas wanted to be elsewhere, doing other things or at least praying in different locations. Some felt pangs of guilt, feelings of betrayal, while others crowed, "I'm not going here after my bar mitzvah, ha!"

While many Brooklyn ex-*shuls* were knocked down (often for space to build public housing or smaller residential edifices), others remained and changed hands, becoming churches or schools or day care sites or medical-social service centers. Some reverted to being private residences. The past lives of these buildings cannot and should not be denied. Why ignore the fact that a Baptist church on Glenmore Avenue used to be a beautiful synagogue, especially when there are many symbols of Judaica remaining, as well as Hebrew words? Why hush up the fact that a huge church on Arlington Avenue used to be Temple Sinai? The past is there to be revealed, to be discussed, to be gawked at. These places show the intersection of different cultural and religious groups and I, for one, think this is fascinating and worth learning more about.

There were churches throughout the United States, within New York City, and even located in Brooklyn that closed, that changed, that even became synagogues. How did the parishioners of these churches feel about this? Did they lament the passing of their churches? In recent years, the Catholic Archdiocese of Brooklyn has closed some Catholic schools and consolidated others due to decreased enrollment at these schools. Some families, students, and faculty protested these changes, cried when they found out that their schools were being phased out, and I sympathized with them. Their disappointment echoed the disappointment of Jewish people who saw their *shuls* depleted and closed. Some of these parish schools have since become public schools; do the former students feel wistful about this? Do they look inside the windows at times and say to themselves, "I used to be there in that chair"?

Do at least some Jewish people drop by their old synagogues, look inside at the church service in progress, and think back to the times they attended Shabbat services there?

The concept of turning a *shul* into a museum has occurred not only in Manhattan but elsewhere, especially in Europe. I have visited ex-*shuls* in Prague, Czech Republic, and Amsterdam, the Netherlands, which are now beautiful, intriguing museums. In a way they have become shrines, and while they are being utilized in a positive way, they are not being utilized in the way they were originally cast. Some European *shuls* are not ex-*shuls*, for although they are under-attended by parishioners they also function as museums, as tourist destinations. The Remuh or Rema Synagogue in Krakow, when I stopped by on a Friday evening/*Erev Shabbos* in 1999, had but a few old men in the chairs. After they left, within minutes singing teenagers came down the street. Soon a group of Israeli teens on a tour were entering the *shul*, and with their teachers they began their own *Kabbalat Shabbat* service. The *shul* had become vibrant and alive, but how frequently would this occur? Is this a synagogue primarily for a few older people or for tourists who pay their respects once or twice in their lifetimes?

Could all the many remaining ex-*shul* buildings in Brooklyn be turned into museums? Could they become spots for enthusiastic teens to pray on a rare occasion? Could at least a few become museums, if not the bulk of them? This is unlikely to occur for many reasons. Real estate is too potent a factor in New York City. How could a non-profit group or governmental agency persuade a Christian congregation to leave the premises so that some nice old building with pretty touches to it could become a museum? That is a far-fetched task.

We should also ask the Christian congregants who now use these buildings if they have any memories of the turnover process, from synagogue to church. The elders may have valuable information about this. We should ask the congregants, as I have done on a small scale, how they react to the Judaic symbols on the walls and windows and pews. What have they learned, surmised, wondered? How have they changed the buildings to make them their own? This is how history evolves.

My interest in the subject of ex-*shuls* in Brooklyn and elsewhere will not conclude with this chapter nor with the publication of this book. I will continue to be fascinated, haunted, delighted by this topic. I know that these buildings and the people and things they represent will stay with me. I live in Brooklyn; I drive by these buildings; I have met several Christian people who now go to church in these buildings; my family and I had relationships with some of these congregations.

My task has been to convince other people to become interested in learning about them and researching and visiting them. If you are Jewish or Christian, if you live in Brooklyn or elsewhere, if you enjoy urban history, if you are a devotee of architecture, if you want to learn about a somewhat off-beat topic that really is quite mainstream, then I hope you have benefitted from this book. Let other people know that Brooklyn's ex-*shuls* live on.

Survey of the Buildings

The ex-*shuls* of Brooklyn fascinate for many reasons, and aesthetics certainly play a role. Since childhood I have had an interest in architecture, partly because my father is a retired structural engineer, and he would always remark upon buildings; thus I became aware of their details. I have scrutinized the decoration, styling of the entrances and doors of buildings, colors, materials, landscaping, and the influences of different ages and cultures.

We can analyze these buildings by their size and their detailing and how they are situated. There are some trends among these buildings that are quickly evident. The majority of them are boxy structures not highly innovative. Most that still retain Judaic detail exhibit fairly typical symbols. There are obvious trends in windows, stairways, and doorways, but each old *shul* does have its particulars; some may appear to be "siblings" of others. A few former synagogues are very distinctive edifices that cannot be overlooked. Many others blend in with their surroundings, so that you have to look carefully for them to appreciate their beauty. A handful are dull, fairly charmless buildings.

The website for the New York City Department of Finance at <http://www.nyc.gov/html/dof/html/property/property_info_bbl.shtml> was of great value to my study of the buildings. By typing the street address of an individual building, one can find out the lot size, building size, estimated market value and other salient real estate facts.

There is one area in the study of these buildings I failed to learn much about: who were the architects and engineers and developers of these buildings? This information is not easy to come by. The New York Landmarks Conservancy was a great aid in locating the names of some of these architects. Another disappointment: I could not find out the site specifics for all the ex-*shuls*. For some reason, about a dozen addresses were unavailable for viewing on the Department of Finance website. Sometimes I would get a screen message that the address in question was out of range, or an incorrect address kept popping up instead of the one I had entered. Bugs in the system? I do not know for sure. Here are some representative neighborhoods by zip code, and the number of ex-*shuls* per zip:

11203 (8) Rugby-East Flatbush
11206 (8) Williamsburg-East Williamsburg
11207 (15) Brownsville
11208 (5) East New York
11211 (3) Williamsburg
11212 (20) Brownsville
11213 (6) Crown Heights
11216 (1) Prospect Heights
11217 (1) Park Slope
11221 (5) Bushwick (east)
11222 (1) Greenpoint
11223 (1) Gravesend
11225 (1) Prospect Lefferts Gardens
11226 (6) Flatbush, Prospect Park South
11229 (1) Marine Park
11233 (5) Weeksville-Bedford-Stuyvesant
11234 (1) Sheepshead Bay
11236 (1) Canarsie
11238 (1) Prospect Heights

The ex-*shuls* that I found real estate information for are located in the above zip codes. These neighborhoods are largely northern, central and eastern Brooklyn. There are synagogues in all the other zip codes throughout Brooklyn, but (1) the synagogues in many of these regions have remained synagogues and have not been converted for other use (although in some instances the synagogues have changed names and degrees of religiosity) (2) there are a few neighborhoods where the ex-*shuls* are just gone—this is particularly true of zip code 11224, Coney Island. These buildings were knocked down or so radically changed they could not be located. Evidence of ex-*shuls* is much greater in Brownsville, East New York, Flatbush, and especially East Flatbush.

Lot Size

How big is the lot size for each former synagogue, and why should this be important? It was easy to find out the lot sizes for most of these edifices through the use of the NYC Department of Finance website. I initially thought that many ex-*shuls* would have lot sizes similar to a residential house plot, or double that. My father long ago told me that a typical New York City side-street lot size is 40x100 feet, so I had assumed that many ex-*shuls* would be on lots that size or some multiple thereof (80x100, 20x100, or even 160x100).

There are six ex-*shuls* which sit on that typical size lot of 40x100, and that was the most frequent lot size listed. As well, there were two ex-*shuls* on lots of 20x100 each and one at 80x100. In general, something times 100 feet was the most common measurement, and some were neat, even numbers: 60x100, 100x100 (three ex-*shuls* stand on lots of that size). But then we see ex-*shuls* on lots measuring 20.25x100, and 39x100 (who shorted them the one foot?) and 45.25x100 (huh?) or 94.42x100. The city is seemingly obsessed with getting those fractional measurements into the archives. The reasons for these oddball sizes could generally be chalked up to the availability at the time, perhaps easements. Parcels of land in Brooklyn are not always standardized. Several ex-*shuls* were considered "irregular" in size by the Finance Department.

Why would the lot size be worthy of discussion? Partly, this shows how much a congregation was able to purchase initially. Also, if a congregation was interested in locating its building in a particular neighborhood, they had to look into the availability of space at the time.

Then there are the building sizes. As far as size, they are varied. Not a single measurement popped up more than once, although several were within striking distance. A few of these old synagogues were quite spacious, especially if they were located on large lots. Examples include the former Temple Sinai on Arlington Avenue, Petach Tikvah on Rochester Avenue, Shaarey Zedek on Kingston Avenue. Some former *shuls* were sizable, such as Bnai Jacob on Glenmore Avenue (especially because of its large columns, it gives off an imposing air). A great number were moderate, the size of a multiple family dwelling. Some were quite small; the synagogue on Louisiana Avenue is certainly modest. We cannot know now what the finances were of each congregation when these buildings were being erected, but you can infer that the very big synagogues were backed by wealthier patrons, or a greater number of contributors.

Market Value

I decided to look at the current estimated market value of these ex-*shuls*. This does not necessarily tell us a great deal about the past, although the bigger ex-*shuls* do tend to be valued at a higher amount now. I wanted to know what these buildings are worth now, and even compared these amounts to older Brooklyn synagogues that are in different Brooklyn neighborhoods. Many of the ex-*shuls* (as opposed to the still-*shuls*) are in poorer regions of Brooklyn. Brownsville and East New York have certainly experienced recent development and are reaping the benefits of a generally stronger economy in recent years. Yet the ex-*shuls* there are still worth less, in general, than synagogues in Midwood, or Sheepshead Bay, Park Slope, and other wealthier neighborhoods.

Taking a Tour:
Photographs and Text on Ex-Shuls of Brooklyn

To a great extent this book is an extension of my photography exhibit at the Brooklyn Historical Society of twenty-two black-and-white photographs of ex-*shuls* around Brooklyn. This exhibit ran from November 15, 2006, to February 12, 2007, with a preview of five photographs on November 1, 2006. I delivered a lecture about the topic and exhibit on Sunday, January 21, 2007.

When I realized that my topic was receiving serious attention and press, I decided to take it further. The research and writing, the continued photographic work, and other planning involved have not been easy, but I feel that there has not been another study quite like this one, as comprehensive and multi-faceted.

I also wanted to offer a "tour guide" which would include photographs, historical background, and architectural discussion for many of these ex-*shuls*. Perhaps readers will make pilgrimages to see these buildings; perhaps some will have information to add about these sites. Anything to shine more light on the history and personality of every ex-*shul* adds to our store of knowledge.

These ex-*shuls* often share certain architectural trends. One obvious structural pattern found among several ex-*shuls* (as well as some older Brooklyn synagogues which are still active) is what can be dubbed the "triptych" style. Similar in ways to a triptych, a three-paneled painting ensemble, some ex-*shul* buildings have a tri-part design. Typically, this means that the middle section of the whole structure is the biggest and/or widest, and it is flanked by two smaller or narrower structures.

This type of design attempts to make a synagogue resemble an opened Torah scroll. There are at least a dozen Brooklyn ex-*shuls* where this is obvious. The two outer segments of the building (at least as seen from the street) appear to be like the two polls of a Torah scroll, with the parchment wrapped around them, and the middle section, which is wider, is the section of the Torah which is being read. The open Torah scroll is also a common symbol of Judaism

This trend can also be seen as reflecting the Romanesque Revival style of a main part of the building flanked by two towers. There are churches from the late 1800s which reflect this style. (See *Identifying American Architecture* by John J.-G. Blumenson, p. 42 for excellent examples.) A number of churches in the United States are in this style or its off-shoots, especially in older urban regions, but in these Brooklyn ex-*shuls,* the outer segments are not typically towers.

Examples of these structures include fairly modest buildings as well as gems. The New Hebrew School building at Stockton Street is a somewhat streamlined example of this style, as is B'nai Abraham on Scholes Street; more elaborate buildings in this vein include Men Of Justice on Park Place and Beth Hemidrish Hagadol on Williams Street. These types of buildings tended to be built expressly as houses of worship, as opposed to renovated residences turned into small *shuls*.

This design trend is well suited to an urban area where synagogues cannot be built as sprawling complexes. There are some Bronx and Manhattan ex-*shuls* that appear to follow this trend; however, although there are some stylistic similarities, overall the Bronx synagogues do not look quite like the Brooklyn ones. In fact, there is discernible individuality amongst a great many ex-*shuls* of Brooklyn and the Bronx, as well as in Manhattan (although the East Village-Lower East Side has modest ex-*shuls* that are easily cousins to Brooklyn ex-*shuls*). Look at the website Shtetlhood.com, about Detroit's "lost" synagogues to see that those ex-*shuls* often look quite different from Brooklyn and Bronx examples.

A particularly important feature of many ex-*shuls,* as well as older *shuls* that remain active, is the rose window. Perhaps many people think of rose windows when they think of major Gothic cathedrals and not of modest 20th-century synagogues, but many ex-*shuls* and active *shuls* showcase this type of window, in some form.

Many of these Brooklyn ex-*shuls* have their own circular rose window (occasionally windows) hovering above the main entrance or near the roof. Now that many of these buildings have been converted into churches, these rose windows have often been spackled over, or covered over with paint or wood paneling. Sometimes a cross has been inserted in the middle. These congregations may have retained much or some other Judaica, but they often wished to include a cross in their decorative scheme for identification purposes. As Deacon Herbert Gandy of Gethsemane Baptist Church explained to me, the glass in the rose window on the front of his ex-*shul*/church had become broken and the cost of repair was prohibitive. Round windows and stained glass windows in general certainly are harder and more costly to repair and replace.

The *shuls* that have these rose windows often have nice brickwork surrounding the windows. Amongst the ex-*shuls* with a typical rose window or place for it are: Macedonia Missionary Baptist Church on Howard Avenue; Little Rock Baptist Church on Chester Street; Greater Bright Light Baptist Church on Sutter Avenue; Christ Apostolic Church on Williams Street; Jones Temple on Hinsdale Avenue; and Messiah Missionary Baptist Church on Sutter Avenue. These rose windows vary in size.

Two of the more remarkable rose windows are at Little Zion Baptist Church on Scholes Street and Faith Chapel Baptist on Prospect Place. Little Zion has special features, one of which is its rose window with a flower-petal motif. The eight petals are in decent shape and are framed by an arch of thin piped columns. Faith Chapel has a half rose window above the entrance, with a wheel motif of eight spokes, segmented into thirds with a half bulls-eye in the center. It too is striking, with nice work within the individual panes. A variation on the rose window can be seen on the Brooklyn Christian Center, formerly Chevra Sphard of Perryslaw. There is no real rose window but a circle of raised brick, and within that still rests a brick Jewish star.

In the past were these modest Jewish stars or bold designs; delicately decorated or starkly simple? It is possible to see what these buildings looked like in the late 1930s and early 1940s, in their Hebraic heyday. At some point, every New York City building, be it private residence, place of business, house of worship or public institution, was captured on film with a number for taxation purposes. Today one can locate these photographs by using the building- block-lot number provided by the New York City Department of Finance.

You can order a black-and-white print of a building for a fee, or you can go to the Municipal Archives, track down the numbers, and look through the microfilm spools that carry the photographs. Besides being able to see what these buildings looked like decades ago, you can see former buildings, as well as anything contemporary that drifted into the photographs (cars, people, advertisements).

In the individual entries for the many synagogues listed here I will describe the architecture, especially if the building is not just a generic converted residence. There were many attractive, even remarkable *shuls* built in Brooklyn before World War II. Manhattan is not the only New York City borough with a healthy helping of handsome houses of worship. Perhaps their good looks helped many of these buildings to survive and become recycled for other uses, for other religions. (However, some highly remarkable synagogues are long gone, due to destruction, fire, and other unfortunate circumstances.) This is a good reason to be interested in and impressed by the ex-*shuls* that still stand: they should be recognized for what they once were and what they still are.

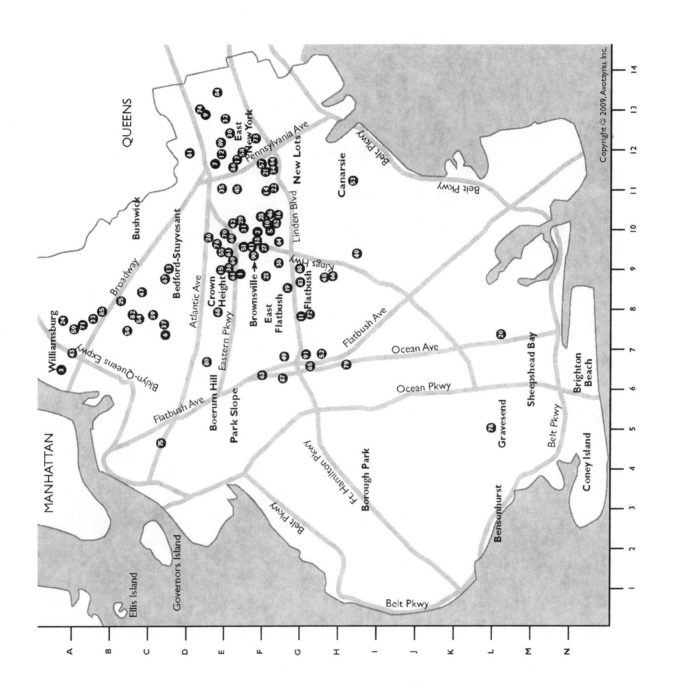

1. Congregation Adath Yeshurun 1403 Eastern Parkway at Lincoln Place, Brownsville (F9)
2. Congregation Agudas Achim Ansche Bobruisk 729 Saratoga Avenue, Brownsville (F10)
3. Agudas Achim Anshei Mishnitz 726 Driggs Avenue, lower Williamsburg (A7)
4. Agudas Achim Anshei New Lots 43 Malta Street, New Lots (G10)
5. Agudath Achim Anshei David Horodok 855 Saratoga Avenue, Brownsville (F10)
6. Congregation Ahavath Achim of Bedford Section 404 (402) Gates Avenue, Bedford-Stuyvesant (C7)
7. Agudath Achim Bnei Jacob of East New York 503 Glenmore Avenue, East New York (E12)
8. Congregation Ahavas Achim B'nai Abraham 394–6 Logan Street, East New York (D13)
9. Congregation Ahavas Achim Brownsville 105 Riverdale Avenue, Brownsville (F10)
10. Ahavath Achim Anshei Brownsville 105 Riverdale Avenue, Brownsville (F10)
11. Congregation Ahavas Achim of East Flatbush 203 East 37th Street, East Flatbush (G8)
12. Congregation Ahavath Chesed Day Nursery 394 Hendrix Street, East New York (E12)
13. Ahavath Chesed 740 (742) Jefferson Avenue, Bedford-Stuyvesant (C9)
14. Ahavath Israel 760 Sackman Street, East New York/New Lots (F11)
15. Ahavath Reyim 209 Rochester Avenue, Northern Crown Heights (E9)
16. Anshei Azaritz/Azaritz Young Friends 885–7 Thomas Boyland (Hopkinson) Street, Brownsville (F10)
17. Anshei Krashnik of East New York Nusach Sfard, 473 Vermont Street, East New York (E12)
18. Congregation Beth Abraham 770 Howard Avenue near Livonia Avenue, Brownsville (F10)
19. Beth Hamedrash HaGadol 777–779 Schenectady Avenue (East 47th Street), East Flatbush (G9)
20. Beth Hamedrash Hagadol Nachloth Zion of South Flatbush 2175 East 22nd Street, Sheepshead Bay (L7)
21. Beth Hemidrash Hagadol 611 Williams Street, East New York New Lots (F12)
22. Congregation Beth Israel 771 Sackman Street, Brownsville (F11)
23. Congregation Beth Israel 8910 Remsen Avenue/ 650 Avenue A, Remsen Heights/East Flatbush (F9)
24. Beth Israel 231–3 Ainslie Street, Williamsburg (A8)
25. Bikur Cholim 3 (or 3–5–7) Lewis Avenue, Northern Bedford-Stuyvesant (B8)
26. Congregation Bikur Cholim Bnai Jacob 2134 Dean Street,Weeksville-Bedford-Stuyvesant (E10)
27. B'nai Israel Jewish Center 9517 Kings Highway, East Flatbush/Brownsville border (F10)
28. Chevra Ahavath Israel Anshei Ostrolenker 375 Bristol Street, Brownsville (F10)
29. Chevra Poelei Tzedek Anschei Glubucker of Brownsville 167–69 Chester Street, Brownsville (E10)
30. Congregation Chevra Tehillim Nusach Ashkenaz 511 Elton Street, East New York (E12)
31. Chevra Torah Anshei Radishkowitz 135–9 Amboy Street, Brownsville (E10)
32. Chevre Anshei Zedek/ Talmud Torah Anshei Zedek of East New York 308–310 Atkins Avenue, East New York (E13)
33. Daughters of Zion 130 Boerum Street, East Williamsburg (B8)
34. Congregation Dorshe Tov Anshei New Lots 21 Louisiana Avenue, New Lots (F12)
35. Congregation Eliezer of East New York 133 Hinsdale Street, East New York (E11)
36. Etz Chaim Machzikei Hadath 1477 Lincoln Place, Brownsville (E9)
37. Ezrath Israel 496 Gates Avenue, Bedford-Stuyvesant (C8)
38. Congregation Friends Oholei Torah 890 Lenox Road, East Flatbush (G9)
39. Gates of Prayer/Community Center Congregation and Talmud Torah/Odessa Benevolent 180–182 Van Buren Street, Bedford-Stuyvesant (C8)
40. Glenwood Jewish Center-Lila R. Korf Talmud Torah 888 East 56th Street, Old Mill Basin (H9)
41. H.E.S. (Hebrew Educational Society) Thomas Boyland (Hopkinson) Street at Sutter Avenue, Brownsville (F10)
42. Hebrew Ladies Day Nursery 521 Thomas Boyland Street, Brownsville (E10)
43. Hebrew School of Williamsburg 310 South 1st Street, Williamsburg (A7)
44. Hessed Ve Emeth Society of Castorialis 69–71 Malta Street, East New York (F12)
45. Independent Chevra Sphard of Perryslaw 247 Snediker Avenue, East New York (E11)

46. Congregation Independent Esrath (or Ezrath) Achim 144 Newport Street, Brownsville (F10)
47. Israel Elice Brethren of Yale 474–6 Kosciuszko Street, upper Bedford-Stuyvesant (C8)
48. Jewish Center of Hyde Park 779 East 49th Street, East Flatbush (H9)
49. Judea Center 2059 Bedford Avenue, East Flatbush (F7)
50. Congregation Kachlow Israel 220–2 Hegeman Avenue, Brownsville-East New York (B7)
51. Kenesseth Israel Beth Jacob 35 Blake Avenue, Brownsville (E10)
52. Kesser Torah 2310 Cortelyou Road at East 23rd Street, Flatbush (H7)
53. "Kevelson's" Shul 1387 East 96th Street, Canarsie (H11)
54. Machzikei Torah Bnei David 175 Hart Street, Bedford-Stuyvesant (C8)
55. Men of Justice 1676–8 Park Place, Brownsville/East New York (E9)
56. New Hebrew School of Brooklyn/ Bnos Israel Malbush Arumim 146 Stockton Street, Bedford-Stuyvesant (F11)
57. New Lots Talmud Torah 330–370 New Lots Avenue at Pennsylvania Ave., East New York (F12)
58. Ohev Shalom (Bais Harav Midrash Eliyahu Anshei Charney?) 744 Dumont Avenue, East New York (E12)
59. Ohev Sholom Anshei Sfard 157 Leonard Street at Stagg Street, East Williamsburg (A8)
60. The Parkway Theater 1768 St. John's Place, Brownsville (E10)
61. Congregation Petach Tikvah 261 Rochester Avenue, Crown Heights (E10)
62. Petrikower Anshe Sfard of Brownsville 493 Herzl Steet, Brownsville (F10)
63. Prospect Park Jewish Center and Yeshiva 153 Ocean Avenue, Flatbush (F6)
64. Rishon L'Zion 409 East 95th Street, East Flatbush (F10)
65. Shaare Torah 305 East 21st Street at Albemarle Road, Flatbush (G7)
66. Shaari Israel 810 East 49th Street, East Flatbush (H9)
67. Shaari Zedek, then Ahavath Achim 765–7 Putnam Avenue, Bedford-Stuyvesant (C9)
68. Shaari Zedek 221 Kingston Avenme, Bedford-Stuyvesant (E8)
69. Sheveth Achim 276 Buffalo Avenue, Brownsville (E9)
70. The Little Temple Beth Jacob 285 Buffalo Avenue, Brownsville (E10)
71. Sons of Abraham 157 Leonard Street at Stagg Street, East Williamsburg (A8)
72. Congregation Sons of Isaac 300 East 37th Street, East Flatbush (G8)
73. Talmud Torah Atereth Eliezer Glovinsky 747 Hendrix Street, East New York (F12)
74. Talmud Torah Atereth Israel 85–87 Fountain Avenue, East New York (D13)
75. Talmud Torah Beth Jacob Joseph 368 Atlantic Avenue, Boerum Hill (C5)
76. Talmud Torah Tifereth Hagro (originally Talmud Torah Tifereth Zion) 425 Howard Avenue, Weeksville (E10)
77. Talmud Torah Tifereth Israel of West Flatbush 1913–1915 West 7th Street, Gravesend (L5)
78. Temple Beth Ohr 1010 Ocean Avenue, Flatbush (H7)
79. Temple Isaac (aka Ohel Yitzhok) 554 Prospect Place, Prospect Heights (E7)
80. Temple Sinai 24 Arlington Avenue, Highland Park (D12)
81. Tifereth Israel 656–8 Willoughby Avenue, Bedford-Stuyvesant (C8)
82. Tifereth Yehuda Nusach Sfard 347 East 49th Street, East Flatbush (F9)
83. Tomchai Torah 1320 Sutter Avenue, East New York (E14)
84. Mystery Jewish establishment on Varet Street 101 Varet Street, East Williamsburg (B8)
85. Congregation Vezras Achim 341 Pennsylvania Avenue, East New York (E11)
86. Woodruff Avenue Temple 151 Woodruff Avenue at East 21st, Flatbush (G6)
87. Yeshivat Rabbi Meyer Simcha HaCohen 309 East 53rd Street, East Flatbush (G9)
88. Yeshivath Torah Chaim of Greater New York (also Young Israel of East New York) 631 Belmont Avenue, East New York (E12)
89. Young Israel of Brownsville and East Flatbush 1091 Winthrop Street at East 94th Street, East Flatbush-Brownsville (F9)
90. Young Israel of Prospect Park 2170 Bedford Avenue, Flatbush (G7)

Congregation Adath Yeshurun
1403 Eastern Parkway at Lincoln Place, Brownsville
(now Universal Temple Church of God)

If you drive westward on Eastern Parkway, this house of worship appears to be at an angle in a dramatic way. The street comes to a sharp point and the building, which has both Christian symbols and two very obvious Jewish emblems, captures your attention. (The two signs of Judaica are a Jewish star near the roof and Decalogue tablets.) There are other interesting features and decorative touches to this building, which looks to be in good shape from the outside. This building was a theater, then a synagogue, and then a church. Additional information about this *shul* can be found in the "Visits" chapter. The WPA made note of this interesting building.

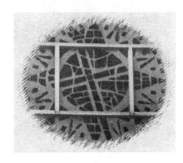

Congregation Agudas Achim Ansche Bobruisk
729 Saratoga Avenue, Brownsville
(now Power Up Faith Fellowship)

There were a good number of Brooklyn *shuls* that were basically converted private residences. This is still the case throughout much of Brooklyn, but the neighborhoods are different. These little synagogues were once prevalent in Brownsville, East Flatbush, and other neighborhoods studied in this book. Now they are found largely in Midwood, Borough Park, Kensington, Sheepshead Bay—mostly in southern and western Brooklyn, aside from Williamsburg. The WPA survey had entries for four Brooklyn *shuls* that were known as Agudas Achim Ansche or Anshei or even Anschei, but each was differentiated by the fourth part of the name. Thus at 729 Saratoga Avenue one would find AAA Bobruisk (the others were Libovitz, Mishnitz, and Stolin—all places in Eastern Europe). It must have just looked like a house then and it still does. Now that it is a nondenominational church, there is one nod to the former persuasion of the premises, a Jewish star on the schedule plaque. An attractive feature of the modest building is the pretty fence wrapped around it.

Agudas Achim Anshei Mishnitz
726 Driggs Avenue, Lower Williamsburg
(now Evangelistic Missionary Temple Inc.)

Architecturally and semantically, this ex-*shul* is a northern sibling of AAA Bobruisk. The building is not special looking, basically a renovated residence with a cross and a sign to designate its Christian mission. Similar to AAA Bobruisk, it also has a fence that stands out against the facade. There appears to be no Judaica markings on this ex-*shul*. AAA Mishnitz was organized in 1880, and the first rabbi was A.J. Katz.

Agudas Achim Anshei New Lots
43 Malta Street, New Lots
(now Church of God of Prophecy)

This quiet residential block once had two synagogues. The building at 71 Malta Street was a Sephardic (Levantine) synagogue, the one at 43 Malta Street an Ashkenazic (Eastern European) synagogue. Did they ever sponsor joint activities? Did people "*shul* hop" along Malta Street? Complimentary *kiddush* to all? Probably not, or not often, considering that their constituents would have had different customs, although they were both traditional, Orthodox synagogues. The ex-*shul* at 71 is more unusual, striking looking, but 43 has quiet charm. Actually, in its Jewish heyday, it was quite a nice-looking smallish building. According to the tax photo circa 1939–1940, it had a rose window with a Jewish star (which is now covered by the church sign) and there were several stylish urns gracing the building. On the roof there were a few, and on the street-level posts. Perhaps these were not maintained, even mutilated or stolen. Whatever the case may be, they all seem to be gone. The church has also added an awning by the front doors. The building had a vague Romanesque look to it, so the arches above the second-story windows have the appearance of eyebrows. This block has seen a lot of development in recent years. New housing (much of it built during 2006) on the block has changed the look quite a bit. At this point, the two ex- *shuls* which are now churches are the oldest buildings on the street. A.A.A. New Lots was dedicated and consecrated in 1911. The rabbi at the time of the WPA survey was

Lippman Levine who came from Russia. Helen Mirell of the WPA described the building as "a two-and-a-half story, red brick building, limestone staircase leading to synagogue on second floor. *Beth Hamedrash* in basement. Balcony second floor. Congregation has 20 (Torah) scrolls." That is an impressive amount, especially for such a small synagogue. If it were a Saturday morning and one were to stand on the street in, the 1920s or 1930s, would one hear competing tunes for prayers? And when the neighborhood's Jews were moving away, which synagogue held on longer? Did they ever think of consolidating?

Agudath Achim Anshei David Horodok
855 Saratoga Avenue, Brownsville
(now Holy Redeemer Baptist Church)

This building features several windows with stained glass "DH" designations standing for David Horodok, a town in today's Belarus. For quite some time, I was not able to identify this former synagogue until I saw that the Museum of Family History website had identified it as A.A.A. Harodic. (The web offers variations on the spelling.) This is a plain boxy building except for the nice stained glass windows in the front and on the side. It was probably a converted residence. The building is in fair shape. Although there seems to be an active church here, they have not fixed it up well and it looks somewhat decrepit.

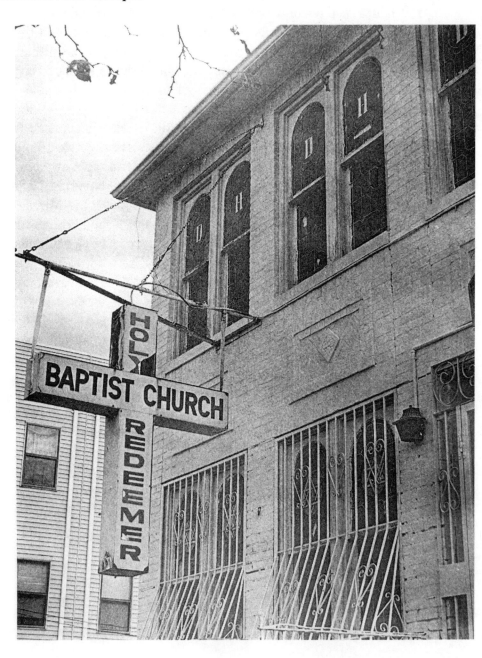

Congregation Ahavath Achim of Bedford Section
404 (402) Gates Avenue, Bedford-Stuyvesant
(now United Pentecostal Faith God ALL

One of many Ahavath Achim *shuls* that once graced Kings County, this "AA" has no overt Judaica left. There are some nice architectural details still embraced by the Christian congregation that took over the space. A semi-rose window is the focal point, flanked by small sets of double pilasters. Beside each set is a pretty, delicate oval window with attractive stone work. These are unusual and charming touches. At Beth David Cemetery, the congregation purchased a section for congregants' burial needs, and the gate columns they erected list the *shul* name and many members. Although the *shul* originated in 1922, the gate was dedicated in 1941. Interestingly, the building had been purchased from the Motion Picture Syndicate and converted. It is not clear how much of the decorative effects were added by the congregation. Their president at the time of the WPA survey was Mr. Harry Fuchs. The two Gates Avenue ex-*shuls* (the other is at 496 Gates) are just two of a number of synagogues that had been part of the Bedford-Stuyvesant landscape. Bedford-Stuyvesant has long been thought of as an African-American neighborhood, but it also had a Jewish population for some years.

Agudath Achim Bnei Jacob of East New York
503 Glenmore Avenue, East New York
(now the Second Calvary Baptist Church)

An absolute gem of an ex-*shul* today. With its bold front entrance columns, large and stately portico, and sheer size and corner location, this was and is a building that has power, a sense of arrival and permanence. Alas, the Jewish congregation that once trod the steps is no longer there, and in its place is a Baptist congregation that has retained the aura of this building, including the majority of stained glass windows, the small Jewish stars and Hebrew name signs. Apparently this congregation had some money. The building held a gallery for the women's section and a vestry for daily services. Frank Rosenblum, a local nonagenarian, more than once told me that this was a beautiful synagogue, a fancy synagogue, one for rich people. This is no modest *shteibe*[5] but a temple. This is formality with museum overtones. This was not a weather-beaten model of Hebraism, but an eye-pleasing in-place to gather. It still is a big statement of a building, even with some scuffed windows and a few spots of graffiti. The plain, small sign that announces the Christian congregation seems at odds with the whole scheme. But it is there and a cut and dry reminder of the change in ecclesiastical hands and hearts.

There are three Jewish stars of sandstone atop the building, somewhat similar to the stone Jewish star atop the former Anshei Zedek on Park Place. I categorize this structure with Shaari Zedek on Kingston Avenue and Temple Sinai on Arlington Avenue as the Grand Dames of Brooklyn ex-*shuls*. They were built specifically as synagogues. They all have big columns and porticos and similarities among the entrance doors. They have their names written in large Hebrew and English letters. All sit on oversize corner lots and are oversize buildings. All retain a great deal of outer detail. (Shaari Zedek has much of the interior detail too, which I viewed. I have not been inside the other two buildings.) They all have original stained glass windows. The exteriors of all three have only a minimum of Christian symbolism or church identification; for the most part they all still look like active synagogues except for the small curious signs announcing their church status. Bnei Jacob and Temple Sinai had the same architects according to the New York Landmarks Conservancy. These two have many stylistic similarities. Temple Sinai and Shaari Zedek were Conservative synagogues. Bnei Jacob was Orthodox. The cornerstones are easily visible on both Sinai and Zedek.

Bnei Jacob's rabbi at the time of the WPA survey was Alexander S. Linchner who began his tenure in 1933. The building was dedicated in 1922 and had two previous nearby locations. It had two classrooms for its Talmud Torah as well as a meeting room and social hall. The founding rabbi was A. Kaplan who served from 1908–1912. It had plots in Acacia and Montefiore cemeteries. A *Brooklyn Eagle* clipping from the late 1940s was "Citizens Organize Vacation School of Jewish Lore." It tells about Sunday morning classes led by then Rabbi Mordechai Lomdinski and Dr. Aaron Chait. Previously the congregation met at two other sites before erecting this four-story gem.

---

[5] A *shteibel* is a small facility, often a room or rooms within a building, that is used as a synagogue.

Congregation Ahavas Achim B'nai Abraham
394–396 Logan Street, East New York
(now Second St. James Church of God Diciples [sic])

You can't keep a good Jewish star down or hidden completely. In so many cases, there are Brooklyn churches and schools that have their Judaica peeking out from a sign or a paint-over or another cover-up. The former Ahavas Achim on Logan Street has a cross on a circular sign that cannot fully cover the Jewish star behind it. There are other places on the front of the building that were probably the sites of Jewish decoration. Way out in East New York, this former synagogue was of a decent size, and the brick work is still nice looking. At the time of the WPA survey, the rabbi was Aaron S. Semensky. The second floor housed the Talmud Torah; the basement was for social functions, and there was a ladies' auxiliary. The congregation had seven Torah scrolls. The building was dedicated and consecrated in 1914, but the congregation previously rented at 149 Fountain Avenue (right near the former Talmud Torah Atereth Israel at 85–87 Fountain Avenue).

Ahavath Achim Anshei Brownsville
105 Riverdale Avenue, Brownsville
(now The Peoples Baptist Church)

From the outside this is a pleasant-looking building although not unusual, more or less a rectangular corner building with decorative touches. Above the entrance is the synagogue's name in Hebrew, which has since been covered over. The inside of the building has more elegant touches. A few sites change their features somewhat as the churches make their marks on the buildings, typically by adding signs which sometimes obscure or cover the Judaica. Peoples Baptist has done that; however, they have kept some of the other Judaica visible, and they are taking good care of the building—look at how well-maintained the brick is here.

Congregation Ahavas Achim of East Flatbush
203 East 37th Street, East Flatbush
(now Northeastern Conference Mt. Zion Church of God)

The former Ahavas Achim is tucked away in the middle of a side street, East 37th Street between Church Avenue and Linden Boulevard. It has typically Romanesque Revival style windows and doors topped by half-rose windows. It is also built in the triptych open Torah style. The building is unusual in that the middle section is set back several feet from the two outer sections. A single set of stairs leads to the two-door entrance. Much Judaica is still retained here on the front of the building (including the *shul* name in Hebrew—written as "Cong. Ahavas Achim of Flatbush") and the front gate still has prominent Jewish stars. The only additions the church made are a sizable sign above the entrance and one smaller sign. The congregation originated in 1923; in 1931 they merged with the B'nai Abraham congregation. The building was consecrated in 1931. There was some kind of split, and another related congregation set up shop at 300 East 37th Street. This congregation may have served people who had a connection to the local hospital. This ex-*shul,* unremarkable today, is a low-key yet quite attractive building on a quiet street.

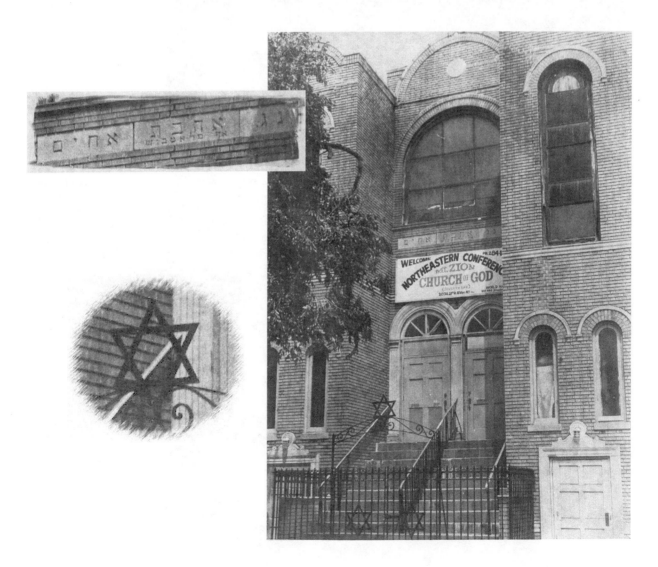

Congregation Ahavath Chesed Day Nursery
394 Hendrix Street, East New York
(now New York Psychotherapy and Counseling Center)

New York City has taken over a few ex-*shuls* of Brooklyn and converted them to public use. The building at 394 is one of them. (The nearby public school at 631 Belmont Avenue, formerly a *shul* and Talmud Torah, has also been converted.) The former Ahavath Chesed now serves adults with mental health needs, rather than religious needs. This building was originally a two-story, two-family house that was converted into a day nursery. Religious services were held in the auditorium on the first floor (once the living room or the dining room or perhaps both?). Brooklyn has a few other former Hebrew day nurseries that also housed congregations—a prominent example is the one on Thomas Boyland Street (then Hopkinson Street). Ahavath Chesed had four Torah scrolls for its congregational purposes. It was established in 1917, according to Alter Landesman. (*Brownsville*, p.280) You can still see Hebrew writing and a few Jewish stars of sculpted stone on the face of the building. The most laudable aspect of the building is the main entrance, which is flanked by fairly simple but nicely maintained columns.

At the crown of the building is written in Yiddish:

> *Ahavas*
> *Chesed Day Nursery*
> *1921 of East New York 5681*

The door's wrought-iron work, with two Jewish stars in circles, one holding a D in the center, the other an N in the center (for Day Nursery).

Ahavath Chesed
740-742 Jefferson Avenue, Bedford-Stuyvesant
(now Universal Baptist Church)

Universal Baptist Church lives up to its name, in a way—its universal approach extends to its Jewish-star-studded fence and windows. Take away the plethora of *Magen Davids*, and the building looks like it belongs in Italy. The arches around the windows and main entrance and the other decorative touches here lend a European flavor. Even the decorations at both corners on the roof are atypical. The filled-in rose window, a sizable space, probably was very eye-catching. When I first visited this ex-*shul*, the Christian congregation was deep into building an extension next door, but it is rare today for workers to recreate the ornate touches of yesteryear. Many speak of ex-*shuls* in Brooklyn, but often the ex-*shuls* of Bedford-Stuyvesant go unmentioned. Mostly the former synagogues of East Flatbush and Flatbush, Brownsville and East New York, and a few in East Williamsburg are recognized. Perhaps people are more familiar with the late 1960s strife in the school district of Ocean Hill-Bedford-Stuyvesant in which Jewish public school teachers felt besieged by a radicalized local school board of African-Americans. That image may linger in some minds, but years before there was a sizable Jewish community here, and this ex-*shul* and others are testimony to that. Today Bedford-Stuyvesant's brownstones are highly desirable and the racial make-up of the area is becoming more varied. Will any ex-*shuls* make a comeback?

Ahavath Israel
760 Sackman Street, Brownsville
(now Church of God/Iglesia De Dios [Mission Board])

 It looks like little more than a two-family home with a sign on the front. I assume that when 760 Sackman was a *shul* it looked pretty much like this but without a church sign. This is a very modest house of worship and likely always was, at least in appearance. The spirit inside, of course, is another story. As Ahavath Israel, the congregation was organized in 1939, so it was not a Jazz Age edifice like many others in the area. The president at the time of the WPA survey was Mr. Hyman Millberg.

Ahavath Reyim
209 Rochester Avenue, Weeksville
(now New Gethseman Baptist Church/Bible Institute)

The Jewish stars come out and not just at night. This is a fairly plain building with a few encircled Jewish stars of sculpted stone that remain as a testament to the former life of this building. The current church was renovated in recent years, but the Jewish stars have been retained in a quiet tribute to the past. Inside, in the basement, there are a few plaques with Jewish names.

Anshei Azaritz/Azaritz Young Friends
885–887 Thomas Boyland (Hopkinson) Street, Brownsville
(now New Life Seventh-Day Adventist Church)

This congregation originated in 1916. In 1926 they erected this three-story brick building. At the time of the WPA survey the rabbi was Morris Mashbaum. The congregation had a ladies' auxiliary. It is a handsome building in that open-Torah-triptych style. Among the interesting features here are thin windows that are paired on the outer sections of the building. There are decorative argyle patterns of brick on each side. (A few other Brooklyn ex-*shuls* display this design.) There are at least four outside plaques with Hebrew names, but they have been painted over a number of times, so the words are not all clear. There are other nice touches, but I am not sure if the eagle statuettes by the stairs are original to the *shul* or were added by the church.

Anshei Krashnik of East New York
Nusach Sfard, 473 Vermont Street, East New York
(now Greater St. John Community Church)

There is nothing unusual about the building that once housed Anshei Krashnik, although there are a few nice Romanesque windows on the side street. One odd feature of the building is that it is more or less flush with the sidewalk; unlike many ex-*shuls* and older Brooklyn *shuls* in general, there is no dramatic set of single or double stairs. The *shul* was organized in 1919. The president at the time of the survey was Simon Silber. Nusach Sfard refers to a style of prayer common among Hassidic Jews and does not imply it was a Sephardic *shul*.

Congregation Beth Abraham
770 Howard Avenue near Livonia Avenue, Brownsville
(now Macedonia Missionary Baptist Church)

This is an atypical block in southern Brownsville, bisected by a strip of land with greenery. Much of the housing on this block is relatively recent, but 770, the site of the former Congregation Beth Abraham, is of the older remaining stock. It is not a remarkable building, basically rectangular with much wear and tear. One remaining symbol of its former life is the large Jewish star on a section of the fence. There are a few other tell-tale signs, such as the filled-in rose window out front (which probably displayed a Jewish symbol years ago) as well as dual staircases, typical of many older synagogues. (A subtle humorous touch is the street number, 770—in light of the Lubavitcher Rebbe's noted residence at 770 Eastern Parkway in Crown Heights.) This Jewish congregation was organized in 1914, and the building was "realtered" in 1920. The first Rabbi was Samuel Rabinowitz. On the east side, at 803, there is recent housing; in the past this was the site of the Brooklyn Hebrew Home and Hospital for the Aged, which was organized in 1907, built and dedicated that same year.

Beth Hamedrash HaGadol
777–779 Schenectady Avenue (East 47th Street), East Flatbush
(now Christian Fellowship Seventh Day Adventist Church)

This church, with the fortunate street number of 777, was not always a church—it was once a synagogue. There is a certain sense of continuity (or is it irony?) in seeing Seventh Day Adventists, with their same-day Sabbath worship, taking over former synagogues. This Beth Hamedrash HaGadol (there were others in Brooklyn, and still are) is of an orange-yellow brick and still looks very attractive. The wings of the building are plain, but the arched main entrance just has to be seen. It features a large rose window with a Jewish star and a trio of braided columns on each side. There is also a Decalogue and the doors are impressive. The current church has discretely added a modest sign with its name just above the doors, so the Magen David still has pride of place here. Two denominational websites each have a listing for this church along with a well-taken color photograph. (Check www.eadventist.net and www. adventistdirectory.org.) The *shul* "emerged from the East Flatbush Jewish Community Center due to a misun-

derstanding of the firing of a Rabbi to which they objected," according to writer Helen Meltzer in the WPA survey. The Rev. S. Gersten officiated from 1936 to at least the time of the survey. The building that housed the East Flatbush JCC on Linden Boulevard no longer stands, but the former Beth Hamedrash HaGadol is still around and looking quite like it did in its Hebraic form.

Beth Hamedrash Hagadol Nachloth Zion of South Flatbush
2175 East 22nd Street, Sheepshead Bay
(now C.C.B. School)

This small, one-story, squat, unattractive building that once had been a school, also was a synagogue at one time. Hagadol means "the great" or "the big," but this building is not big, it does not look great now, and there is no Judaica on the outside. Perhaps the one and only vestige is scarring on the front near the current sign, where perhaps a *shul* sign or even Hebrew letters once were displayed. The scarring could have been from the previous school's sign. It is peculiar that a *shul* went out of commission in this area, somewhat like the case of the West Flatbush *shul* on West 7th Street. (Both of these ex-*shuls* had names connecting in a tenuous way to Flatbush.) This area should not be called South Flatbush by any stretch. There are many active synagogues of varying sizes in this area, so it is a mystery as to why this *shul* became inactive. Although it did not become a church, it has had a few incarnations as a school. The *shul* had been organized and dedicated in 1930. It does not appear to have been a converted private home, as are other small *shuls* in the neighborhood. There are some pretty, striking synagogues near here such as Pri Eitz Chaim on Ocean Avenue near Avenue U and the Young Israel of Kings Bay with its exotic "Oriental" style front by Jerome Avenue. Somehow Nachloth Zion did not survive the way some others did.

Beth Hemidrash Hagadol
611 Williams Street, East New York/New Lots
(now Christ Apostolic Church Mosem)

This ex-*shul* is a quaint and quietly attractive building. It lacks Judaica outside (there are several spackled-over circles to suggest where the Hebrew symbols once appeared), but the building was obviously a former synagogue, by the look of the windows and covered circles, big and small. The thin Romanesque windows topped by small arches and circles are the stand-out features here. The building sits on a calm street, very residential. The lot size is unusual in its depth (40' by 117'). The *shul* was organized in 1923, the same year the building was dedicated and consecrated. They had no rabbi, but the Protocol Secretary was a Mr. L. Feingin (sp?). There were ten Torah scrolls, a surprising number for a building that looks ample but not vast.

Congregation Beth Israel
771 Sackman Street, Brownsville
(now United Missionary Baptist Church)

So many *shuls* used to dot the many blocks of Sackman Street, similar to Williams Street and others. These streets were *shul*-magnets. They were modest spiritual centers. Today many of those buildings are gone, with newish housing in their places, but 771 Sackman is still a house of worship. The former Beth Israel did not make it into the WPA survey. Perhaps the building was erected after 1940. The front of the structure may have been changed at some point, and much of the building may not look as it did when it was a *shul*. The remaining Judaica included a few memorial stones that had Jewish names written in English, and there was some faded Hebrew lettering on at least one. Until the early years of the 2000s, the building was still in the name of Congregation Beth Israel. This is not a spectacular building but there is some nice brickwork. The name is short and common, compared to some of the longer and more exotic names that graced some ex-*shuls*.

Congregation Beth Israel
8910 Remsen Avenue/ 650 Avenue A, Remsen Heights/
East Flatbush
(now Grace Deliverance Tabernacle Church of God)

There are a number of Brooklyn *shuls* and ex-*shuls* that are rather plain and boxy, stream-lined constructions of brick and concrete. They are not stunning works of art, but most of them do feature some pleasant, straight-forward examples of Judaica. Some of the still-active synagogues in this mold are the Avenue Z Jewish Center near Coney Island Avenue and former-Reform, now-Orthodox, Beth Hillel on Ralph Avenue, as well as another in Canarsie. An ex-*shul* that falls into this category is Congregation Beth Israel at the corner of Remsen Avenue and Avenue A. (Another is the Glenwood Jewish Center.) It became a church during the summer of 2006, but it still retains much Judaica—metal Stars of David on upper windows, smaller ones on the main doors; a Decalogue built into a wall that features two engraved lions, a more modern version of that seen at the former Ezrath Achim on Newport Street; small showcases with "Congregation Beth Israel" and a menorah behind glass; and a Decalogue that has an engraved quote, in Hebrew and English translation, from the Ethics of the Fathers ("Al Shloshah D'varim..."—The world is based on three pillars...) The ex-*shul* also has an attached building which has housed senior centers for

some years. JASA, a Jewish communal group, had a branch there. They renamed the center, but it still provides services for seniors. These are post World War II buildings, worth viewing to see the style that came about for modest Jewish synagogues in contrast to many that were built in the 1910s and 1920s. The craftsmanship is of not nearly the same quality, but this particular site has its unusual touches.

Beth Israel
231–233 Ainslie Street, Williamsburg
(now San Cono Di Teggiano Catholic Association)

The vast majority of ex-*shuls* that have been converted into churches are now Baptist, Church of God in Christ, Seventh Day Adventist, and various evangelical congregations. This is probably due to the neighborhoods they are found in, which are predominantly African American and Latino. This is the only Roman Catholic group that I found located in a former *shul*, but it is not exactly a church—and it is also a former church building. (This is not the only church-*shul*-church flip found in Brooklyn.) Another factor is that Catholic churches in Brooklyn tend to start as and stay as Catholic churches. This building appears to have been a *shul* with dual staircases flanking a trapezoid and details around the windows. Two Jewish stars were poorly spackled over. The Jewish congregation was organized in 1913; they took over this church building and altered it. The first rabbi was Malech Gordon, and the rabbi in the late 1930s was Simon Brenner. This *shul* may not have been particularly close to any other *shul*, as this is eastern "Italian" Williamsburg, not very close to the main drag of "hipster" Williamsburg, nor to Hasidic Williamsburg either. There is a very distinct Italian-American flavor here evidenced by the stores and eateries.

Bikur Cholim
3 (or 3–5–7) Lewis Avenue, Northern Bedford-Stuyvesant
(now Brooklyn Temple Church of Seventh Day Adventists)

This large ex-*shul* is at the northernmost tip of Lewis Avenue, right near an elevated train line. It is well maintained and has good detailing and some raised brick patterns. There are two types of ornamental scallop designs running the length of the building and thin Romanesque style windows. The one specifically Jewish cue is the cornerstone located near a gated entrance (not the main entrance) which reads: "Org. 1899 Erected 1928 Donated By Ph. Fleisher" with two small Jewish stars flanking "Erected 1928".

Congregation Bikur Cholim Bnai Jacob
2134 Dean Street, Weeksville-Bedford-Stuyvesant
(now Glover Memorial Baptist Church)

Oddly the front of the former Bikur Cholim on Dean Street resembles the cover of a Led Zeppelin rock 'n roll album which shows a building with numerous small windows (some editions feature windows that flip open like a child's book). Bikur Cholim featured eight small, somewhat Romanesque windows in a row above a wood-covered rose window and the main entrance. There are four sets of doubled Romanesque windows on each side. This *shul*'s main features, therefore, are these windows, and most are still in good condition. This is still a handsome building with a few visible Jewish stars, others that are barely visible, and nice brickwork patterns. It has the triptych, three-part open Torah look to it also, with a stream-lined portico on top. The building dates from 1915, and the rabbi at the time of the WPA survey was Mathias Jacob Laks. The *shul* had burial plots at Beth David Cemetery in Elmont, New York, and in a helpful gesture to generations to come, they placed the *shul* name and address on the gate. Among the families represented here are the Goldin, Harnick and Weiser families. Some of the tombstones here have interesting carvings including menorah designs and lions of Judah.

B'nai Israel Jewish Center
9517 Kings Highway, East Flatbush/Brownsville border
(now P.S. 219 Annex #2)

The building in Brooklyn with the biggest Decalogue symbol could be the former B'nai Israel Jewish Center, now Public School 219 Annex #2. There are two big, bold tablets on the front of the building, but they now appear unadorned and ungainly. Basically they are two concrete arches with noticeable wear and tear. There is no other ex-*shul* quite like this one, but this is not exactly a compliment. The Department of Education is not maintaining this building well. On the north side, there is another entrance with a few steps, which is certainly humbler but which has a quiet grace, even with its uninspired paint job. If anyone could make a former synagogue look like an industrial blunder, the New York City Department of Education has done so. In its past this was a more prosperous synagogue than other neighboring houses of worship. As a *shul*, it not only had a brash entrance, it also was located on a high-profile spot, on Kings Highway near Rockaway Parkway. It was at the border between East Flatbush and Brownsville, and the congregants (or at least the architect) wanted this house of worship to look stream-lined and modern. Unfortunately, now it does not have the grace of many other ex-*shuls* that were more modest in scope. It should be noted that the estimated market value of this building was over $2.7 million dollars in 2007, considerably more than almost any other Brooklyn ex-*shul*.

Chevra Ahavath Israel Anshei Ostrolenker
375 Bristol Street, Brownsville
(now Little Rock Baptist Church)

This is another ex-*shul* with no obvious exterior Judaica, but the building has something of the style of some ex-*shuls* in the vicinity. With at least five windows capped with arches, there is a slight Romanesque Revival feel to the front. The blank circle in the center of the main section of the building likely was the site of a Jewish symbol. There is an unusual, subtle decorative touch that seems eerie on a building that was actually built in 1922; flanking the blank circle and a sign for the current church are two sets of raised brick figures, and each set contains six raised-brick line figures. This building was built before the Holocaust, and I doubt the two sets of six were inserted after 1945. An odd coincidence... The *shul* was organized in 1906 and actually merged in 1918 with another *shul*. There are a number of other ex-*shuls* around Brooklyn that resulted from mergers with other congregations. Even today some active synagogues, such as the East Midwood Jewish Center, included mergers with other *shuls* (in that case Shaare Torah and two other congregations).

Chevra Poelei Tzedek Anschei Glubucker of Brownsville
167–169 Chester Street, Brownsville
(now Mt. Hebron Church of Christ, Disciples of Christ)

There really is no Judaica left at 167 Chester Street these days, because the ex-*shul*'s elements have been covered over by refacing and painting. The one visual cue that tips off its Jewish roots is the trapezoidal staircase, with two sets of stairs, typical of so many old ex-*shuls*. However, the church's name is a tip of the hat to Judaism. If you stare intently at the upper part of the building, just under the roof, you may discern the remnants of a Hebrew letter or two.

Congregation Chevra Tehillim Nusach Ashkenaz
511 Elton Street, East New York
(now East New York Seventh-Day Adventist Church)

The old Chevra Tehillim was large enough to be included on a comprehensive chart of Brooklyn in 1929 called the *Desk Atlas Borough of Brooklyn*, found at the Municipal Archives at 31 Chambers Street. Although its name was not written out on the map page, there is a spot that has "synagogue" written on it. Not every synagogue was included on this map, as many were too small, but the synagogue at 511 Elton was deemed significant enough to get credit. Today it is one of several ex-*shuls* that still have Saturday observances on site, as it is a Seventh Day Adventist Church. There must be a special connection for SDA folk to be praying in a former *shul*. The *shul* was organized in 1910 and the building was dedicated in 1925; the congregation had met at two previous locations, in addition to 511 Elton. It is a well-kept, modestly attractive building of brick with nice details. Among them are a sandstone sign displaying the *shul* name in Hebrew letters that are not at all faded. Near the tip of the pointed roof is a Decalogue with Hebrew letters from aleph to yud standing in for the first ten numbers. There is a slight Romanesque Revival influence here found in the rounded arches above some windows and the main entrance. This is one of the ex-*shuls* that has a stair railing which features Judaic symbols. It sits on a lot that is almost a double-sized residential plot. In the late fall of 2007 the brick looked particularly well maintained.

Chevra Tehillim
1925 Nusach Ashkenaz 1910
Of ENY

Chevra Torah Anshei Radishkowitz
135–139 Amboy Street, Brownsville
(now St. Timothy's Holy Church/Cathedral and Love Tabernacle Fellowship)

Gaze at the former Anshei Radishkowitz and you can discern a once-stately synagogue which still shows forth its exceptional features, yet also reveals a distressing amount of wear and tear. You can read more about this congregation in the "Sunday Visits" chapter, and it was written up in a *New York Times* article early in 2008. The outside still has its intricate brick facing, symbols of Judaica and decorative touches. Attention was lavished on this building when it was built, but now you also see broken windows from the street. The sanctuary in particular is in pitiful shape, but the lower level and corridors are somewhat better. This is one site that begs to be restored to its former glory. The congregations that meet here would benefit also from the renovations.

Chevre Anshei Zedek/
Talmud Torah Anshei Zedek of East New York
308–310 Atkins Avenue, East New York
(now New Ammie's Church, F.B.H. Church of God of the Americas)

It is the arched entrance, with a column connecting the two archways, that makes this a notable ex-*shul*. The effect of the sweeping entrance is now marred by the current church's sign, which blocks the tops of the two arches. With no visible Judaica from the outside, one might overlook this building, however, it does seem to have that "open Torah" look to it, with the slightly in-set middle section of the building flanked by outer segments. Inside, however, there is a good deal of Jewish content. Inside, there are four remaining tablets with names and dates that were left by the Jewish congregation. These tablets appear to list names of donors and once-active members. The Holy Ark is still inside the main sanctuary, topped by a Jewish star. Many of the chairs and pews are from the *shul*'s days. Occasionally people come by to photograph the interior for historical purposes. The Hebrew congregation was begun in 1907, and the building was dedicated and consecrated in 1919. The rabbi at the time of the WPA survey was Lazar Cohen. The WPA survey writer took pleasure in describing the details of this *shul*, noting the seven sets of Florentine glass windows, the two-column marble archway which led to the second floor and the red

brick with its white limestone finish. The *shul* had a considerable Talmud Torah, with about 150 students and six classrooms. They also had ten Torah scrolls, a surprising number.

Daughters of Zion
130 Boerum Street, East Williamsburg
(now Spanish Central Brooklyn Seventh Day Adventist Church)

This institutional building with a nice brick pattern and a date of 1925 was once the home of Daughters of Zion. The name seems to be in English only, not in Hebrew.

Congregation Dorshe Tov Anshei New Lots
21 Louisiana Avenue, New Lots
(now Gospel Tabernacle Association)

This congregation is located on the lowest section of Louisiana Avenue, one of the streets in this area that are named for states. (Alabama, Georgia, New Jersey, Vermont and the main artery named Pennsylvania Avenue are nearby.) The former Dorshe Tov was housed in a small building that still displays some interesting Judaica. A small Jewish star rests near the peak of the roof, and some granite tablets with Hebrew writing remain in the corners. Some of the writing has faded even though it was engraved. In some ways, this humble house of worship resembles the small ex-*shul* on Herzl Street; perhaps they are architectural kin. Even with its small physical stature this synagogue housed nine Torah scrolls.

Congregation Eliezer of East New York
133 Hinsdale Street, East New York
(now Jones Temple of the First Born)

According to the WPA survey, the Hinsdale Street of old had a good number of *shuls*. Beth Zedek Anshei New Lots was located at 665; Jehiel Talmud Torah Isaac Joseph was at 285; Chevra Gemilath Chasidim B'nai Reb Leib Ber Anshei Piesk was at 420; Congregation Athereth Israel was at 535; the Sephardic Congregation of New Lots was at 621–623. Not one of these has survived, but somehow the northernmost of the Hinsdale synagogues, Congregation Eliezer, has managed to remain standing. Now known as the Jones Temple, this building looks eerie and forlorn due to its very shoddy condition. Of a modest size and surrounded by weeds, there is no obvious Judaica outside, but the style of decoration, especially near the roof, although simple, bears the stamp of a Brooklyn *shul* of yesteryear. There is a large blank circle near the top-center which must have once had a Jewish symbol. Basic design was delineated by slightly raised brickwork resembling a windmill cookie. The congregation was organized in 1906. In 1926 the building was rebuilt in brick. This woebegone building has managed to make itself known on the

website The East New York Project which can be contacted at tapeshare@yahoo.com. Demetrius Pestun supplied a photograph of this building as well as one on Snediker Avenue, which is in better condition.

Etz Chaim Machzikei Hadath
1477 Lincoln Place, Brownsville
(now a private residence)

In Europe there are many synagogues situated on side streets or tucked into corners off the beaten path. A primary reason for this is to avoid anti-Semitism. Jews congregating for prayer typically attract attention to themselves, so there are a good number of synagogues that are less conspicuous or are confusing to find. Certainly not all European synagogues are like this; many make bold statements with their Judaica, their architecture, their location, or all three. Jews in America have faced anti-Semitism, to be sure, but it has not been as severe as in Europe or in many Middle Eastern locales. Jewish houses of worship, especially those with some depth of funding, have been much more upfront, proud and eager to be on display. It is easier to be Jewish and to go to services, at least from a standpoint of security. Even the poorer *shuls* have not been so much hidden, just less extensive in their size and decoration. That is why the former Etz Chaim Machzikei Hadath, a small *shul* with a big name, is a genuine curiosity. The building that

once housed it is hidden from view on Lincoln Place; you must make an effort to see it, since it is easy to pass by. The entrance is set back, and the only noticeable sign of former Judaica is a space above the entrance where there are Hebrew letters that once graced it. Etz Chaim (Tree of Life) definitely reminds one of some Euro-*shuls*, such as the one in Lisbon, Portugal, which is tucked behind a gate. Lincoln Place's secretive synagogue is a curio among curios.

Ezrath Israel
496 Gates Avenue, Bedford-Stuyvesant
(now Ebenezer Faith Temple Holy Church)

This former shul which originated in 1919 has been changed so much that you would really have no idea that it was once Jewish. The Christian congregation removed all traces of Judaica and put up different facing. It should still be noted that this was once a Jewish congregation, one of a few others that were located along Gates Avenue. It is actually a bit surprising that this ex-*shul* as well as one at 404, are still standing, because Gates Avenue is now dominated by big public housing complexes. Somehow this smallish former synagogue still stands even though it does not stand out as such.

Congregation Friends Oholei Torah
890 Lenox Road, East Flatbush
(Later known as Maple Leaf Academy)

In the early 2000s, when this ex-shul was a daycare facility, there was no visible sign of Judaica, but there were signs that it had been a *shul,* such as the style of the windows and the spackled-out area above the three arched windows on the second floor. It had been a decent-sized synagogue with nice brickwork, although it is not obvious when it was built, because a private home had been on this site when the tax photo was snapped around 1940. The formal name on the Department of Finance website for the property was still the name of the congregation. By the summer of 2007, the building had been torn down, and a large construction job was there instead. So this *shul* really is no more; not a trace seems to be left. Some ex-*shuls* stick around in different forms; others are erased from the scene.

Gates of Prayer/Community Center Congregation and Talmud Torah/Odessa Benevolent
180–182 Van Buren Street, Bedford-Stuyvesant
(now Upper Room Full Gospel Baptist Church)

This large old church on Van Buren Street has little more than a hint of Judaica. A few Hebrew letters, painted over many times, peek out through sheer will. This large corner church began life as a church, became a *shul* for quite some time, and then became a church again. This is not the only such example in Brooklyn (witness such specimens as the Bedford Avenue-Martense Street ex-Young Israel, and others in Williamsburg). The Mosaic evidence is very limited here, present only on the avenue side. Careful observance yields a yud and a hay (two letters) and a few other shapes that must be Hebrew letters, but it's difficult to determine due to so many layers of paint. This is a sprawling church with certain nice details such as big windows, but inside and out you see wear and tear. The Jewish congregation was organized in 1892 and had three sites previous to this large one on Van Buren Street. It arrived here in the second decade of the 1900s. The first rabbi was Abraham Joseph Dalginus, and the rabbi at the time of the WPA survey was Morris E. Gordon. There is a large food pantry and kitchen here now for the community and active youth-group programs.

Glenwood Jewish Center-Lila R. Korf Talmud Torah
888 East 56th Street, Old Mill Basin
(now Harvest Army [Church])

Here is probably one of the youngest ex-*shuls* in Brooklyn (and therefore is not listed in the WPA survey). This lengthy ranch-style synagogue is basically a rectangular, one-story building, not particularly graceful, except for the unusual beach-club style wavy cement awning above the main entrance. But this synagogue has interesting stories surrounding it. It is on a wide two-way side street, so there is a good amount of traffic. The building is nothing outstanding in looks, but it still has some Jewish touches. The most prominent are the big letters that read "Lila R. Korf Talmud Torah." There are a few small Jewish stars yet on the facade, and the main doors show the "ghosting" of two removed Jewish stars. A marble plaque reads "Dedicated 1958," so this is decades younger than most ex-*shuls* in this book. There is another plaque dedicated to "Our War Dead" with a date in the 1950s. The Glenwood Jewish Center had an illustrious rabbi, Shlomo Drillman. German-born, he came to the United States after World War II and studied at REITS, Yeshiva University. He was a noted scholar as well as the pulpit rabbi here. Carl Kruger, a local politician, listed this *shul* as one he belonged to. A Marjorie Posner who died in 1997 was one of the founding members of the congregation, according to her *New York Times* obituary. But the most interesting tale surrounds the current Glenwood Jewish Center—which is located in an Is-raeli town. Confused? According to *A Brooklyn Shul In Israel,* by Daphne Berman, in the Eng-lish-version of the Israeli paper *Haaretz:*

> The building is named after the Glenwood Jewish Center in Brooklyn, an aging synagogue that closed its doors because it could barely get a *minyan*....After the building was sold, the synagogue leadership trans-ferred the majority of the funds to the construction of the synagogue in Hashmonaim....In exchange, memo-rial plaques from Brooklyn were brought over to Israel...

These people now participate in the *mitzvah*, the good deed of recalling and memorializing the dead of the Brooklyn *shul*. Just as the Conservative synagogue Shaari Israel has been reborn in Israel, so has the Orthodox Glenwood Jewish Center. Some current members even have a con-

nection to the original. As of 2007 the Department of Finance listed the owner of this building as Sutlingar Realty Corp. Current occupant Harvest Army has catchy graphics for its banner (and a busy-looking website) which now waves across the front of the building. Stylistically this block-like *shul* somewhat resembles ex-*shul* Congregation Beth Israel on Remsen Avenue (which also became a church only in the 2000s) and the former Beth El on Ralph Avenue in the nearby Georgetowne neighborhood. However, the boxy, utilitarian Beth El is still a *shul*, having morphed into an Orthodox *shul*, Beit Hillel. There is also a plain, boxy Reform synagogue in Canarasie on Rockaway Parkway that resembles Glenwood Jewish Center. Sad to say, these 1950s synagogues are not beautiful structures adorned with folksy or commanding details. Some have changed religions; some have changed denominations; some have stuck around as is.

H.E.S. (Hebrew Educational Society)
Thomas Boyland (Hopkinson) Street at Sutter Avenue,
Brownsville
(now a community center)

The H.E.S. building, not strictly a *shul*, held religious services here at times, especially for certain holidays. Often called "the H", it was very important to the Jewish community of Brownsville and other nearby neighborhoods. It was an important site for Jewish and secular education, recreation and culture. It was Brooklyn's settlement house. This boxy brick building, rather institutional looking but with subtle detailing, looks quite a bit as it did when it was built in the 1910s, although somewhat weather- and time-beaten. From the outside, it really did not have much to mark it as a Jewish building, except for the cornerstone which (still) reads "5674–1913" (the Hebrew year being placed first). A contemporary Brownsville organization is now located there, and the H.E.S. still exists—in Canarsie, by the Belt Parkway. The first incarnation of the H.E.S. was incorporated at the end of 1899. It soon moved to a building on Pitkin Avenue and Watkins Street. Then they moved the facility to the building described here at Hopkinson (Boyland Street) and Sutter Avenue. The architect of this building was Simeon B. Eisendrath. This building included such amenities as an auditorium, a gym, club and classrooms, a roof garden, and more. Several *shuls* were within walking distance, as was a large public park facility (the Betsy Head Recreation center) and a public elementary school. Yeshivas were also nearby. When the neighborhood's Jews left, the people in charge of the H.E.S. decided to build a new facility in Canarsie. Canarsie actually has a lengthy history in certain sections, but there was much new housing built there after World War II, and many Jews who left Brownsville and wanted to stay in Brooklyn migrated to this area, not too far from Brownsville but further south. The current H.E.S. is a nice facility from the late 1950s and 1960s, with certain things added on later. This neighborhood is no longer predominantly Jewish (although more Jews have been moving in recently), so the current H.E.S is not exclusively Jewish.

Hebrew Ladies Day Nursery
521 Thomas Boyland Street, Brownsville
(now Bethany Gospel Chapel)

The Jewish community set up and supervised a few day nurseries for the families of Brownsville and East New York. The Ahavath Chesed Day Nursery on Hendrix Street in East New York was a smaller site than the Hebrew Ladies Day Nursery on Hopkinson Street, now better known as Thomas Boyland Street. Both Ahavath Chesed and Hebrew Ladies Day Nursery also had space for religious services. This building is institutional looking but stately, and is well kept. The only noticeable Judaica is the group's name in English, which tops the main entrance in an arc. Part of that sign is blocked by a modern sign for the Christian church which now meets here. It is not a fancy building but there are nice brick details around many of the windows. Even in the early part of the 1900s, Jewish philanthropic groups saw the need to provide day care for the working woman, and this site is situated on a large but somewhat residential street. Of course many synagogues were nearby, and the Hebrew Educational Society, the H.E.S., was also nearby. According to Alter Landesman, the Day Nursery was established in 1909 and "maintained until 1961 its very large and well-equipped building" (p.280, *Brownsville*). Day care is so commonplace today, but it was more unusual in the early part of the 1900s.

Hebrew School of Williamsburg
310 South 1st Street, Williamsburg
(now Damon House, New York)

This stern, institutional-looking building retains its sandstone sign with the words "Hebrew School of Williamsburg" engraved in it. Along with a large American flag on a pole, these are the remarkable features of this plain edifice. It is a bit difficult to find this building, because some of the streets are cut at odd angles. Williamsburg has its Orthodox Jewish segment, which is expanding, and there are plenty of synagogues there, including some very old ones, but some other old *shuls* and Jewish institutions that had been located at South 2nd and South 3rd Streets are gone. The school was organized in 1913, and a new building was built on the site in 1921. According to the Eighth Annual Report of the Brooklyn Federation of Jewish Charities, it received a $230 allotment that year.

Hessed Ve Emeth Society of Castorialis
69–71 Malta Street, East New York
(now West Baptist Church)

This mid-block house of worship, on a quiet residential street in lower East New York, has some very interesting features that help it to stand out. (Just down the block there was another synagogue which now is also a church.) There is a long, narrow triangle, as well as two white triangles and a large circle which may have had Jewish detailing. The lot size here is that of a home and the building size is too, so it is not large. But admire the two upper windows, topped by half-circles and small touches. The most intriguing aspects of the building are near the roof with its three lanterns or lamp-like features. They are similar to the lighting fixtures on some older New York City subway stations. Hessed Ve Emeth was a Sephardic synagogue, atypical of most of the *shuls* in Brownsville and East New York. Perhaps this is the reason for the different styling and details on the building. The building was dedicated in 1930. The red brick is still in nice shape and except for a few spots where a paint touch-up would be worthwhile, it is a handsome, compact building. "Hessed Ve Emeth" translates to "loving-kindness and truth" and is a particularly beautiful name.

Independent Chevra Sphard of Perryslaw
247 Snediker Avenue, East New York
(now Brooklyn Christian Center)

BCC, formerly Chevra Sphard of Perryslaw, is quite a attractive structure and in fairly good shape, but it sticks out like a sore thumb on this street which is dominated by an industrial firm. There are trucks constantly loading and unloading, lots of busy, noisy work and drilling. This site has the triptych style, with raised brickwork that is a bit intricate. The pseudo rose window of raised brick and a Magen David are focal points. On the outer sections of the building, you can clearly read the ex-*shul*'s name in English and in Hebrew. Some parts need painting or fine tuning or cleaning. There are a few other Judaic symbols outside. Inside there are Jewish items too. A chandelier is suspended from a ceiling molding which depicts a Jewish star and bunches of grapes. There were a few plaques in the building, and the Christian congregation is working on interior renovations. The present congregants, who are Latino, expressed interest in preserving at least some of the Jewish material, for the messianic connection they felt it imparted. Originally the Jewish synagogue tore down a one family dwelling and built this brick structure. It was dedicated in 1929. The first rabbi was Rabbi Bluestone, and the rabbi at the time of the WPA survey was Rabbi Abraham Yormark.

Congregation Independent Esrath (or Ezrath) Achim
144 Newport Street, Brownsville
(now Gethsemane Baptist Church)

Above the main entrance of the former Esrath Achim, flanking the largest rectangular window on the front of the building, are two lion figures. These lions have their front limbs raised up against this window, and they seem about to stand up. Their tails are upright and their mouths are open wide and roaring. This symbol is actually a very common one in older synagogues in Europe, the United States and Canada. More typically it is seen inside the synagogue, as the Holy Ark pediment, up on the stage where the Torah scrolls are kept. In *Gilded Lions and Jeweled Horses, The Synagogue to the Carousel—Jewish Carving Traditions,* by Murray Zimiles, which was also an exhibit at the American Folk Art Museum in Manhattan, there are many splendid examples of these lions, representing the Lion of Judah. Aside from the lions this building is not too unusual. It has some features seen in other ex-*shuls* located nearby. Near the roof there is a scalloped design of brick that runs the length of the roof similar to the decorative motif at the former Rishon L'Zion on East 95th Street. There are recessed pilasters of a classical style at the front entrance, which can be seen at the former Talmud Torah Tifereth Hagro and a few other sites. A large circular window has been spackled over, a feature present at many ex-*shuls*. On the side street (Bristol Street), there is another unusual feature—an original gate, painted over many

times, with an arched sign that bears the names of "Mr. & Mrs. Chas. Katz." There are also some small Jewish stars on the Bristol Street side. Inside, there are a number of plaques with Hebrew writing and names. Above the space where the Ark is (it is closed up though) there are Hebrew words which can be seen partially.

Israel Elioe Brethren of Yale
474–476 Kosciuszko Street, upper Bedford-Stuyvesant
(now Church of God in Christ Jesus)

Short and kind of sweet is how to categorize the building that once housed Israel Elioe Brethren of Yale. Although dowdier by now, this building, even with its overpainted white front, has charm along with its two Jewish stars. One is atop the front gate and the other, less conspicuous, sits upon the top of a stone gate entrance. The rose window is just plain glass now, but above it is a scalloped design pattern that is seen on many other 1920s-era *shuls*. The congregation originated in 1920, and the building was built, occupied and dedicated that year too. The WPA survey writer described its style as "Florentine cement" which is a way of conveying the vaguely Italianate styling.

Jewish Center of Hyde Park
779 East 49th Street, East Flatbush
(now a special education preschool)

Many Brooklyn ex-*shuls* have Hebrew names; some have both Hebrew and English names; a few had only English names, and usually they reflected the neighborhood they were located in. Even today, in Brooklyn, you will find many synagogues with Hebrew names only. They tend to be Orthodox institutions. Conservative and Reform synagogues often have the English names, such as the Conservative East Midwood Jewish Center. But the name fits because the Center is located in East Midwood. So how did Jewish Center of Hyde Park get such a name? The neighborhood it was located in is most certainly East Flatbush. Hyde Park is elsewhere in New York State, as is New Hyde Park. But this *shul*, organized in 1929, and led by Rabbi Isaacs, gave itself a confusing name. It is across the street from a public elementary school, as well as the Conservative ex-*shul* Shaari Israel. The building itself is basically boxes with a few remarkable features: the grand, arched main entrance flanked by two large arched windows (there are also a few arched windows on the south side of the main building) and a thought-provoking mural of the biblical burning bush, dedicated by a member of the congregation. It is a colorful and well-maintained mural that is an unusual, unique feature to this ex-*shul*.

Judea Center
2059 Bedford Avenue, East Flatbush
(now Bethanie Seventh Day Adventist Church)

The Judea Center is a quietly handsome building with four semi-inlaid columns and decorative features that make it seem like a more modest, smaller version of the Brooklyn Jewish Center, the noted Conservative synagogue on Eastern Parkway which is now a Chabad Lubavitch building. The cornerstone indicates that it was built in 1926. The two main doors feature several Jewish stars, but the ones placed on the outside of the doors have been painted over many times and are less obvious. There is also a cornerstone that has been painted over a great many times; therefore, it is hard to make out all the Hebrew words on it.

Congregation Kachlow Israel
220–222 Hegeman Avenue, Brownsville
(now Cedar of Lebanon Baptist Church)

This modest ex-*shul*, now a church with a biblically influenced name, is a plain building with no real Judaica presence outside. Perhaps in the past there was a lot more Hebraic enhancement to this squat box. There are two pleasant looking doorways, and it has the appearance of a modern, stream-lined house of worship that lacks the little touches of craftsmanship that older ex-*shuls* (and older churches) seem to have.

Kenesseth Israel Beth Jacob
35 Blake Avenue, Brownsville
(now Grace Church of God)

The Museum of Family History has identified this structure on a list of Brooklyn's former synagogues. There are remnants of Judaica here, most notably on the railings that lead to the front entrance: these feature Jewish stars that can be seen from a distance. There is at least one other Star of David on the side street of the building. Once inside, the location of the Torah Ark can be seen. Perhaps the most interesting aspect of this building, which is not fancy but has nice touches and well-kept brickwork, is its location. It sits on a junction of three streets: Blake Avenue, Howard Avenue and Tapscott Street. The WPA survey does not list this synagogue with its stream-lined style; perhaps it was built after the survey and even after World War II.

Kesser Torah
2310 Cortelyou Road at East 23rd Street, Flatbush
(now Pentecostal Church of East Flatbush)

The former Kesser Torah is a nice-looking building, not stunning, but it has its dignified demeanor. It is cramped by the narrow side street placement; Cortelyou Road is narrow in this area (east of Flatbush Avenue). Inside there is still Judaica to be seen, but I am saddened by the fact that the church has hidden the outside Judaica. In 1999, there was still some Judaica to be seen—the cornerstones with the *shul* name in phonetic English, the English rendition of the Jewish year, and a Jewish star in a circle. Now it is all covered up, spackled over, but you can still make out the Magen David above the entrance, covered by layers of paint. The outline is still discernable. A small note: although there were no other Kesser Torah *shuls* in Brooklyn, the expression or the initials K.T. can be seen in a few places elsewhere. In some synagogues (past and present) you can see carved lions of Judah above the Holy Ark, and they often include the K.T. designation in English or in Hebrew letters. (Kesser Torah is the Ashkenazic pronunciation; Keter Torah is the Sephardic pronunciation, which mean "crown of the Torah".) Kesser Torah was one of the many Flatbush synagogues in a neighborhood that was once regarded as solidly Jewish. Flatbush itself has a storied history, and there are many other landmarks in the vicinity—several churches, including the Dutch Reform church and graveyard that leant the name to Church Avenue (formerly Church Lane), as well as grand (but no longer active) movie theaters, the Sears store, and even a few old residences.

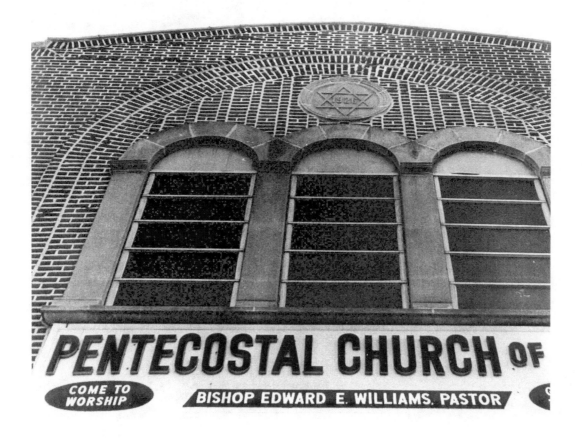

"Kevelson's" Shul
1387 East 96th Street, Canarsie
(now Liberty Hall Church of God)

This is a big building with a great deal of remaining Judaica—Jewish stars on the front, on doors, on windows, the old announcement board encased by glass, and more. Around the corner on the avenue there is the old Hebrew school, with letters intact that spell "Talmud Torah R. Morris Kevelson." The church that is there now has signs with three variations of their name, but the Kevelson letters remain as a tribute to a synagogue that had a big reputation in Canarsie. The proper name of the synagogue was Congregation Talmud Torah Ohev Shalom, and it was organized in 1923 as Talmud Torah B'nai Elihui. (The WPA survey has the street number as 1381, but this is certainly the same building.) This is not the only Ohev or Ohav Shalom in Brooklyn. Kevelson's was one of the sinking synagogues profiled in a mournful 2004 article in the *Canarsie Courier*, an old local publication of the neighborhood. In "Jewish Community Shrinking, But Surviving," December 23, 2004, by Shlomo Greenwald, there is an article about the fading Jewish population of Canarsie and how it affected synagogues and other Jewish institutions. Kevelson's was not the only *shul* in the area to close around that time. Many of the Jews who lived in Canarsie had migrated southward from older Jewish precincts such as Brownsville and East New York; however, there are still Jews and synagogues left in Canarsie, whereas there are virtually no Jews in Brownsville today.

Machzikei Torah Bnei David
175 Hart Street, Bedford-Stuyvesant
(now Mt. Zion Pentecostal Holy Church)

This humble building, a dwelling that was converted into a synagogue in 1936, appears to have no Judaic indications remaining. There are decorative stained glass windows, however, which may be from the days of the synagogue. The name of the church is a nod to the Old Testament. Machzikei Torah was included in the WPA survey, and is further evidence of the Jewish community that once existed in Bedford-Stuyvesant.

Men of Justice
1676–1678 Park Place, Brownsville
(now Bright Light Baptist Church)

There is still something regal and visually arresting about this ex-*shul*. It sits on a side street where it seems too grand for its site; it belongs on a parkway, a boulevard. There are details, decorative and Judaic, that are a step above the typical synagogue built in the early 1900s. The hybrid style is somewhat different than many other Brooklyn ex-*shuls*. In a way it is a minor enigma. The church at this site now, a Baptist Church, has put up a few signs, painted some doors a bright red, and changed a few windows; but they have left a great many Jewish symbols, writing and more. There are eye-catching details here, such as the lion heads placed in diamond-shaped niches, and at the highest point of the roof, a Jewish star of stone that has the appearance of a medallion or a lollipop. These free-standing Magen Davids are not typical of most ex-*shuls,* but variations can be seen at the ex-*shul* B'nai Joseph on Glenmore Avenue. There are other ways in which this building stands out, such as the handsome brickwork and the tops of windows which are unusual. Unlike many ex-*shuls* which exhibit variations on the Romanesque Revival style, this building has a different style. Perhaps it could be described as vaguely Moorish. There is a large, stylish old apartment building complex on Ocean Avenue and Church Avenue (the southwest corner) called Cathedral Arms that has this pointed feature over some windows and the main entrance. A building on one of the westernmost blocks of Blake Avenue also has an entrance topped by a similar stylized arch. Men of Justice was organized in 1907, and this building was occupied and dedicated in 1912. The rabbi at the time of the WPA survey was Rabbi H. Gerchikof. Today this block has some recently built houses, a few empty lots, and older housing.

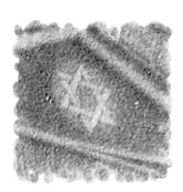

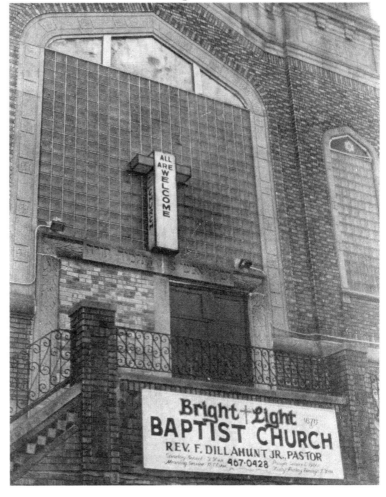

New Hebrew School of Brooklyn/
Bnos Israel Malbush Arumim
146 Stockton Street, Bedford-Stuyvesant
(now Greater Free Gift Baptist Church)

Approach this unassuming building and gaze carefully at the area just under the portico out front. In faint letters you will see "BREW SCHOOL." The HE has faded away with time, but this is an ex-*shul* and a school of some renown. The front of the building is plain, but the two vaguely Romanesque Revival windows are a nice touch. Inside the building has been redone, but there is a remaining Jewish star above the choir loft. The "Faith in the City" column in the Sunday *New York Daily News* provides a good profile of the current church. The Brooklyn Historical Society has other documents with information about the Jewish former life of this building. In a late 1910s edition of the Brooklyn Federation of Jewish Charities, Eighth Annual Report, it is said that this New Hebrew School of Brooklyn received an allotment of aid, as did other Talmud Torah schools such as the Hebrew Free School of Brownsville and three other educational institutions that year. The listed allotment for New Hebrew was $2,333.33. Another group that met there, Bnos Israel, received $10 from the Federation that year. This school was organized in 1909, or 5669 by the Jewish calendar. The building originally housed nine classrooms and the synagogue with gallery. It was also "equipped with all modern appliances and improvements." This was certainly notable in a time when many Jewish children received religious instruction in cramped, sub-par quarters. About 600 children came for schooling here, and many did not pay tuition.

New Lots Talmud Torah
330–370 New Lots Avenue at Pennsylvania Ave., East New York
(now Bishop Gregory Day Care Center)

"My Brooklyn is ENY (East New York)," writes Jack M. Purvis on the website "My New York." He name-drops many of the things he remembers including "New Lots Talmud Torah, Nino's Pizzeria, the Biltmore Theater..." Schooling, eating (not always the kosher variety) and entertainment were all part of the East New York Jewish experience. This is a big, somewhat ungainly and oddly shaped building because it rests at the junction of two streets that are not quite at a right angle. Primarily known as a school, it did hold services, especially under the leadership of Rabbi S. Grossbein. The school that is there now has altered the windows and other features, so that much of the charm the building may have had before has been muted. With the bricked-over windows and such, it looks a bit prison-like.

Ohev Shalom (Bais Harav Midrash Eliyahu Anshei Charney?)
744 Dumont Avenue, East New York
(now House of David, First Temple of the House of David)

The story of this ex-*shul* and current house of worship is somewhat unusual for a number of reasons. The WPA survey offered no clues about the history of this modest-looking building with its interesting outdoor Judaica and fascinating collection of Judaica inside. The congregation is Hebrew-Christian, and they have retained a great deal of the former synagogue's ritual items for their own use. At least two objects reveal the name of the ex-*shul*: the burgundy velvet curtain that covers the Holy Ark for the Torah scrolls and a plaque dated 1949. Both state the name of the congregation as Ohev (or Ohav?) Shalom. One of the oldest and earliest synagogues in Brownsville had a similar name, but it is unknown whether a connection existed between this synagogue and the Ohab Sholom of Brownsville founded in the 1800s. Ohab or Ohev or Ohav Shalom is not an uncommon name for a synagogue; it means "Lover of Peace," a generically positive and pleasant name. The Ohab Sholom of Brownsville has a section in the Beth David Cemetery in Elmont, Long Island, but the congregants' names on the gate pillars do not match the congregants' names on a plaque at the 744 Dumont Avenue ex-*shul*. The Ohev Shalom of 744 Dumont was originally, of all things, "Katz's Appetizing Dairy and Grocery." Yes, it was an appe-

tizing shop, according to the tax photograph at the NYC Municipal Archives. It certainly is the same building, judging by the brickwork design on the top of the second floor windows. That explains why the three windows of the second floor were modified from rectangular to arched on top.

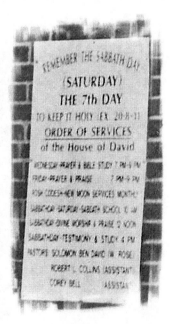

As well, the brickwork on the first floor seems somewhat different than the rest of the building. The congregants must have had the store windows removed and different doors installed. The building overall is not remarkable outside, but there are a few attractive stained glass windows out front. One unusual touch is found on the main entrance, where two Lions of Judah had been painted onto two glass panes. Inside you find the Torah Ark, velvet curtains and altar covers which may very well be

originals, a pretty stained glass door to the backyard (which features a large elongated Jewish star), pews and carvings that appear to be originals, and most telling, on the second floor there is the 1949 plaque which states the officers, building committee, and other people whose "generous donations... helped build this shool (sic)." The names listed are mostly typical Ashkenazic Jewish surnames such as Levine, Feldman, Rosen, Newman. Outside, there is a lamp hanging by the front entrance with a plaque bearing the name of Sylvia (Shifra) Pinsker. The House of David celebrates the range of Jewish holidays including the *Rosh Chodesh*, the New Month ceremonies. While they have moved some contemporary items into the sanctuary, such as an electronic keyboard, they have gone to great lengths to preserve much of the interior of the former synagogue, and they use the items left there with reverence. They also keep a little garden, a Green Thumb pocket park, next door and sell produce in season.

Ohev Sholom Anshei Sfard
157 Leonard Street at Stagg Street, East Williamsburg
(now Iglesia Accion En Cristo)

Time has not been kind to the former Ohev Shalom Anshei Sfard. The outside is quite weathered. This is a fairly old ex-*shul*, in Williamsburg, and the architectural style is not quite like many of the Brownsville, East Flatbush and East New York ex-*shuls*. However, on the front of the buildings there are two Romanesque windows and a partial one atop the main entrance. You can also make out a partial rose window above the doors. If you look carefully, you can locate the three small Jewish stars that run the length of the building, which are the primary clues to its Jewish past. Ohav Shalom Anshei Sfard (according to the WPA survey) originated in 1894. It has a portico on the roof and the brickwork seems to be pretty good for the most part. Other elements of the building need work. Sfard refers to a style of prayer common among Hassidic Jews and does not imply it was a Sephardic *shul.*

The Parkway Theater
1768 St. John's Place, Brownsville
(now Holy House of Prayer for all People)

This theater was one of the most popular and highest profile Yiddish theaters in Brooklyn. The building is quite pretty, but over the top in its abundance of decoration at the front. This building with its odd shape and plot has a commanding appearance. It stands at an unusual, angled intersection of St. John's and Eastern Parkway. (There are a number of buildings that have irregular shapes due to the curves of Eastern Parkway, such as the former Adath Yeshurun at 1403 Eastern Parkway.) While the outside does not feature particularly Jewish symbols, there is much delicately carved stonework, handsome rounded arches (somewhat similar to many ex-*shuls*), and stylish, multi-colored brickwork. Animals, flowers and other plants are the dominant motifs. The side is quite nice looking too, if not as vivid as the entrance. Brooklyn still has some of its old lavish theater palaces, as does Manhattan and the Bronx, and many of them have become churches. The church that is there now has put up a sign and a very modest cross. The cross seems to be overpowered by the rich decoration surrounding it. Alter Landesman writes about this site:

"In 1927 the Rolland, or Parkway Theatre at 1768 Saint John's Place was erected at a cost of about a million dollars. It was a large and well-equipped playhouse. For some thirty years both theatres [the other was the Hopkinson at Hopkinson and Pitkin Avenues– Ed.] functioned simultaneously. Then the Hopkinson Theatre was torn down to make room for the parking lot of the East New York Savings Bank, and the Parkway Theatre was taken over for a church." (*Brownsville*, p. 153)

"[During World War II] thousands of people jammed the theatre to hear the famous Russian Jewish dramatists and poets, Michaels and Pfeffer, speak." (Ibid, p. 322)

Congregation Petach Tikvah
261 Rochester Avenue, Crown Heights
(now Greater Bibleway Temple)

Taking up a full block of Rochester Avenue, the former Petach Tikvah (which is the name of a city in modern Israel) is an impressive site. The focal point of this well-designed structure is the main entrance to the synagogue, on Lincoln Place. The doors and stairs (a single set, not the trapezoidal style found on many other Brooklyn ex-*shuls*) are at an angle with the street. There are a few other New York Jewish institutions with this type of grand entrance—the Garfield Temple (Beth Elohim) on Eighth Avenue in Park Slope and one of the entrances to the Jewish Theological Seminary in Manhattan's Upper West Side are two notable examples. Above the main entrance are four Romanesque windows and a Jewish star inside a portico. The entrance makes a dramatic statement and the paint job is quite good. Other areas of this large former synagogue-center are in nice shape, but the northern section of the building is not quite as well-kept. There is visible wear and tear here. This was once a high-profile Conservative synagogue with a large membership and illustrious rabbis in the Conservative movement. The Brooklyn Jewish Center on Eastern Parkway was nearby, another flagship Conservative synagogue of cen-

tral Brooklyn. Today Brooklyn Jewish Center has been re-named and is used by the Chabad Lubavitch Hassidic organization; Petach Tikvah is now a Christian church with a high-profile mission, a snazzy web-site and videos on YouTube. Congregation Petach Tikvah was organized in 1914. Alter Landesman in his Brownsville study remarks that it "enjoyed a remarkable growth" due to the magnetic Rabbi Israel Levinthal, as well as its tradi-tional service which still pro-moted mixed-gender seating and a mixed choir. It was the closest example of a Conserva-tive, modern *shul* for those liv-ing in Brownsville, so it became attractive to a number of fami-lies. Eventually even the "mod-ern" Petach Tikvah saw its de-cline when its membership was depleted and the neighborhood became both African-American and Orthodox Chasidic Jewish. The church takes good care of the main sanctuary and the outside of the southern part of the building, but other parts of the building need work and paint. Edward M. Adelsohn, who designed a wing of the Brooklyn Hebrew Maternity Hospital, was the architect for this building. The source for this information was the Central Branch of the Brooklyn Public Library.

Petrikower Anshe Sfard of Brownsville
493 Herzl Street, Brownsville
(now Iglesia Congregacional "El Verbo" (Congregational Church "The Word"))

This tiny ex-*shul* is a very modest edifice, but the front of the building still has quite a bit of Jewish evidence. There is a Decalogue with Hebrew words near the very basic portico; there are at least two cornerstones with Hebrew names and words; and the sign of the current church covers up more engraved words from the old *shul*. You do see "Org. 1916" and the Hebrew date, because the sign doesn't cover these. Outside there is a decrepit wooden thing that may have been a charity box; it looks like a doll house in its style. The building is detached and has a footpath on each side. This ex-*shul* is minutes away from Brookdale Hospital, formerly known as Beth El Hospital, a hospital with a Jewish foundation. It bares a resemblance in size and in certain decorative features to the ex-*shul* (and current church) at 21 Louisiana Avenue. Perhaps the builders were the same. Sfard refers to a style of prayer common among Hassidic Jews and does not imply it was a Sephardic *shul*.

Prospect Park Jewish Center and Yeshiva
153 Ocean Avenue, Flatbush
(now John Hus Moravian Church)

Many Brooklynites are aware of the changeover at this ex-*shul*, the Prospect Park Jewish Center and Yeshiva, because of its location. It is near the northern end of Ocean Avenue, across the street from Prospect Park, and near the Brooklyn Botanic Gardens, the Brooklyn Museum, the general Park Slope, Prospect Heights and Lefferts Gardens areas. The basic shape of the building is not remarkable, but the entrance has a certain grandeur and what is perhaps the choicest aspect of this site is its spot across from the greenery of Brooklyn's premier park. The current Christian congregation removed the last vestiges of Judaica from the outside of the building. The spots where Judaica and symbols must have been located are obvious, where the decorations were removed or spackled over (as in the three rectangular spots above the main entrance). This was a fairly large synagogue with an attractive interior and pleasant schoolrooms. Peculiarly, this ex-*shul* and another Ocean Avenue ex-*shul* several blocks south were not listed in the WPA survey. Were they overlooked or were they congregations formed after 1940?

Rishon L'Zion
409 East 95th Street, East Flatbush
(now Church of God of East Flatbush)

On a quiet street of northeastern East Flatbush, not far from Brookdale Hospital (once known as Beth El Hospital, with Jewish communal origins) sits the former Rishon L'Zion (First of Zion), a well-maintained building which now houses a church. What is most interesting about this former synagogue is the gate at the front which features Jewish stars and intricate scroll work. Look closely and read the many names and words, in Hebrew and Yiddish, which when translated relate aspects of the old *shul*'s history. Most of the names are of a similar size, but there are some smaller words, somewhat fainter too, which seem to have been added as afterthoughts. There is some nice scalloping near the roof of contrasting brick color, and there are stained glass windows on the side of the building which have Judaic symbols. Read more about this congregation in the "Interviews" and "Visits" chapters for a fuller story.

Shaare Torah
305 East 21st Street at Albemarle Road, Flatbush
(previous location 2252 Bedford Avenue, Flatbush)
(now Salem Missionary Baptist Church)

Brooklyn is the hometown of a good number of impressive ex-*shuls*, edifices that still stir the soul, one of which is the former Shaare Torah. This building, which is in very good condition inside and out, has a striking feature in a metal sculpture of the Biblical burning bush. (Exodus 3:2. "And the angel of the Lord appeared unto [Moses] in a flame of fire out of the midst of a bush; and [Moses] looked, and, behold, the bush burned with fire, and the bush was not consumed.") (*The Pentateuch and Haftorahs*, Hertz, 2nd Edition. London: Soncino Press, 1970. p. 213) This sculpture has eight flame-like extensions, positioned asymmetrically around two unequal tablets—an unusual depiction of the Decalogue. The Hebrew words "Shaare Torah" (Gates of Torah) are woven into the bottom portion. This sculpture is unusual on its own, and certainly is an unique draw among Brooklyn's former synagogues. Many ex-*shuls* of Brooklyn are in the Romanesque Revival style or a variation of that, while others have classical themes, or are mere boxy buildings of a modest style. Shaare Torah is none of these; it really has its own style (perhaps there are hints of Classicism here and there.) The front of Shaare Torah is of sandstone, segmented to appear perhaps like the rungs of a ladder (think of the patriarch Jacob's ladder in Genesis) or perhaps like a net, especially a massive fishing net (which has a connection to Christian theology). There is a small fence at the corner of the building that features a menorah pattern (a modest version of the trapezoidal, dual staircase fronts of several former synagogues), and the Albemarle

Road side of the building has handsome stained glass windows and plantings. This formidable building was not the first site of Shaare Torah. An earlier site was on Bedford Avenue, not far away (close to the back entrance of Erasmus Hall High School, the oldest secondary school in North America). In its heyday that was a handsome building, although it did not resemble the East 21st Street site. In its later years it became decrepit and was knocked down; now a public elementary school resides on the plot.

Shaari Israel
810 East 49th Street, East Flatbush
(now United Pentecostal Deliverance Church)

Shaari Israel is the best documented ex-synagogue of Brooklyn, without a doubt. Suffice to say here that there is still some Judaica left to be seen on the outside and even some inside. On the outside near the roof you can see a version of the Decalogue with an engraved menorah between the halves. There are Hebrew words near a banister which had been partially chipped away. The full letters are not clear, but it is obvious that they were Hebrew letters. It is still a good-looking building with slight Romanesque Revival touches. Originally there was a Jewish star in a rose window out front, which is gone.

Shaari Zedek, then Ahavath Achim
765–767 Putnam Avenue, Bedford-Stuyvesant
(now St. Leonard's Church)

This very impressive building has a convoluted history, and is part of a hopscotch-like tale of changing congregations. It is situated in the middle of one of the classiest blocks of Bedford-Stuyvesant. Some streets in Bedford-Stuyvesant have a regal bearing, showcasing ornate houses that have been coddled for years. More and more buildings in this neighborhood are undergoing renovations so that it is slowly being restored to its former glory of sumptuous living quarters. There are still, of course, many buildings that need work, and the public housing here ranges from neat but institutional to poorly maintained and desultory. Today the building features no Judaica, although it has the look particular to a number of Brooklyn ex-*shuls*, with its neat brickwork, trio of big Romanesque windows, and classy portico and main entrance. It looks somewhat like the front of a pipe organ (as a matter of fact, it has two pipe organs inside). Plop a Jewish star somewhere on the front or a free-standing menorah near the entrance, and you would identify it as a Jewish congregation. Today it houses a Protestant Christian congregation, but in the past it played host to two different *shuls* at different times. Somehow these two *shuls* followed each other around. Let us start with Shaari Zedek, the same congregation that built the

amazing edifice on Kingston Avenue. Before they were at Kingston Avenue they were located at Quincy Street near Stuyvesant Avenue. They are listed in the November-December 1905 edition of the *Jewish Review of Brooklyn*, and at that time G. Taubenhaus was rabbi and A. Eisenberg was cantor. They then built a structure nearby on Putnam Avenue and, according to Samuel P. Abelow in his *History of Brooklyn Jewry* (1937), "this Putnam Avenue building was later acquired by Ahavas Achim when Shaari Zedek in 1922 built its home on Kingston Avenue." But Ahavath Achim had also been at the Quincy Street building, as noted in the WPA survey! So they both made parallel moves—when the first one left Quincy Street the second moved in; and when the first one left Putnam Avenue the second moved into that one too. When Ahavath Achim was still on Putnam, its rabbi was Joseph Paymer (the first rabbi was Isaac Hess). They categorized the *shul* as "semi-Reform," certainly not typical to Brooklyn. They went from traditional Orthodox to Conservative in 1910, and then they drifted leftward to "semi-Reform." This is certainly in contrast to the majority of Orthodox ex-*shuls* and the few Conservative ex-*shuls*. The few very old Reform synagogues still standing (Garfield Temple in Park Slope and Beth Emeth in Flatbush) have held on because they were fortunate enough to be surrounded by a Jewish population. There are very few Jewish people in Bedford-Stuyvesant today, and most likely they are recent arrivals from other neighborhoods or states or countries. According to the church history presented in the *Daily News* "Faith in the City" column, the Christian congregation purchased the building "in October 1944," and "its unique and very attractive sanctuary has high and low altar settings as well as upper and lower level seating..." Whoever has resided at 767 has worshipped in a beautiful building with notable features.

Shaari Zedek
221 Kingston Avenue, Weeksville
(now Historic First Church of God in Christ)

Without a doubt the former Shaari Zedek is one of Brooklyn's grandest houses of worship. It is a huge structure that fits its plot nicely. Inside is an awesome interior, with well-preserved highlights and details that recall the interiors of opulent movie palaces. There have been some changes made since its days as a Jewish site, but for the most part this is a house of worship to stroll through slowly, while soaking up the art and craft and atmosphere. The outside design is a brand of neo-classicism, and the inside features painted designs of various types, and so much more. It is important to note that the earlier site of Shaari Zedek, on Putnam Avenue, is also a nice-looking structure but not nearly as notable and sizable as this one. As fate would have it, the Great Depression hit not long after the Kingston Avenue building was done. Historic First Church certainly pays homage to the building's Jewish past by its placement of one modest sign advertising the church name. Otherwise this still really does look like a synagogue center of magnitude.

Sheveth Achim (?)
276 Buffalo Avenue, Brownsville
and The Little Temple Beth Jacob
285 Buffalo Avenue, Brownsville
(now Greater Friendship Baptist Church)

Jews and Christians are alike for obvious reasons (monotheistic beliefs, reverence for the Ten Commandments) and obscure reasons. A particular, even peculiar way in which Jews and Christians in Brooklyn follow similar trends: they support multiple houses of worship on the same street. There are certain blocks in East New York, Bedford-Stuyvesant and East Flatbush where there are three or more Christian churches on the same side of the street. They service different denominations, yet they are sort of competing for parishioners. There are also certain streets in Midwood, Borough Park, Williamsburg and elsewhere on which there are more than one synagogue, and they may all be Orthodox synagogues. There are a few streets where there are multiple ex-*shuls* to be found, such as Malta Street (where 43 and 71 were once *shuls* and are now churches). Another example is Buffalo Avenue, the first block just north of Eastern Parkway. There are two ex-*shuls* here, on either side of the street. At 285, once known as The Little Temple Beth Jacob, there is no identifiable Judaica outside (other than the trapezoidal staircase). The church congregation re-did the facing and more, so that unless you were to tap away at the facade with a chisel you would find no clues to its past. That ex-*shul* originated in 1939. At 276, on the southwest corner, there is a *shul* that was not in the WPA survey, but it was most certainly a Jewish institution. There is a strip of cast stone that has the ghosting shapes of Hebrew letters. It was so thoroughly scrubbed of the letters that is difficult to make out any words. There are some other ex-*shuls* that have these marks, such as 658 Willoughby. That one can at least be identified, this one cannot. The faded letters are but a sad testament to a vague past.

Yes, it was Jewish, but what was its name? Arched windows have also been filled in with brick, so you cannot get much of a sense of the look here other than dark brick. Thanks again to the Museum of Family History website for providing the likely name of this former synagogue.

Sons of Abraham
157 Leonard Street at Stagg Street, East Williamsburg
(now Little Zion Baptist Church)

This is a building that was once stunning. Its glory is faded, literally, because the brick needs a thorough cleaning, and that lends an unfortunate shabbiness to an otherwise striking edifice. According to the New York Landmarks Conservancy Sacred Sites program, the roof is in danger of collapsing. To quote a long-ago writer from the *Brooklyn Eagle*, "the new edifice is a handsome two story structure... of India sandstone, with terra cotta trimmings. A gilded dome is a prominent feature of the building." That dome is still the main eye-catcher, but notable also are the second floor Romanesque windows ringed by inset columns, the large rose window in the middle as well as two smaller rose windows, the scalloped design near the roof that features miniature columns, and other niceties. There is no overt Jewish symbol present, but the writing on a few plaques was spackled out long ago. This is one of the triptych synagogues; however, the middle section of the building is pushed forward, and the outer parts are set back slightly, therefore, it does not look quite like an opened Torah scroll. The *Brooklyn Eagle* article, dated December 16, 1895, describes the opening ceremony for the

shul and lists important persons involved with the congregation such as "the Rev. K. Solomon" (the *Brooklyn Eagle* in the late 1800s and early 1900s referred to rabbis as Reverends) and the congregational president S. Freudenthal. This congregation was among the older *shuls* in Brooklyn, as was its nearby neighbor, Ohev Shalom on Leonard Street. In fact, Sons of Abraham split off from another *shul*, Beth Jacob. Comparing the older *shul* buildings from East Williamsburg to those of Brownsville and East New York, you can see noticeable differences in style. However, that Romanesque theme proved to be very popular over the years with many a synagogue building.

Congregation Sons of Isaac
300 East 37th Street, East Flatbush
(now Church of God and Saints of Christ)

If Brooklyn has a humble, plain-looking church, then this is it. It is just a bit south of the stylish Ahavas Achim at 203 East 37th Street. Brooklyn has its formerly Jewish gems, as well as its formerly Jewish diamonds in the rough.

Congregation Sons of Judah
864 Sutter Avenue, East New York
(now Messiah Missionary Baptist Church)

This former synagogue, an attractive building, has elements similar to many other Brooklyn ex-*shuls*: a "triptych" three part layout, a large (and now filled in) rose window, a scalloped design of slightly raised brick, and a Decalogue near the roof. The Decalogue of Sons of Judah seems to be the solitary remaining symbol of its Jewish past, and this one has Hebrew words for the Ten Commandments (other old synagogues had Roman numerals or other notations). The congregation originated in 1907, and the rabbi at the time of the WPA survey was Herman Martel. They had burial plots at the Beth David cemetery in Elmont, Nassau County. It is noteworthy that this synagogue had 20 Torah scrolls, quite a collection.

Talmud Torah Atereth Eliezer Glovinsky
747 Hendrix Street, East New York
(now The House of David Pentecostal Apostolic Church of God)

The former Glovinsky *shul* is a fine example of how, in Brooklyn's not-so-distant past, even small structures in modest precincts could boast of handsome brickwork and architectural detailing. Unlike the many boring brick boxes that dot Brooklyn's landscape more and more, this one-story building has some fine attributes. The brickwork still looks well maintained, and the variegated colors hold up well. The arches over the windows in the front are gracious and frame well-kept stained glass windows. The gate is in good shape, and Jewish stars grace a few points. For the WPA survey, the building, given the address of 745, was dedicated and consecrated in November 1926. Why the name Glovinsky? A "Mr. Glovinsky had donated land and necessary funds to erect the synagogue." Although it had a Talmud Torah designation, it had only two classrooms. They had six Torah scrolls. The congregation had purchased cemetery plots at the Beth David Cemetery in Elmont, Long Island, just over the Queens County border. The WPA survey often mentions where particular synagogues held their plots, and Beth David is frequently mentioned. This is one of the best maintained and largest Jewish cemeteries which is not too far from Brooklyn. The Glovinsky *shul* plots are fronted by an entrance consisting of two pillars and an engraved step, and not surprisingly there are a number of headstones here that have the Glovinsky name. The WPA survey was done by Morris Addleman.

Talmud Torah Atereth Israel
85–87 Fountain Avenue, East New York
(now Ninth Tabernacle)

This ex-*shul* still seems to be more synagogue than church, by virtue of its very minimal Christian decoration (a lone small showcase and a wall sign about parking on the side street, at Wells Street), contrasted with much remaining Judaica. This corner building has a box shape, but there are pleasant touches such as stained-glass windows with Jewish stars and a few vaguely Romanesque Revival window toppings. The building's fence is in good shape. Atereth Israel is the eastern-most Brooklyn ex-*shul* of this study, close to Queens. The Jewish congregation was organized in 1912. The building was built, dedicated and occupied in 1923. The first spiritual leader was Rabbi Isaac Zaks. The *shul* had six Torah scrolls.

Talmud Torah Beth Jacob Joseph
368 Atlantic Avenue, Boerum Hill
(now Deity, a bar/club)

Here is an exception to the *shul*-to-church trend. This ex-*shul* spent years as an antiques and collectibles shop known as Time Trader and in 2006–07 was changed into the cheekily named Deity, a wine bar. Much Judaica on the front of the building has been preserved. It is a handsome building with a great deal of detail. On top is the Decalogue with Roman numerals up to ten (this can be seen on many ex-*shuls*). There are several small Jewish stars set on circles, in a medallion fashion. The old synagogue name is written in Hebrew in raised letters above the doorway. The doorway itself is a focal point, with its pointed arch. "1917" sits just above the door. Near the top are attractive, thin Romanesque Revival windows. You can easily read this building's past. The congregation was organized in 1903, the building dedicated in 1917. It was named for a famous rabbi, Rabbi Jacob Joseph, who was the first and only Chief Rabbi of New York City. The Rabbi, who lived from 1840–1902, was invited to come to the City from Eastern

Europe. Among his achievements was his role in establishing the Etz Chaim Yeshiva, the first yeshiva on the Lower East Side. Now the Jacob Joseph schools are in Staten Island and New Jersey. The interior has been redone. This "conversion" to a social site was documented in a *New York Sun* article dated Thursday, January 11, 2007, ("Synagogue Gets New Identity as Wine Bar", p.10). Apparently, this former synagogue may have been a beer hall in an even earlier incarnation.

Talmud Torah Tifereth Hagro
(originally Talmud Torah Tifereth Zion)
425 Howard Avenue, Weeksville
(now Mt. Ararat Baptist Church)

This was a pretty big school building in its time, with an institutional yet stately air. The building has held up well and retains much of its earlier decorative detail, but the only Judaica left is a small Jewish star set into a scrolled stone piece, near the top of the building. The front shows some semi-pillars capped with Corinthian-influenced capitals, so this building bears the influence of the neo-classical style. The school and congregation originated in 1907; the name change came in 1917. The building itself dates from 1919, and it contained 15 classrooms in its three stories. This building also fills out the complete plot (58.42' by 100 feet), unlike most Brooklyn ex-*shuls* and schools.

Talmud Torah Tifereth Israel of West Flatbush
1913–1915 West 7th Street, Gravesend
(now New Jerusalem Christian Church)

This has to be one of the more peculiar ex-*shuls* of Brooklyn. The majority of ex-*shuls* covered here are found in Brownsville, East New York, Flatbush and East Flatbush. To a lesser degree they are in East Williamsburg and Bedford-Stuyvesant; Canarsie and Sheepshead Bay and Sunset Park have a few. As neighborhood demographics continue to change, certain other synagogues lose their congregants and then become lost. It had stopped being a synagogue years earlier, perhaps in the late 1960s or early 1970s. Some decorative scrolling and a date remain—1925? 1926? There were tablets with Hebrew writing, at sidewalk level, but some letters seemed to be faded, which struck me as odd. I found out the name and some information via the WPA survey. Why was this *shul* placed in "West Flatbush"? There is no way to describe this area as West Flatbush, because it is nowhere near Flatbush proper. Was this a case of wishful thinking on the congregation's part? Flatbush is miles away, East Flatbush even more so.

Was this a desirable designation, meant to appeal to Jewish Brooklynites' affections for Flatbush? The congregation, with its curious name, originated in 1925. The writer described it as "modified Florentine brick" which is generous. It really is not a remarkable building. It does resemble a number of other 1920s ex-*shuls* with its "modified" triptych style and an arched but filled in space above the main entrance. The first rabbi, who also officiated at the time of the WPA survey, was Dr. Meyer Sharff. It is quite clear that Jews left eastern and central Brooklyn neighborhoods, and that the synagogues there disbanded. Why this *shul* faded out is a true mystery, when there are many other synagogues and Jewish businesses nearby.

Temple Beth Ohr
1010 Ocean Avenue, Flatbush
(Later Redemption Gospel)

A wonderful book about houses of worship in Manhattan is *From Abyssinian to Zion,* by David Dunlap. Ah, for such a book about Brooklyn's houses of worship. Dunlap's book features discussions on the artistic, architectural, and historical aspects of just about every known house of worship in Manhattan. Many Gotham houses of worship have gone through at least two, if not three, four or more incarnations, running the gamut of religions as well as degrees within a particular religion. Sometimes churches became synagogues that later became different churches. For a tangled history, look at that of 1010 Ocean Avenue. A *New York Times* Sunday Real Estate section article, dated September 23, 2007, presents its saga. This mansion and the one next door were designed by George Palliser, and 1010 served as a residence for a few decades. By 1940, 1010 had become a synagogue. It was still a synagogue, a reform congregation called Temple Beth Ohr, at least through the 1980s. Years later, there was a sign on the lawn for a Christian

church. In 2007, the *New York Times* relates that a doctor bought the building. In 2008, apparently the doctor sold it to a church group. So this Colonial Revival edifice, a gorgeous and stunning corner building will once again be serving a congregation. So it goes in the world of Brooklyn real estate.

Temple Isaac (aka Ohel Yitzhok)
554 Prospect Place, Prospect Heights
(now Faith Chapel Baptist Church)

There are a number of Brooklyn synagogues, including some still active, which have a front that is adorned but basically flat, a single plane of decoration. In contrast to the "open Torah" triptych style of many *shuls*, these have a front that is pretty but seems to be propped up in front of a typical boxy building. There may be a rounded roof segment, nice doors and windows, well-shaped pilasters, but the front is like a set placed on a stage. Temple Isaac has this kind of layout. There are not too many former or current synagogues in this area so it stands out by dint of its location. There are some pleasing elements to the front of this house of worship. The argyle pattern of brickwork is unusual. The half arc of windows above the three Romanesque Revival doors is a handsome touch, and if you look carefully you can discern further details within the individual glass panels. There are two pilasters topped with globes, and the synagogue name is rendered

in English. The gate and entrance are in good shape. The congregation was organized in 1904, and the building was built and occupied in 1920. Rabbi Leon S. Essex officiated at the time of the WPA survey. This was one of the few Conservative synagogues at this time and in this vicinity, and the congregational name is a clear tipoff to that. This ex-*shul* has attracted a bit of notice. It has been mentioned in a few other contemporary articles.

Temple Sinai
24 Arlington Avenue, Highland Park
(now Misionario Cristiano)

This is another stunning ex-*shul*, sitting in a quietly regal fashion on its corner lot. Upon first glimpse, it seems to be synagogue; but there is a small sign bearing the name of the current church. The Christian congregation could have just called it Temple Sinai Church, since the name is still prominently displayed in English (and in Hebrew for those in the know). Located in a pleasant area of mostly one and two family houses with gardens, it is close to Highland Park. Compared to a number of other ex-*shuls* in East New York, this one seems to have a small-town feel due to its location. Temple Sinai has a lengthy history and Alter Landesman covers it in his *Brownsville* tome. First the congregation, originally known as Bikur Cholim (Visiting the Sick), met at a former church at 101 Wyona Street. It was a predominantly German Jewish group, as opposed to the many Russian and Polish Jewish congregations in the area. Finally in April 1920, they had the groundbreaking at Arlington Avenue; the cornerstone was placed in June of that year and in September 1921 the building was dedicated. It was the priciest *shul* in the neighborhood; later it took over the adjacent lots and built a religious school (that building is not nearly as sophisticated in design and has that boxy modern appearance). The congregational name morphed from Bikur Cholim to the folksy Old Wyona Street Synagogue to Temple Sinai, perhaps a nod to its hilly location. If you are traveling around East New York and Brownsville looking for ex-*shuls*, this one is harder to find and further away. It did last as a Jewish house of worship into the early 1980s, according to Oscar Israelowitz.

Tifereth Israel
656–8 Willoughby Avenue, Bedford-Stuyvesant
(now Aguadilla Day Care Center)

The former Tifereth Israel became not a church but a day care center, which puts it in the minority of ex-*shul* conversions (along with the New Lots Talmud Torah and a few others). The front of the building has mostly been redone, but you can easily see where the Hebrew lettering was once set. Were there individual metal letters, for example, that were removed? Did someone also try to cover up the lettering? In any case, the "ghosts" of Hebrew words remain, along with a two-sided cornerstone that reads "5672" on one side the Hebrew letters representing that year on the other. There are a few other ex-*shuls* that have on display the faded spots where the Hebrew letters once stood. However, Tifereth Israel has one of the clearer sets of "ex-letters" that can be seen. The congregation was organized in 1912; the building was built and dedicated in 1917, making it a bit older than many of the Brooklyn ex-*shuls* of the 1920s.

Tifereth Yehuda Nusach Sfard
347 East 49th Street, East Flatbush
(now New Life Tabernacle)

The New Life Tabernacle looks pretty new and reflects little or nothing of its Jewish past. Its fortress-like gate, with its name, guard a building, or at least a plot, that was once an ex-*shul*. The Jewish congregation was organized in 1929 as Ohev Shalom of East Flatbush, and the name was changed in honor of Rabbi Yehuda Silverberg, to Tifereth Yehuda Nusach Sfard. This *shul* was built or organized in 1929, on the eve of the Great Depression. Brooklyn has some ex-*shuls* that came about in that year, and a number of others that started within a year or two of that fateful time. Nusach Sfard refers to a style of prayer common among Hassidic Jews and does not imply it was a Sephardic *shul*.

Tomchai Torah
1320 Sutter Avenue, East New York
(now Greater Bright Light Baptist Church)

There is something motel-like to this wide building that once housed a *shul* but is now a church since around 1990. Made of yellow brick with a spacious archway, it is not a highly styled building, although the six-door entrance lends a spacious feel to the entrance. The outside still features a Decalogue with brief Hebrew words. Etched in sandstone near the roof is the ex-shul's name and basic information in Hebrew. There is no remaining Judaica inside the building. As a *shul*, Tomchai Torah had six Torah scrolls. The building was dedicated and consecrated in 1927. There are also two remaining Jewish cornerstones as testament to the old congregation.

Mystery Jewish establishment on Varet Street
101 Varet Street, East Williamsburg
(now Varet Street Market)

Was this a *shul* at some point? Or a kosher butcher or grocery shop? There are a few tantalizing clues left here—the year "1918" in sculpted stone near the roof, a Jewish star design of brick in a shade darker than the rest of the brick, and what was probably a sign that has been covered over, just beneath the 1918 designation. There was a synagogue on Varet Street but at a different number (now gone) and nearby streets also had synagogues. Obviously this was part of the Jewish life of this neighborhood, but in which capacity is not clear.

Congregation Vezras Achim
341 Pennsylvania Avenue, East New York
(now Mt. Moriah Baptist Church)

Shuls and ex-*shuls* usually do not have signs with catchy phrases on their lawns or raised above their main entrances. They have small, discrete panels announcing the times for services and the name of the bar or bat mitzvah of the week. There are no thought-provoking or humorous tag lines with religious themes. The slogan at Mt. Moriah Baptist Church is: "Small Church with a Big Vision through Christ—To Teach the Lost at Any Cost." This is a small church; it was once one of the smaller two-story *shuls*. Congregation Vezras Achim once stood on a major thoroughfare, mid-block. It originated in 1925 and was formerly a three-family building (albeit at two stories). The style of the building is plain, with a few nice touches over the windows and one Jewish star near the roof.

Woodruff Avenue Temple
151 Woodruff Avenue at East 21st, Flatbush
(now Calvary Pentecostal Church)

The identifying Jewish symbols are the many Jewish stars that run up the side of the building. There is a photograph of this synagogue at the Brooklyn Collection in the Central branch of the Brooklyn Public Library, which revealed an unusual artistic feature of this ex-*shul*. Twelve small decorative windows represented the Twelve Tribes, and the layout resembled a high priest's breast plate. You can still see the spaces for several of these windows; the windows were removed and some of the spaces have been bricked in. The shape resembles a Decalogue. This ex-*shul* is on a side street, but it has an interesting position because another street dead-ends right by it.

Yeshivat Rabbi Meyer Simcha HaCohen
309 East 53rd Street, East Flatbush
(now medical offices)

This building has been altered so much, but it remains a rather nice-looking building with charming details. The picture here will give some idea what it used to look like when it served souls and not medical roles. This ex-*shul* is a bit unusual in that it did not become a church. Before the major renovation into a medical complex, it had served as a community center. It retained the bulk of its detail up until the developers of the medical center began their work. This was one of the ex-*shuls* that had been named after a specific sage. Anther example in this book includes the Talmud Torah Jacob Joseph on Atlantic Avenue. Who was Rabbi Meyer (or Meir) Simcha HaCohen? According to Wikipedia and a Jewish learning website, this rabbi lived from 1843–1926. He was born in Lithuania and spent most of his adult life as the rabbi in Dvinsk, Latvia. He is known for two books he penned, *Or Sameach* (Light of Happiness) and *Mesech Chochma.* There are yeshivas in the United States, Canada and Israel named for Or Sameach. This ex-*shul* was organized in 1926, and perhaps that is the reason the congregation adopted the name in the year of his demise. This synagogue has been described as a handsome one, some-

what more sumptuous than others in the area. Until 2006 it still had a trio of large Romanesque windows flanked by ribbed columns. Underneath was a series of smaller arched columns of brick, built into the face of the building. There were still Jewish stars and a menorah in sculpted stone. The stained glass panes were not in great shape, however. The adjacent building that had housed the Hebrew school was fenced in by barbed wire at that time, and mounds of dirt and rock sat in front of it. It still had its Jewish star too.

Yeshivath Torath Chaim of Greater New York
(also Young Israel of East New York)
631 Belmont Avenue, East New York
(now a Public School building)

There is little about this nice looking but clearly institutional building to suggest that it was a synagogue or a yeshiva, but it certainly looks like a stately if unremarkable school. It was a school, then of a Jewish nature, now a Department of Education building with a nice entrance, tweed-like brick work, simple but tasteful window decorations, and a few other good details. Other than a Hebrew year somewhere on the building (spelled out in letters), any Judaica that may have once been present has been removed or covered over. At the top of the building, there is evidence of where a Decalogue probably was exhibited in the past. At the time of the WPA survey, the school was licensed as a public school, so it had a dual curriculum. As of December 2007, there was no evidence of Judaica in the building, which was known at the time as the Belmont Academy, a suspension school for high school students.

Young Israel of Brownsville and East Flatbush
1091 Winthrop Street at East 94th Street, East Flatbush-Brownsville
(now 2nd St. John Missionary Baptist Church)

The Young Israel movement of modern Orthodox Judaism had a few Brooklyn outposts that are now ex-*shuls*. The Prospect Park branch was a former church on Bedford Avenue, while the Brownsville-East Flatbush division met at a renovated private residence that was at the border of East Flatbush and Brownsville. This congregation had met at a few other sites before landing on Winthrop Street in 1957 (they had spent more than 30 years at the Hebrew Educational Society, H.E.S. building on Sutter and Hopkinson). By setting up shop in 1957, this Young Israel was doomed pretty quickly, for the exodus of Jews from this area of Brooklyn was already beginning and would be a major demographic factor within a handful of years. Alter Landesman mentions this in his dry, recitative fashion in *Brownsville*, but does not explore the motives for a congregation to move to a space that the congregants probably already sensed was precarious and not too desirable in the long run. The building is unremarkable in style, but there are several Jewish stars in the stained glass windows on both the Winthrop Street and East 94th Street sides. Inside there is not much remaining Judaica but there are a few *mezuzot* painted over a number of times, remaining affixed to doorways.

Young Israel of Prospect Park
2170 Bedford Avenue, Flatbush
(now Faith Assembly of God)

This former synagogue looks a lot like a church because originally it was a church, that became a synagogue—and it later became a church again. The main aspect of Judaic interest here is the large rose window on the Bedford Avenue side, which has the Young Israel symbols, sort of like a Seder plate design.

Appendix A:
Known Architects for Brooklyn's Former Synagogues

Most of the architects of Brooklyn's former synagogues, as well as many that still survive, are unknown today, as they were not recorded on the building plans. However, the New York Landmarks Conservancy, through the work of their Sacred Sites program lead by Ann Friedman, has located the names for a group of these buildings. Among these ex-shuls are some of the most impressive buildings surveyed in this book. As well, a few more modest structures are included here because someone made the effort to include the names of architects on the plans.

Edward M. Adelson was the architect for at least four ex-shuls in Brooklyn:

1. Petach Tikvah at 261 Rochester Avenue (Mentioned in the entry for the congregation earlier in the text)
2. AA Bnei Jacob of East New York at 503 Glenmore Avenue
3. Sons of Judah at 864 Sutter Avenue
4. Temple Sinai at 24 Arlington Avenue

Abraham Farber was the architect for at least two ex-shuls in Brooklyn:

1. Chevra Sphard of Perryslaw at 247 Snediker Avenue
2. Men of Justice at 1678 Park Place

S. Millman and Son were the architects for these:

1. Chevra Ahavath Israel Anshei Ostrolenker at 375 Bristol Street
2. AAA Brownsville at 105 Riverdale Avenue
3. Congregation Kachlow Israel at 220 Hegeman Avenue

There may be a connection to the architect Peter Millman who was the architect for Congregation Agudath Achim of East Flatbush at 203 East 37th Street

Other architects known to have designed at least one ex-shul in Brooklyn are:

F. Jack Fein who worked on Congregation Dorshe Tov Anshei New Lots at 21 Louisiana Avenue

Axel S. Hedman and Eugene Schoen who worked on Shaare Zedek at 767 Putnam Avenue

Moses Mendelsohn who worked on Kevelson's Shul at 1387 East 96th Street

Henry J. Nurick who worked on Bikur Cholim at 3 Lewis Avenue

H.G. Savran who worked on Shaare Torah at 305 East 21st Street

Martyn N. Weinstein who worked on Temple Isaac at 554 Prospect Place

These synagogues were located in several neighborhoods around Brooklyn. Several are among the larger structures featured in this book, but a few, such as Kachlow Israel and Dorshe Tov, are smaller. Edward M. Adelson seems to have been one of the more prolific synagogue architects in Brooklyn. The four buildings listed include some of the grandest former synagogues, congregations that had more wealth.

Perhaps someday the names of more of these architects will be uncovered. I would be especially interested to find out who was the architect of Shaare Zedek on Kingston Avenue, still a magnificent site, but as time passes, it is less likely that this information will come to light.

Appendix B:
Using This Book as a Teaching Tool for
Various Grade Levels

The material covered in this book can be utilized by teachers for their students and by parents for their children. There are a number of ways to integrate the themes and information contained within *The Lost Synagogues of Brooklyn*. Below are suggestions for different grade levels and content areas. While this book focuses on Brooklyn, these lessons can be used in a similar fashion for other regions throughout the United States, Canada, Europe, the Caribbean, and South America, where there are former synagogues that can be examined for educational purposes. Related field trips can be a wonderful idea too. These teaching points are based on my years as a New York City public high school and middle school teacher, primarily teaching social studies as well as photography and writing curriculum packages for high school courses.

Judaic Studies

This book offers much to explore for those who teach about Judaism. There are religious and cultural aspects that can be explored. Students can learn about synagogues; what happens in a synagogue as well as how congregants use the synagogue, and this book can be tied into that. The majority of Jews who went to these Brooklyn ex-*shuls* were of Eastern European backgrounds; that is another avenue to explore with students. A lesser number were of Iberian or Middle Eastern extraction, and that can provide for a lesson in comparative sub-ethnic groups. Although some of these topics may be more appropriate for middle school and above, even younger children can appreciate certain themes if tied in with oral history, especially of family members and neighbors. Students can also study the Hebrew meanings of the old congregational names, which range from those we even see today (Bnai Israel, Shaare Torah) to those that are more obscure.

Christian Studies

There are many Christian congregations that have adopted and adapted the former synagogue buildings to their use as churches. Students can learn about and compare the denominations that are prevalent in these buildings, such as Baptist and Pentecostal. Students can learn how the Christians use the buildings in similar or different ways. Students can also study the meanings behind the names of the Christian churches such as Gethsemane, Calvary, etc.

Interfaith Relations and Studies

This book can be useful in conducting lessons on interfaith relations and studies. Students can compare and contrast aspects of the Jewish and Christian congregations that have occupied the buildings at different times. Students can discuss the similarities and differences among the two major religious folds. One suggestion is to compare the prayer books of a Jewish and a Christian congregation: what are the similar prayers and words; which are different? What scriptural trends can be seen in both types of congregations? How are the prayers sung differently? For some students this could involve visits to different houses of worship—perhaps even visits to the buildings described and analyzed in this book.

Art and Architecture

There is a great deal that this book offers for lessons in art and architecture and even preservation arts. Students at different levels can study the photographs here and describe the Jewish and Christian elements of the buildings. They can discuss why a Christian congregation may have retained elements of the Judaica on an old building, or why and how they changed things. Advanced students can tease out the stylistic trends exhibited on these buildings, such as Neo-Classical, Romanesque Revival, etc., and the individual parts such as columns, window dressings, doorways, arches and such. If students are brought on field trips, they can photograph or sketch the art and design of these buildings.

Urban History

The Lost Synagogues of Brooklyn is a study of demographic change in an urban setting. Students can engage in "expeditionary learning" (hands-on investigative studies) about the changes happening in a neighborhood, using this book as a starting point. They can study how buildings are used in different ways, at different times, using the idea of religious changes at houses of worship. They can ask questions about why buildings change hands, how their use differs, how people adapt space to their own needs.

Research Methods: Locating and Using Resources

At certain points in the text, I discuss my methods of research for this book—which are many. Students can tour municipal and regional archives to learn what types of materials are available and to what uses they can be employed. They can learn how to "read" a building as I did in many cases when examining these buildings (although in these cases, knowledge of Hebrew, Yiddish and Roman numerals was quite important). Students can learn what to look for when touring a historical site or any building being examined; the awareness of architecture as a form of language is stressed here.

As well, students can learn how to use the Internet in their research, through formulating and asking questions, locating appropriate sites, and mining various archives and dictionaries.

Interviewing Techniques and Using Oral History

Learning how to construct useful interviews is an important skill for students, and at each grade level they should be able to refine the process further. *The Lost Synagogues of Brooklyn* features a variety of interviews based on peoples' affiliations (members of synagogue or *shul*, members of church, clergy, and such), and students can learn how to organize and group their questions to maximize the actual interviews. They can also learn how to document the information and fact-check for accuracy (or analyze why oral history has certain drawbacks as well as benefits). They can come to realize that when they interview people of older generations they can learn much from them.

Socials studies classes. This book has much to do with history and geography. Students can learn ethnic history, urban studies, and similar fields. It can be helpful for students to use the map and learn how to navigate an urban area, especially targeting particular sites.

English Language Arts. There are narratives within this book, especially when reading the interviews. Autobiographical elements can be explored. This book can be paired with memoirs of people who grew up in Brooklyn or who are currently living in Brooklyn, as well as fictional works; these books include story books for the younger grades. Students can also read the sources listed in the bibliography, especially the books and newspaper articles. They can use this book as an inspiration for their own creative writing or artistic projects (short stories, poems, plays, paintings and drawings, dioramas, etc).

Arts courses. Students can engage in drawing, painting, photography, model making of the houses of worship featured in this book or similar ones in other cities and countries. Consult the bibliography for information on artists and photographers whose work I viewed during my research.

Sample Lesson Plan

This is included based upon my years as a teacher in the New York public school system, working mostly with high school and middle school students, and as a mentor for two student teachers.

AIM: What can we learn from examining houses of worship that have served more than one religion?

Grade levels: Appropriate for middle school and above, even college level

Instructional Objective: Students will be able to discern visual cues that signify meaning for different religions; students will be able to discuss the differences between and similarities among more than one house of worship.

Materials used: Students can use the photographs within *The Lost Synagogues of Brooklyn*; students may go on a supervised field trip to visit such buildings, using this text as a guide.

Among the questions a teacher/instructor may pose to students include:

• What symbols and words signify a Jewish congregation? A Christian congregation?

• How are the names of the congregations similar and different?

• Why might a Christian congregation hold onto Jewish building decorations and accessories?

• Why might a Christian congregation move into a former Jewish house of worship?

• Most of these buildings were built before the 1930s. How do these buildings look different from more modern buildings? How are they similar?

Follow-up activity: Students can pick a particular building to do further research on; they can draw, paint, or make a 3D model of a building in the study; they can pose further questions about the buildings and people using the buildings.

I welcome commentary and look forward to hearing about how teachers and students use the book. Contact me through the publisher or e-mail at bigsis464@yahoo.com.

Appendix C:
Non-English Words Used in Synagogue Names

Below is a list of non-English words used in names of synagogues. Most are from Hebrew, the language of the Torah. There are various schemes to transliterate Hebrew or Yiddish into the Latin alphabet and spelling variants below are obvious (Ahavas/Ahavath, Ansche/Anschei). Unless specified otherwise, the word is from the Hebrew language.

Achim. Brothers
Agudas. Society
Ahavas. Lover of
Ahavath. Lover of
Ansche. People of
Anschei. People of
Anshe. People of
Anshei. People of
Ashkenaz. Describing Jews from Central or Eastern Europe
Atereth. Glory of
Azaritz. Probably the town of Ozarichi, Belarus
B'nai. Sons of, people of
Beth. House of
Bikur. Visitors (as in Bikur Cholim which means visiting the sick)
Bnai. Sons of, people of
Bnei. Sons of, people of
Bobruisk. A city in Belarus.
Chesed. Loving-kindness
Chevra. Society
Chevre. Society
Cholim. The sick (as in Bikur Cholim which means visiting the sick)
Dorshe. Seekers
Eliezer. Biblical male name
Eliyahu. Elijah
Emeth. Truth
Esrath. Variant of ezrath, the help of
Etz Chaim. Tree of life
Ezrath. Variant of esrath, the help of
Glubucker. Probably the town of Glebokie, Belarus
HaCohen. The priest; religious designation
Hadath. Assembly
Hagadol. The great
Hagro. A title for genius, Gaon
Hamedrash. As in Bet/Beit Hamedrash, house of

prayer/study
Harav. The rabbi
Hemidrash. Variant of hamedrash
Hessed. Variant of chesed
Kachlow. Name of an unknown town
Kenesseth. When preceded by the word "Beth" it means house of worship
Kesser. Crown, variant of keter
Krashnik. Probably the town of Krasnik, Poland.
Machzikei. From chazak,— Upholders (as in "Machzikei Torah")
Midrash. Learning portion
Mishnitz. Probably the town of Myszyniec, Poland
Nachlot Inheritance, as in "Nacholoth Zion," Inheritance of Israel
Nusach. Style of prayer
Ohel. Tent
Ohev. Lover of
Oholei. Tents
Ohr. Light
Ostrolenker. From the town of Ostrolenka, Poland
Petach Tikvah. A city in Israel; literally the opening of hope
Petrikower. From the town of Petrikow
Poelei. Workers
R. Abbreviation for "rabbi."
Radishkowitz. Probably the town of Radoshkovichi, Belarus.
Reyim. Friends, revered title for
Rishon L'Zion. A city in Israel; literally, the first of Zion
Sfard. A type of ritual common among Hassidic Jews (not to be confused with Sephardic)
Shaare. Gates of (variant of

shaari)
Shaari. Gates of (variant of share)
Shalom. Peace
Sholom. Peace
Shul. Yiddish for synagogue
Sinai. Mount Sinai of biblical importance
Snediker. Dutch name, a street in Brooklyn
Sphard. Variant of sfard
Talmud. The Oral Law in Judaism
Talmud Torah. Religious school
Tehillim. Psalms
Tifereth. Praising
Tomchai. Supporters
Torah. The Five Books of Moses, literally "law"
Torath. Plural of Torah
Tov. Good
Tzedek. Righteous
Ve. And
Vezras. And the help of
Yehuda. Judah; a tribe of Israel; often used to designate the Jewish people
Yeshiva. Jewish school of learning
Yeshivat. Plural of yeshiva
Yeshivath. Plural of yeshiva
Yeshurun. Jeshurun, of Biblical importance
Yitzhok. Issac
Zedek. Variant of Tzedek
Zion. A designation for the Jewish people

Bibliography

Books

Abelow, Samuel. *History of Brooklyn Jewry*. Brooklyn: Scheba Publishing, 1937.

Abramovitch, Ilana and Sean Galvin, editors. *Jews of Brooklyn*. Hanover, N.H: University Press of New England, 2001.

Appel, Rabbi Gersion. *The Concise Code of Jewish Law. Volume One: A Guide to Prayer and Religious Observance in the Daily Life of the Jew*. New York: Ktav, 1977.

Blumenson, John J.-G. *Identifying American Architecture. A Pictorial Guide to Styles and Terms, 1600–1945*. Walnut Creek, Calif: AltaMira Press, 1995.

Chatenow, Gerald and Bernard D. Schwartz. *Another Time, Another Place: A Neighborhood Remembered*. Philadelphia: Xlibris Corp, 2000.

Dimont, Max I. *Jews, God and History*. New York: Signet Books, 1962.

Dunlap, David W. *From Abyssinian to Zion: A Guide to Manhattan's Houses of Worship*. New York: Columbia University Press, 2004.

Ford, Carole Bell. *The Girls: Jewish Women of Brownsville, Brooklyn 1940–1995*. New York: State University Press of New York, 1999.

Fox, Muriel. *A Girl from The Home*. Philadelphia: Xlibris Corp, 2000.

Goodman, Fred. *The Secret City: Woodlawn Cemetery and the Buried History of New York*. New York: Random House, 2004.

Gutman, Joseph, editor. *The Synagogue: Studies in Origins, Archaeology and Architecture*. New York: Ktav, 1975.

Hamill, Pete. *Downtown: My Manhattan*. New York: BackBay Books, 2005.

Hertz, Dr. J.H., editor. *Pentateuch and Haftorahs. Hebrew Text English Translation and Commentary*, 2nd ed. London: Soncino Press, 1976.

Ierardi, Eric J. *Brooklyn in the 1920s. Images of America Series*. Charleston, S.C.: Arcadia Publishing: 1998.

Israelowitz, Oscar. *Synagogues of New York City: A Pictorial Survey*. New York: Dover Publications, 1982.

Kaufman, David. *Shul with a Pool: The "Synagogue Center" in American Jewish History*. Hanover, N.H.: Brandeis University Press, 1999.

Kazin, Alfred. *A Walker in the City*. New York: Harcourt Brace Jovanovich, 1951, 1977.

Krinsky, Carol Herselle. *Synagogues of Europe*. New York: Dover, 1996.

Landesman, Alter. *Brownsville: The Birth, Development and Passing of a Jewish Community in New York*, 2nd. ed. New York: Bloch Publishing Co, 1971.

Mirsky, Jeannette. *Houses of God*. Chicago: University of Chicago Press, 1976, c1965.

Packer, Robert A. *Chicago's Forgotten Synagogues. Images of America Series*. Charleston, S.C.: Arcadia Publishing: 2007.

Pritchett, Wendell. Brownsville, *Brooklyn: Blacks, Jews, and the Changing Face of the Ghetto*. Chicago: University of Chicago Press, 2002.

Raphael, Marc Lee. *Judaism in America*. New York: Columbia University Press, 2003.

Rieder, Jonathan. *Canarsie: The Jews and Italians of Brooklyn Against Liberalism*. Cambridge, Mass.: Harvard University Press, 1985.

Rosenblum, Robert. *My Bar Mitzvah*. William Morrow, 1985.

Roth, Henry. *Call It Sleep*. New York: Avon Books, 1964, 1934.

Thabit, Walter. *How East New York Became a Ghetto*. New York: New York University Press, 2003.

Zimiles, Murray. *Gilded Lions and Jeweled Horses: The Synagogue to the Carousel, Jewish Carving Traditions*. Waltham, Mass.: Brandeis University Press, 2007.

Zucker, David J. *American Rabbis: Fact and Fiction*. Northvale, N.J.: Jason Aaronson, 1998.

Newspaper and Magazine Articles

Berman, Daphna. "A Brooklyn Shul in Israel." *HaAretz*. November 16, 2007.

Berger, Joseph. "Small Jewish Congregations Attracting More Worshipers." *New York Times*. August 5, 1986. B1, B6.

Birkner, Gabrielle. "Synagogue Gets New Identity as Wine Bar." *New York Sun*. January 11, 2007. 10.

"Brownsville Fasting." *Brooklyn Eagle*. September 17, 1896. 4.

Chambers, Marcia. "Brooklyn Synagogue to Hear Sound of Shofar Last Time." *New York Times*. October 4, 1976. 30.

"Citizens Organize Vacation School of Jewish Lore." *Brooklyn Eagle*. August 10, 1948.

DeWees, Gayle, compiled by. "Faith in the City. Greater Free Gift Baptist Church." *New York Daily News*. November 12, 2006. KSI

DeWees, Gayle, compiler. "Faith In The City: Power Up Faith Fellowship." New York Daily News. September 23 2007. KSI 3.

DeWees, Gayle, compiler. "Faith in the City: St. Leonard's Church." *New York Daily News*. June 24, 2007. KSIL 45.

Dickter, Adam. "Not Sold on Synagogue Sale." *Jewish Week*. June 18, 2004.

Gonzalez, David. "Once a Synagogue, Now a Church, and Ailing Quietly." *New York Times*. January 28, 2008. B1, B6.

Gray, Christopher. "Kissing Cousins at 100: Only One Shows Its Age. Streetscapes/Ocean Avenue, Brooklyn." *New York Times*. September 23, 2007. Real Estate section 6.

Harrison, Rick. "Cash-strapped Synagogue Weighs Sale to Messianic Congregation." *Forward*. October 8, 2004.

Jacobs, Andrew. "Two Miles in Newark That Run from Long Decline to Rebirth." *New York Times*. January 5, 2007. A1, B2.

Joselit, Jenna Weissman. "Museum Woe. The Wonders of America." *Forward*. January 4, 2008. B3.

"Lemon Dismissed the Case." *Brooklyn Eagle*. April 13, 1900. 11.

"New Synagogue Dedicated." *Brooklyn Eagle*. December 16, 1895. 9.

"Synagogue for Sale Down South..." *Kesher Talk*. September 22, 2003.

Websites and Website Articles

Boileau, Lowell. "The Lost Synagogues of Detroit." <www.shtetlhood.com>.

Breger, Marshall J. "Soloveitchik's 'Confrontation': A Reassessment." posted on <www.escholarship.bc.edu/scjr/vol1/iss1/18/>.

"East Brooklyn: Synagogues Turn Churches." posted comments to article, January 28, 2008. Yeshiva World: Frum Jewish News. <www.theyeshivaworld.com>.

Fine, Rabbi David J. "On the Sale of Holy Property." OH 153:2.2005a. Jewish Theological Seminary of America. <www.jtsa.edu>.

ICCJ. International Council of Christians and Jews. Home page. <www.iccj.org>.

Jacobs, Louis. "Respect in the Synagogue." posted on MyJewishLearning.com, the Personal Gateway to Jewish Exploration. <www.MyJewishLearning.com/daily_life/Prayer/TO_Synagogue/Respect_for_Synagogue>.

Jewish News of Greater Phoenix Online. Contact information. <www.jewishaz.com>.

Museum of Family History. Home Page and "The Synagogues of New York City, Former Synagogue List, Brooklyn." <www.museumoffamilyhistory.org>.

New York City Department of Finance. website. "Property: Find Borough, Block & Lot." <http://www.nyc. gov/html/dof/html/property/property_info_bbl.shtml>

Perlin, Seymour J., Ed.D. "Remembrance of Synagogues Past. The Lost Civilization of the Jewish South Bronx." <www.bronxsynagogues.org>.

"Rose Window." Wikipedia article.

Rosen, Jeremy. "Jeremy Rosen Online: Halachic Q & A. Entering Churches." <www.jeremyrosen.com/halacha/entering_churches.html>.

Schechter, Leah. E-mail response. August 22, 2006. Library of the Jewish Theological Seminary of America. <www.jtsa.edu>.

Silberberg, Rabbi Naftali. Posting. <www.askmoses.com>.

<www.webshas.org/tefillah/kedushah.html>. Intelligent Topical Index to the Talmud: Prayer, Holiness of a Synagogue.

Zsurlo Film Ltd. "Synagogue for Sale" by Zsuzsanna Geller-Varga. <www.zsurlofilm.com>.

Archives

Congregation Shaari Israel, Brooklyn, New York Records, 1929–1991.

Joseph and Miriam Ratner Center for the Study of Conservative Judaism, the Jewish Theological Seminary, New York. Gift of Rabbi Abraham Feldbin, 1996.

Papers of Rabbi Joseph Miller. 1920s–1967. The Joseph and Miriam Ratner Center for the Study of Conservative Judaism, the Jewish Theological Seminary, New York. Gift of Amos Miller, December 1990.

Works Progress Administration (WPA) Federal Writers Project. Survey of State and Local Histories. Church and Synagogue Records for New York City, 1939–1940. Housed at the New York City Municipal Archives, 31 Chambers Street, Manhattan.

The 1939–1940 "Tax" Photograph Collection, New York City Municipal Archives, Department of Records and Information Services, 31 Chambers Street, Manhattan. [individual photographs of 1678 Park Place, Brooklyn; 71 Malta Street, Brooklyn; 765–7 Putnam Avenue; 144 Newport Avenue; 744 Dumont Avenue; 890 Lenox Road, Brooklyn].

New York Landmarks Conservancy, *Sacred Sites* Program.

Calendars

"Hebrew-Christian Calendar of the House of David, 2006–2007." House of David, 744 Dumont Street, Brooklyn, New York.

August 2007 Calendar of Events, Universal Church of God In Christ. 1403 Eastern Parkway, Brooklyn, New York.

Pamphlets

"Forgotten Heritage: Uncovering New York's Hidden Jewish Past." Photographs by Julian Voloj. 2007.

New York Supreme Court, Appellate Division: Second Department. Record on Appeal for Congregation House of Abraham. 1968. Provided by Robert S. Hammer.

"Welcome! To the Salem Missionary Baptist Church." 2007. Brooklyn, New York.

Journals

Jewish Communal Survey of Greater New York. Report of Executive Committee, October 1929. Brooklyn, New York.

Brooklyn Federation of Jewish Charities: 1917, pp. 16–17; 130–131 1918, pp. 72, 101, 125 1919, pp. 5–6

Jewish Review of Brooklyn. November-December 1905. p. 16.

Map

Map, Beth David Cemetery. Elmont, New York. 2007.

Thesis

Halpert, Max. "The Jews of Brownsville, 1880–1925." 1958. pp. 21, 171, 176. Microfilm, New York Public Library.

CPSIA information can be obtained at www.ICGtesting.com
Printed in the USA
BVOW062217020112

279648BV00002B/1/P